Collins

D0522553

Collins
French
Verbs

HarperCollins Publishers
Westerhill Road
Bishopbriggs
Glasgow
G64 2QT
Great Britain

First Edition 2005

Reprint 12 11 10 9

© HarperCollins Publishers 2005

ISBN 978-0-00-720324-6

Collins® and Bank of English® are
registered trademarks of
HarperCollins Publishers Limited

www.collinslanguage.com

A catalogue record for this book is available
from the British Library

Typeset by Davidson Pre-Press, Glasgow

Printed in Italy by LEGO Spa, Lavis (Trento)

Acknowledgements
We would like to thank those authors and
publishers who kindly gave permission for
copyright material to be used in the Collins
Word Web. We would also like to thank
Times Newspapers Ltd for providing
valuable data.

PUBLISHING DIRECTOR
Lorna Knight

EDITORIAL DIRECTOR
Michela Clari

MANAGING EDITOR
Maree Airlie

CONTRIBUTORS
Wendy Lee
Gaëlle Amiot-Cadey
Di Larkin
Laurent Jouet
Cécile-Aubinière Robb

William Collins' dream of knowledge for all began with the publication of his first book in 1819. A self-educated mill worker, he not only enriched millions of lives, but also founded a flourising publishing house. Today, staying true to this spirit, Collins books are packed with inspiration, innovation, and practical expertise. They place you at the centre of a world of possibility and give you exactly what you need to explore it.

Language is the key to this exploration, and at the heart of Collins Dictionaries is language as it is really used. New words, phrases, and meanings spring up every day, and all of them are captured and analysed by the Collins Word Web. Constantly updated, and with over 2.5 billion entries, this living language resource is unique to our dictionaries.

Words are tools for life. And a Collins Dictionary makes them work for you.

Collins. Do more.

Contents

Contents

Introduction

The *Easy Learning French Verbs* is designed for both young and adult learners. Whether you are starting to learn French for the very first time, brushing up your language skills or revising for exams, the *Easy Learning French Verbs* and its companion volume, the *Easy Learning French Grammar*, are here to help.

Newcomers can sometimes struggle with the technical terms they come across when they start to explore the grammar of a new language. The *Easy Learning French Verbs* contains a glossary which explains verb grammar terms using simple language and cutting out jargon.

The text is divided into sections to help you become confident in using and understanding French verbs. The first section looks at verb formation. Written in clear language, with numerous examples in real French, this section helps you to understand the rules which are used to form verb tenses.

The next section of text looks at certain common prepositions which are used with a number of verbs. Each combination of verb plus preposition is shown with a simple example of real French to show exactly how it is used.

The Verb Tables contain 115 important French verbs (both regular and irregular) which are given in full for various tenses. Examples show how to use these verbs in your own work. If you are unsure how a verb goes in French, you can look up the Verb Index at the back of the book to find either the conjugation of the verb itself, or a cross-reference to a model verb, which will show you the patterns that verb follows.

The *Easy Learning French Grammar* takes you a step further in your language learning. It supplements the information given in the *Easy Learning French Verbs* by offering even more guidance on the usage and meaning of verbs, as well as looking at the most important aspects of French grammar. Together, or individually, the *Easy Learning* titles offer you all the help you need when learning French.

Glossary of Verb Grammar Terms

ADVERB a word usually used with verbs, adjectives or other adverbs that gives more information about when, where, how or in what circumstances something happens, for example, *quickly, happily, now*.

AGREE (to) to change word endings according to whether you are referring to masculine, feminine, singular or plural people or things.

AGREEMENT changing word endings according to whether you are referring to masculine, feminine, singular or plural people or things.

ARTICLE a word like *the, a* and *an*, which is used in front of a noun. See also **definite article** and **indefinite article**.

AUXILIARY VERB a verb such as *be, have* and *do* when it is used with a main verb to form tenses, negatives and questions.

BASE FORM the form of the verb without any endings added to it, for example, *walk, have, be, go*. Compare with **infinitive**.

CLAUSE a group of words containing a verb.

CONDITIONAL a verb form used to talk about things that would happen or would be true under certain conditions, for example, *I would help you if I could*. It is also used to say what you would like or need, for example, *Could you give me the bill?*

CONJUGATE (to) to give a verb different endings according to whether you are referring to *I, you, they* and so on, and according to whether you are referring to past, present or future, for example, *I have, she had, they will have*.

CONJUGATION a group of verbs which have the same endings as each other or change according to the same pattern.

DEFINITE ARTICLE the word *the*. Compare with **indefinite article**.

DEMONSTRATIVE PRONOUN one of the words *this, that, these* and *those* used instead of a noun to point out people or things, for example, *That looks fun*.

DIRECT OBJECT a noun referring to the person or thing affected by the action described by a verb, for example, *She wrote her name.; I shut the window*. Compare with indirect object.

DIRECT OBJECT PRONOUN a word such as *me, him, us* and *them* which is used instead of a noun to stand in for the person or thing most directly affected by the action described by the verb. Compare with indirect object pronoun.

ENDING a form added to a verb, for example, *go > goes*, and to adjectives and nouns depending on whether they refer to masculine, feminine, singular or plural things.

FEMININE a form of noun, pronoun or adjective that is used to refer to a living being, thing or idea that is not classed as masculine.

FUTURE a verb tense used to talk about something that will happen or will be true.

IMPERATIVE the form of a verb used when giving orders and instructions, for example, *Shut the door!; Sit down!; Don't go!*

IMPERFECT one of the verb tenses used to talk about the past, especially in descriptions, and to say what was happening or used to happen, for example, *I used to walk to school; It was sunny at the weekend*. Compare with **perfect**.

IMPERSONAL VERB one which does not refer to a real person or thing and where the subject is represented by *it*, for example, *It's going to rain; It's 10 o'clock*.

INDEFINITE ARTICLE the words *a* and *an*. Compare with **definite article**.

INDEFINITE PRONOUN a small group of pronouns such as *everything, nobody* and *something*, which are used to refer to people or things in a general way, without saying exactly who or what they are.

INDIRECT OBJECT a noun used with verbs that take two objects. For example, in *I gave the carrot to the rabbit, the rabbit* is the indirect object and *carrot* is the direct object. Compare with **direct object**.

INDIRECT OBJECT PRONOUN when a verb has two objects (a direct one and an indirect one), the indirect object pronoun is used instead of a noun to show the person or the thing the action is intended to benefit or harm, for example, *me* in *He gave me a book* and *Can you get me a towel?* Compare with **direct object pronoun**.

INDIRECT QUESTION used to tell someone else about a question and introduced by a verb such as *ask, tell* or *wonder*, for example, *He asked me what the time was; I wonder who he is.*

INFINITIVE the form of the verb with *to* in front of it and without any endings added, for example, *to walk, to have, to be, to go*. Compare with **base form**.

IRREGULAR VERB a verb whose forms do not follow a general pattern or the normal rules. Compare with **regular verb**.

MASCULINE a form of noun, pronoun or adjective that is used to refer to a living being, thing or idea that is not classed as feminine.

NEGATIVE a question or statement which contains a word such as *not, never* or *nothing*, and is used to say that something is not happening, is not true or is absent, for example, *I never eat meat; Don't you love me?*

NOUN a 'naming' word for a living being, thing or idea, for example, *woman, desk, happiness, Andrew.*

NUMBER used to say how many things you are referring to or where something comes in a sequence. See also **ordinal number** and **cardinal number**.

OBJECT a noun or pronoun which refers to a person or thing that is affected by the action described by the verb. Compare with **direct object**, **indirect object** and **subject**.

OBJECT PRONOUN one of the set of pronouns including *me*, *him* and *them*, which are used instead of the noun as the object of a verb or preposition. Compare with **subject pronoun**.

PART OF SPEECH a word class, for example, *noun*, *verb*, *adjective*, *preposition*, *pronoun*.

PASSIVE a form of the verb that is used when the subject of the verb is the person or thing that is affected by the action, for example, *we were told*.

PAST HISTORIC one of the verb tenses used to talk about the past when referring to completed actions, whether they happened recently or a long time ago and regardless of how long they lasted.

PAST PARTICIPLE a verb form which is used to form perfect and pluperfect tenses and passives, for example, *watched*, *swum*. Some past participles are also used as adjectives, for example, *a broken watch*.

PERFECT one of the verb tenses used to talk about the past, especially about actions that took place and were completed in the past. Compare with **imperfect**.

PERSON one of the three classes: the first person (*I*, *we*), the second person (*you* singular and *you* plural), and the third person (*he*, *she*, *it* and *they*).

PERSONAL PRONOUN one of the group of words including *I*, *you* and *they* which are used to refer to yourself, the people you are talking to, or the people or things you are talking about.

PLUPERFECT one of the verb tenses used to describe something that <u>had</u> happened or had been true at a point in the past, for example, *I'd forgotten to finish my homework*.

PLURAL the form of a word which is used to refer to more than one person or thing. Compare with **singular**.

PREPOSITION is a word such as *at*, *for*, *with*, *into* or *from*, which is usually followed by a noun, pronoun or, in English, a word ending in *-ing*. Prepositions show how people and things relate to the rest of the sentence, for example, *She's <u>at</u> home; a tool for cutting grass; It's <u>from</u> David*.

PRESENT a verb form used to talk about what is true at the moment, what happens regularly, and what is happening now, for example, *I'm a student; I travel to college by train; I'm studying languages*.

PRESENT PARTICIPLE a verb form ending in -ing which is used in English to form verb tenses, and which may be used as an adjective or a noun, for example, *What are you doing?*; *the setting sun*; *Swimming is easy!*

PRONOUN a word which you use instead of a noun, when you do not need or want to name someone or something directly, for example, *it, you, none*.

PROPER NOUN the name of a person, place, organization or thing. Proper nouns are always written with a capital letter, for example, *Kevin, Glasgow, Europe, London Eye*.

REFLEXIVE PRONOUN a word ending in -self or -selves, such as *myself* or *themselves*, which refers back to the subject, for example, *He hurt himself.*; *Take care of yourself.*

REFLEXIVE VERB a verb where the subject and object are the same, and where the action 'reflects back' on the subject. A reflexive verb is used with a reflexive pronoun such as *myself, yourself, herself*, for example, *I washed myself.*; *He shaved himself.*

REGULAR VERB a verb whose forms follow a general pattern or the normal rules. Compare with irregular verb.

SINGULAR the form of a word which is used to refer to one person or thing. Compare with plural.

STEM the main part of a verb to which endings are added.

SUBJECT the noun in a sentence or phrase that refers to the person or thing that does the action described by the verb or is in the state described by the verb, for example, *My cat doesn't drink milk.* Compare with object.

SUBJECT PRONOUN a word such as *I, he, she* and *they* which carries out the action described by the verb. Pronouns stand in for nouns when it is clear who is being talked about, for example, *My brother isn't here at the moment. He'll be back in an hour.* Compare with object pronoun.

SUBJUNCTIVE a verb form used in certain circumstances to express some sort of feeling, or to show doubt about whether something will happen or whether something is true. It is only used occasionally in modern English, for example, *If I were you, I wouldn't bother.*; *So be it.*

TENSE the form of a verb which shows whether you are referring to the past, present or future.

VERB a 'doing' word which describes what someone or something does, what someone or something is, or what happens to them, for example, *be, sing, live*.

Introduction to Verb Formation

The three conjugations

Verbs are usually used with a noun, with a pronoun such as *I*, *you* or *she*, or with somebody's name. They can relate to the present, the past and the future; this is called their <u>tense</u>.

Verbs are either:

> <u>regular</u>; their forms follow the normal rules
> <u>irregular</u>; their forms do not follow the normal rules

Regular English verbs have a <u>base form</u> (the form of the verb without any endings added to it, for example, *walk*). The base form can have *to* in front of it, for example, *to walk*. This is called the <u>infinitive</u>. You will find one of these forms when you look a verb up in your dictionary.

French verbs also have an infinitive, which ends in -er, -ir or -re, for example, **donner** (meaning *to give*), **finir** (meaning *to finish*), **attendre** (meaning *to wait*). <u>Regular</u> French verbs belong to one of these three verb groups, which are called <u>conjugations</u>. We will look at each of these three conjugations in turn on the next few pages.

English verbs have other forms apart from the base form and infinitive: a form ending in -s (*walks*), a form ending in -*ing* (*walking*), and a form ending in -*ed* (*walked*). French verbs have many more forms than this, which are made up of endings added to a <u>stem</u>. The stem of a verb can usually be worked out from the infinitive.

French verb endings change, depending on who you are talking about: je (*I*), tu (*you*), il/elle/on (*he/she/one*) in the singular, or nous (*we*), vous (*you*) and ils/elles (*they*) in the plural. French verbs also have different forms depending on whether you are referring to the present, future or past.

For further explanation of grammatical terms, please see pages 8-11.

Some verbs in French do not follow the normal rules, and are called <u>irregular verbs</u>. These include some very common and important verbs like **avoir** (meaning *to have*), **être** (meaning *to be*), **faire** (meaning *to do, to make*) and **aller** (meaning *to go*). There is information on many of these irregular verbs in the following sections.

The following sections give you all the help you need on how to form the different verb tenses used in French. If you would like even more information on how French verbs are used, the *Easy Learning French Grammar* shows you when and how numerous different verbs are used when writing and speaking modern French.

The present tense

Forming the present tense of regular -er (first conjugation) verbs

If an infinitive in French ends in -er, it means the verb belongs to the <u>first conjugation</u>, for example, donner, aimer, parler.

To know which form of the verb to use in French, you need to work out what the stem of the verb is and then add the correct ending. The stem of -er verbs in the present tense is formed by taking the <u>infinitive</u> and chopping off -er.

Infinitive	Stem (without -er)
donner (*to give*)	donn-
aimer (*to like, to love*)	aim-
parler (*to speak, to talk*)	parl-

Now you know how to find the stem of a verb, you can add the correct ending. Which one you choose will depend on whether you are referring to je, tu, il, elle, on, nous, vous, ils or elles.

Here are the present tense endings for -er verbs:

Pronoun	Ending	Add to stem, e.g. donn-	Meanings
je (j')	-e	je donn<u>e</u>	I give I am giving
tu	-es	tu donn<u>es</u>	you give you are giving
il elle on	-e	il donn<u>e</u> elle donn<u>e</u> on donn<u>e</u>	he/she/it/one gives he/she/it/one is giving

For further explanation of grammatical terms, please see pages 8-11.

Pronoun	Ending	Add to stem, e.g. donn-	Meanings
nous	-ons	nous donn<u>ons</u>	we give we are giving
vous	-ez	vous donn<u>ez</u>	you give you are giving
ils elles	-ent	ils donn<u>ent</u> elles donn<u>ent</u>	they give they are giving

Marie <u>regarde</u> la télé.   Marie is watching TV.

Le train <u>arrive</u> à deux heures.   The train arrives at 2 o'clock.

Note that there are a few regular -er verbs that are spelled slightly differently from the way you might expect.

Forming the present tense of regular -ir (second conjugation) verbs

If an infinitive ends in -ir, it means the verb belongs to the <u>second conjugation</u>, for example, finir, choisir, remplir.

The stem of -ir verbs in the present tense is formed by taking the <u>infinitive</u> and chopping off -ir.

Infinitive	Stem (without -ir)
finir (to finish)	fin-
choisir (to choose)	chois-
remplir (to fill, to fill in)	rempl-

Now add the correct ending, depending on whether you are referring to je, tu, il, elle, on, nous, vous, ils or elles.

Here are the present tense endings for -ir verbs:

Pronoun	Ending	Add to stem, e.g. fin-	Meanings
je (j')	-is	je finis	I finish I am finishing
tu	-is	tu finis	you finish you are finishing
il elle on	-it	il finit elle finit on finit	he/she/it/one finishes he/she/it/one is finishing
nous	-issons	nous finissons	we finish we are finishing
vous	-issez	vous finissez	you finish you are finishing
ils elles	-issent	ils finissent elles finissent	they finish they are finishing

Le cours <u>finit</u> à onze heures.   The lesson finishes at eleven o'clock.

Je <u>finis</u> mes devoirs.   I'm finishing my homework.

The **nous** and **vous** forms of -**ir** verbs have an extra syllable.

vous fi|ni|ssez   (*three syllables*)

tu fi|nis   (*two syllables*)

Forming the present tense of regular -re (third conjugation) verbs

If an infinitive ends in -re, it means the verb belongs to the underline{third conjugation}, for example, attendre, vendre, entendre.

The stem of -re verbs in the present tense is formed by taking the underline{infinitive} and chopping off -re.

Infinitive	Stem (without -re)
attendre (*to wait*)	attend-
vendre (*to sell*)	vend-
entendre (*to hear*)	entend-

Now add the correct ending, depending on whether you are referring to je, tu, il, elle, on, nous, vous, ils or elles.

Here are the present tense endings for -re verbs:

Pronoun	Ending	Add to stem, e.g. attend-	Meanings
je (j')	-s	j'attend<u>s</u>	I wait I am waiting
tu	-s	tu attend<u>s</u>	you wait you are waiting
il elle on	-	il attend elle attend on attend	he/she/it/one waits he/she/it/one is waiting
nous	-ons	nous attend<u>ons</u>	we wait we are waiting
vous	-ez	vous attend<u>ez</u>	you wait you are waiting
ils elles	-ent	ils attend<u>ent</u> elles attend<u>ent</u>	they wait they are waiting

J'<u>attends</u> ma sœur.   I'm waiting for my sister.

Chaque matin nous <u>attendons</u> le train ensemble.

Every morning we wait for the train together.

Spelling changes in -er verbs

Learning the patterns shown on pages 14–17 means you can now work out the forms of most -er verbs. A few verbs, though, involve a small spelling change. This is usually to do with how a word is pronounced. In the tables below the forms with the irregular spelling are <u>underlined</u>.

Verbs ending in -cer

With verbs such as lancer (meaning to throw), which end in -cer, c becomes ç before an a or an o. This is so the letter c is still pronounced as in the English word ice.

Pronoun	Example verb: lancer
je	lance
tu	lances
il/elle/on	lance
nous	<u>lançons</u>
vous	lancez
ils/elles	lancent

Nous lançons le ballon aussi haut que possible.

We throw the ball as high as we can.

Nous avançons sans bruit.   We move forward without a noise.

Nous les devançons de plusieurs kilomètres.

We're several kilometres ahead of them.

For further explanation of grammatical terms, please see pages 8-11.

Verbs ending in -ger

With verbs such as manger (meaning *to eat*), which end in -ger, g becomes ge before an a or an o. This is so the letter g is still pronounced like the s in the English word *leisure*.

Pronoun	Example verb: manger
je	mange
tu	manges
il/elle/on	mange
nous	mangeons
vous	mangez
ils/elles	mangent

Nous mangeons à huit heures du soir.   We eat at eight.
Nous ne les dérangeons pas.   We aren't disturbing them.
Nous rangeons la cuisine.   We're tidying up the kitchen.

Verbs ending in -eler

With verbs such as appeler (meaning *to call*), which end in -eler, the l doubles before -e, -es and -ent. The double consonant (ll) affects the pronunciation of the word. In appeler, the first e sounds like the vowel sound at the end of the English word *teacher*, but in appelle the first e sounds like the one in the English word *pet*.

Pronoun	Example verb: appeler
j'	appelle
tu	appelles
il/elle/on	appelle
nous	appelons
vous	appelez
ils/elles	appellent

Il appelle son frère pour son anniversaire.
He calls his brother for his birthday.
Nous vous rappelons que le bus part à sept heures.
May we remind you that the bus leaves at seven.

The exceptions to this rule are geler (meaning *to freeze*) and peler (meaning *to peel*), which change in the same way as lever.

Verbs like this are sometimes called '1, 2, 3, 6 verbs' because they change in the first person singular (je), second person singular (tu), and third person singular and plural (il/elle/on and ils/elles).

Verbs ending in -eter

With verbs such as jeter (meaning *to throw*), which end in -eter, the t doubles before -e, -es and -ent. The double consonant (tt) affects the pronunciation of the word. In jeter, the first e sounds like the vowel sound at the end of the English word *teacher*, but in jette the first e sounds like the one in the English word *pet*.

Pronoun	Example verb: jeter
je	jette
tu	jettes
il/elle/on	jette
nous	jetons
vous	jetez
ils/elles	jettent

Tu jettes l'enveloppe à la poubelle.   You put the envelope in the bin.

The exceptions to this rule include acheter (meaning *to buy*), which changes in the same way as lever.

For further explanation of grammatical terms, please see pages 8-11.

Verbs ending in -yer

With verbs such as **nettoyer** (meaning *to clean*), which end in **-yer**, the y changes to i before **-e**, **-es** and **-ent**.

Pronoun	Example verb: nettoyer
je	nettoie
tu	nettoies
il/ell/on	nettoie
nous	nettoyons
vous	nettoyez
ils/elles	nettoient

Ils nettoient leurs bureaux chaque semaine.
They clean their desks every morning.
Tu essuies tes lunettes avant le début du film.
You clean your glasses before the film starts.
Il balaie le trottoir devant sa porte.
He sweeps the pavement outside his door.

Verbs ending in **-ayer**, such as **payer** (meaning *to pay*) and **essayer** (meaning *to try*), can be spelled with either a y or an i. So **je paie** and **je paye**, for example, are both correct.

Changes involving accents

With verbs such as **lever** (meaning *to raise*), **peser** (meaning *to weigh*) and **acheter** (meaning *to buy*), e changes to è before the consonant + **-e**, **-es** and **-ent**. The accent changes the pronunciation too. In **lever** the first e sounds like the vowel sound at the end of the English word *teacher*, but in **lève** and so on the first e sounds like the one in the English word *pet*.

Pronoun	Example verb: lever
je	<u>lève</u>
tu	<u>lèves</u>
il/elle/on	<u>lève</u>
nous	levons
vous	levez
ils/elles	<u>lèvent</u>

Il achète le journal.   He buys the paper.

Nous achetons des pommes pour faire une tarte.

We buy apples to make a pie.

On pèse le bébé à sa naissance.   The baby is weighed after its birth.

Nous pesons trop lourd pour prendre cet ascenseur.

We're too heavy to take this lift.

With verbs such as espérer (meaning *to hope*), régler (meaning *to adjust*) and préférer (meaning *to prefer*), é changes to è before the consonant + -e, -es and -ent.

Pronoun	Example verb: espérer
j'	<u>espère</u>
tu	<u>espères</u>
il/elle/on	<u>espère</u>
nous	espérons
vous	espérez
ils/elles	<u>espèrent</u>

Elle règle sa montre avant de se coucher

She sets her watch before going to bed.

Nous réglons la pendule de la cuisine.   We set the kitchen clock.

For further explanation of grammatical terms, please see pages 8-11.

Je préfère lire plutôt que de regarder la télévision.
I prefer to read rather than to watch television.
Nous préférons la mer à la montagne.
We like the sea better than mountains.
J'espère te revoir bientôt.   I hope to see you soon.
Nous espérons que vous allez tous bien.   We hope you're all well.

Irregular -ir verbs

Many irregular verbs that end in -ir, such as partir (meaning *to go*) and tenir
(meaning *to hold*), have a common pattern in the singular. The je and tu forms
often end in -s, and the il/elle/on form often ends in -t.

Pronoun	partir	tenir
je	par<u>s</u>	tien<u>s</u>
tu	par<u>s</u>	tien<u>s</u>
il/elle/on	par<u>t</u>	tien<u>t</u>

Je <u>pars</u> demain.   I'm leaving tomorrow.
Elle <u>tient</u> le bébé.   She is holding the baby.

All the most important irregular verbs are shown in full in the **Verb Tables** at the
back of the book.

The imperative

Forming the present tense imperative

For regular verbs, the imperative is the same as the **tu**, **nous** and **vous** forms of the present tense, except that you do not say the pronouns **tu**, **nous** and **vous**. Also, in the **tu** form of -**er** verbs like **donner**, the final -**s** is dropped.

Pronoun	-er verbs: donner	Meaning	-ir verbs: finir	Meaning	-re verbs: attendre	Meaning
tu	donne	give	finis	finish	attends	wait
nous	donnons	let's give	finissons	let's finish	attendons	let's wait
vous	donnez	give	finissez	finish	attendez	wait

> <u>Donne</u>-moi ça!   Give me that!
> Finissez vos devoirs et <u>allez</u> vous coucher.
> Finish your homework and go to bed.
> <u>Attendons</u> le bus.   Let's wait for the bus.

Where to put the object pronoun

An object pronoun is a word like **la** (meaning *her/it*), **me/moi** (meaning *me*) or **leur** (meaning *to them*) that is used instead of a noun as the object of a sentence. In orders and instructions, the position of these object pronouns in the sentence changes depending on whether you are telling someone <u>TO DO</u> something or <u>NOT TO DO</u> something.

If you are telling someone <u>NOT TO DO</u> something, you put the object pronouns <u>BEFORE</u> the verb.

> Ne <u>me</u> dérange pas.   Don't disturb me.
> Ne <u>leur</u> parlons pas.   Let's not speak to them.

Ne le regardez pas. Don't look at him/it.

If you are telling someone <u>TO DO</u> something, you put the object pronouns <u>AFTER</u> the verb and join the two words with a hyphen. The word order is the same as in English.

Excusez-<u>moi</u>. Excuse me.
Aide-<u>nous</u>. Help us.
Attendons-<u>la</u>. Let's wait for her/it.

Orders and instructions telling someone to do something may contain <u>direct object</u> and <u>indirect object pronouns</u>. When this happens, the pronouns go in this order:

Direct		Indirect
le		moi
la	**BEFORE**	toi
les		lui
		nous
		vous
		leur

Prête-<u>les moi</u>! Lend them to me! or Lend me them!
Donnez-<u>la-nous</u>! Give it to us! or Give us it!

Reflexive verbs

Forming the present tense of reflexive verbs

To use a reflexive verb in French, you need to decide which reflexive pronoun to use. The forms shown in brackets in the table are used before a word starting with a vowel, most words starting with h, or the French word y.

Subject pronoun	Reflexive pronoun	Meaning
je	me (m')	myself
tu	te (t')	yourself
il	se (s')	himself
elle		herself
on		itself
		oneself
nous	nous	ourselves
vous	vous	yourself (*singular*)
		yourselves (*plural*)
ils	se (s')	themselves
elles		

Je <u>me lève</u> tôt.   I get up early.

Elle <u>s'habille</u>.   She's getting dressed.

Ils <u>s'intéressent</u> beaucoup aux animaux.   They're very interested in animals.

The present tense forms of a reflexive verb work in just the same way as an ordinary verb, except that the reflexive pronoun is used as well.

For further explanation of grammatical terms, please see pages 8-11.

Reflexive forms	Meaning
je me lave	I wash (myself)
tu te laves	you wash (yourself)
il se lave	he washes (himself)
elle se lave	she washes (herself)
on se lave	it washes (itself)
	one washes (oneself)
nous nous lavons	we wash (ourselves)
vous vous lavez	you wash (yourself) (*singular*)
	you wash (yourselves) (*plural*)
ils se lavent	they wash (themselves)
elles se lavent	

Nous nous amusons beaucoup.   We have a lot of fun.

Ils se voient de temps en temps.   They sometimes see each other.

Le dimanche, il se repose.   On Sundays, he has a rest.

Il se regarde dans le miroir.   He looks at himself in the mirror.

Elle ne se souvient pas de leurs noms.   She can't remember their names.

Some reflexive verbs, such as s'asseoir (meaning *to sit down*), are irregular. Some of these irregular verbs are shown in the **Verb Tables** at the back of the book.

Where to put the reflexive pronoun

In the present tense, the reflexive pronoun almost always comes <u>BEFORE</u> the verb.

Je me couche tôt.   I go to bed early.

Comment t'appelles-tu?   What's your name?

When telling someone <u>NOT TO DO</u> something, you put the reflexive pronoun <u>BEFORE</u> the verb as usual.

Ne <u>te</u> lève pas.   Don't get up.

Ne <u>vous</u> habillez pas.   Don't get dressed.

When telling someone <u>TO DO</u> something, you put the reflexive pronoun <u>AFTER</u> the verb and join the two words with a hyphen.

> Lève-<u>toi</u>!   Get up!
> Dépêchez-<u>vous</u>!   Hurry up!
> Habillons-<u>nous</u>.   Let's get dressed.

Each other and one another

We use *each other* in English when we are talking about two people, and *one another* when we are talking about three or more people. The French reflexive pronouns nous, vous and se can all mean two or more people.

> Nous <u>nous</u> parlons tous les jours.   We speak to <u>each other</u> every day.
> On <u>se</u> voit demain?   Shall we see <u>each other</u> tomorrow?
> Les trois pays <u>se</u> ressemblent beaucoup.
> The three countries are really like <u>one another</u>.

For further explanation of grammatical terms, please see pages 8-11.

The imperfect tense

Forming the imperfect tense of -er verbs

To form the imperfect tense of -er verbs, you use the same stem of the verb as for the present tense. Then you add the correct ending, depending on whether you are referring to je, tu, il, elle, on, nous, vous, ils or elles.

Pronoun	Ending	Add to stem, e.g. donn-	Meanings
je (j')	-ais	je donn<u>ais</u>	I gave I was giving I used to give
tu	-ais	tu donn<u>ais</u>	you gave you were giving you used to give
il elle on	-ait	il donn<u>ait</u> elle donn<u>ait</u> on donn<u>ait</u>	he/she/it/one gave he/she/it/one was giving he/she/it/one used to give
nous	-ions	nous donn<u>ions</u>	we gave we were giving we used to give
vous	-iez	vous donn<u>iez</u>	you gave you were giving you used to give
ils elles	-aient	ils donn<u>aient</u> elles donn<u>aient</u>	they gave they were giving they used to give

Il <u>portait</u> toujours un grand chapeau noir.   He always wore a big black hat.
Nous <u>habitions</u> à Paris à cette époque.   We were living in Paris at that time.
Pour gagner un peu d'argent, je <u>donnais</u> des cours de français.
To earn a little money I used to give French lessons.

Forming the imperfect tense of -ir verbs

To form the imperfect tense of -ir verbs, you use the same stem of the verb as for the present tense. Then you add the correct ending, depending on whether you are referring to je, tu, il, elle, on, nous, vous, ils or elles.

Pronoun	Ending	Add to stem, e.g. fin-	Meanings
je (j')	-issais	je finissais	I finished I was finishing I used to finish
tu	-issais	tu finissais	you finished you were finishing you used to finish
il elle on	-issait	il finissait elle finissait on finissait	he/she/it/one finished he/she/it/one was finishing he/she/it/one used to finish
nous	-issions	nous finissions	we finished we were finishing we used to finish
vous	-issiez	vous finissiez	you finished you were finishing you used to finish
ils elles	-issaient	ils finissaient elles finissaient	they finished they were finishing they used to finish

Il finissait souvent ses devoirs avant le dîner.
He often finished his homework before dinner.
Cet après-midi-là ils choisissaient une bague de fiançailles.
That afternoon they were choosing an engagement ring.

For further explanation of grammatical terms, please see pages 8-11.

Forming the imperfect tense of -re verbs

To form the imperfect tense of **-re** verbs, you use the same stem of the verb as for the present tense. Then you add the correct ending, depending on whether you are referring to **je**, **tu**, **il**, **elle**, **on**, **nous**, **vous**, **ils** or **elles**. These endings are the same as for **-er** verbs.

Pronoun	Ending	Add to stem, e.g. attend-	Meanings
j' (j')	-ais	j'attend<u>ais</u>	I waited I was waiting I used to wait
tu	-ais	tu attend<u>ais</u>	you waited you were waiting you used to wait
il elle on	-ait	il attend<u>ait</u> elle attend<u>ait</u> on attend<u>ait</u>	he/she/it/one waited he/she/it/one was waiting he/she/it/one used to wait
nous	-ions	nous attend<u>ions</u>	we waited we were waiting we used to wait
vous	-iez	vous attend<u>iez</u>	you waited you were waiting you used to wait
ils elles	-aient	ils attend<u>aient</u> elles attend<u>aient</u>	they waited they were waiting they used to wait

Christine m'<u>attendait</u> tous les soirs à la sortie.

Christine used to wait for me every evening at the exit.

Je <u>vivais</u> seule après mon divorce.   I was living alone after my divorce.

Spelling changes in -er verbs

As with the present tense, a few -er verbs change their spellings slightly when they are used in the imperfect tense. The forms with spelling changes have been underlined in the tables.

With verbs such as lancer (meaning *to throw*), which end in -cer, c becomes ç before an a or an o. This is so that the letter c is still pronounced as in the English word *ice*.

Pronoun	Example verb: lancer
je	lançais
tu	lançais
il/elle/on	lançait
nous	lancions
vous	lanciez
ils/elles	lançaient

Il lançait des boules de neige sur les passants.
He threw snowballs at passers-by.
Il prononçait les mots d'une façon particulière.
He had a peculiar way of pronouncing words.
La professeur fronçait les sourcils quand les élèves étaient trop bruyants.
The teacher frowned when the pupils were too noisy.

With verbs such as manger (meaning *to eat*), which end in -ger, g becomes ge before an a or an o. This is so the letter g is still pronounced like the s in the English word *leisure*.

For further explanation of grammatical terms, please see pages 8-11.

Pronoun	Example verb: manger
je	<u>mangeais</u>
tu	<u>mangeais</u>
il/elle/on	<u>mangeait</u>
nous	mangions
vous	mangiez
ils/elles	<u>mangeaient</u>

Elle changeait toujours de travail.   She kept changing jobs.
Nous échangions des cadeaux au moment de partir.
When it was time to part, we exchanged presents.
Tu arrangeais toujours tout par avance.
You always arranged everything in advance.

These verbs follow the 1,2,3,6 *pattern*. That is, they change in the first, second and third person singular, and in the third person plural.

Reflexive verbs in the imperfect tense

The imperfect tense of reflexive verbs is formed just as for ordinary verbs, except that you add the reflexive pronoun (me, te, se, nous, vous, se).

Subject pronoun	Reflexive pronoun	Example with laver	Meaning
je	me (m')	lavais	I washed I was washing I used to wash
tu	te (t')	lavais	you washed you were washing you used to wash
il/elle/on	se (s')	lavait	he/she/it/one washed he/she/it/one was washing he/she/it/one used to wash

Subject pronoun	Reflexive pronoun	Example with laver	Meaning
nous	nous	lavions	we washed we were washing we used to wash
vous	vous	laviez	you washed you were washing you used to wash
ils/elles	se (s')	lavaient	they washed they were washing they used to wash

Tu t'amusais beaucoup à l'école.   You had a lot of fun at school.

Nous nous demandions ce qu'il fallait faire.

We were wondering what was to be done.

Ils s'écrivaient toutes les semaines.   They wrote to each other every week.

Irregular verbs in the imperfect tense

The only verb that is irregular in the imperfect tense is **être**.

Pronoun	être	Meaning
j'	étais	I was
tu	étais	you were
il/elle/on	était	he/she/it/one was
nous	étions	we were
vous	étiez	you were
ils/elles	étaient	they were

J'<u>étais</u> heureux.   I was happy.

Mon père <u>était</u> instituteur.   My father was a primary school teacher.

For further explanation of grammatical terms, please see pages 8-11.

The future tense

Forming the future tense

To form the future tense in French, you use:

- the <u>infinitive</u> of -er and -ir verbs, for example, donner, finir
- the <u>infinitive without the final e</u> of -re verbs: for example, attendr-

Then add the correct ending to the stem, depending on whether you are talking about je, tu, il, elle, on, nous, vous, ils or elles. The endings are the same for -er, -ir and -re verbs.

Pronoun	Ending	Add to stem, e.g. donner-, finir-, attendr-	Meanings
je (j')	-ai	je donner<u>ai</u> je finir<u>ai</u> j'attendr<u>ai</u>	I will give I will finish I will wait
tu	-as	tu donner<u>as</u> tu finir<u>as</u> tu attendr<u>as</u>	you will give you will finish you will wait
il/elle/on	-a	il/elle/on donner<u>a</u> il/elle/on finir<u>a</u> il/elle/on attendr<u>a</u>	he/she/it/one will give he/she/it/one will finish he/she/it/one will wait
nous	-ons	nous donner<u>ons</u> nous finir<u>ons</u> nous attendr<u>ons</u>	we will give we will finish we will wait
vous	-ez	vous donner<u>ez</u> vous finir<u>ez</u> vous attendr<u>ez</u>	you will give you will finish you will wait
ils/elles	-ont	ils/elles donner<u>ont</u> ils/elles finir<u>ont</u> ils/elles attendr<u>ont</u>	they will give they will finish they will wait

Elle te <u>donnera</u> mon adresse.   She'll give you my address.

Le cours <u>finira</u> à onze heures.   The lesson will finish at eleven o'clock.

Nous t'<u>attendrons</u> devant le cinéma.   We'll wait for you in front of the cinema.

Nous attendrons que la cloche sonne pour sortir.

We'll wait until the bell rings to go out.

Tu donneras la clef à ma sœur.   You'll give the key to my sister.

Spelling changes in -er verbs

As with the present and imperfect tenses, a few -er verbs change their spellings slightly in the future tense. The forms with spelling changes have been <u>underlined</u> in the tables.

With verbs such as appeler (meaning *to call*), which end in -eler, the l doubles throughout the future tense. The double consonant (ll) affects the pronunciation of the word. In appeler, the first e sounds like the vowel sound at the end of the English word *teacher*, but in appellerai the first e sounds like the one in the English word *pet*.

Pronoun	Example verb: appeler
j'	<u>appellerai</u>
tu	<u>appelleras</u>
il/elle/on	<u>appellera</u>
nous	<u>appellerons</u>
vous	<u>appellerez</u>
ils/elles	<u>appelleront</u>

S'il n'est pas chez lui ce soir je le rappellerai demain.

If he's not in tonight I'll call him again tomorrow.

Ils appelleront leur fille Lara.   They'll call their daughter Lara.

The exceptions to this rule are geler (meaning *to freeze*) and peler (meaning *to peel*), which change in the same way as lever.

With verbs such as jeter (meaning *to throw*), that end in -eter, the t doubles throughout the future tense. The double consonant (tt) affects the pronunciation of the word. In jeter, the first e sounds like the vowel sound at the end of the English word *teacher*, but in jetterai the first e sounds like the one in the English word *pet*.

Pronoun	Example verb: jeter
je	jetterai
tu	jetteras
il/elle/on	jettera
nous	jetterons
vous	jetterez
ils/elles	jetteront

Je jetterai tous ces journaux si tu ne les lis pas.
I'll throw all these newspapers away if you're not reading them.

The exceptions to this rule include acheter (meaning *to buy*), which changes in the same way as lever.

Ils achèteront une nouvelle voiture l'année prochaine.
They'll buy a new car next year.

With verbs such as nettoyer (meaning *to clean*), that end in -yer, the y changes to i throughout the future tense.

Pronoun	Example verb: nettoyer
je	nettoierai
tu	nettoieras
il/elle/on	nettoiera
nous	nettoierons
vous	nettoierez
ils/elles	nettoieront

Je nettoierai la voiture quand j'aurai le temps.
I'll clean the car when I have time.
Ils nettoieront la cuisine le plus tôt possible.
They'll clean the kitchen as soon as possible.

Verbs ending in -ayer, such as payer (meaning *to pay*) and essayer (meaning *to try*), can be spelled with either a y or an i. So je paierai and je payerai, for example, are both correct.

With verbs such as lever (meaning *to raise*), peser (meaning *to weigh*) and acheter (meaning *to buy*), e changes to è throughout the future tense. In lever the first e sounds like the vowel sound at the end of the English word *teacher*, but in lèverai and so on the first e sounds like the one in the English word *pet*.

Pronoun	Example verb: lever
je	lèverai
tu	lèveras
il/elle/on	lèvera
nous	lèverons
vous	lèverez
ils/elles	lèveront

For further explanation of grammatical terms, please see pages 8-11.

Nous payerons le repas pour tout le monde.

We'll pay for everybody's meal.

Nous paierons au début du mois prochain.

We'll pay at the beginning of next month.

Elle lèvera la tête en entendant la cloche.

She'll look up when she hears the bell.

Reflexive verbs in the future tense

The future tense of reflexive verbs is formed in just the same way as for ordinary verbs, except that you have to remember to give the reflexive pronoun (me, se, nous, vous, se).

Subject pronoun	Reflexive pronoun	Example with laver	Meaning
je	me (m')	laverai	I will wash
tu	te (t')	laveras	you will wash
il/elle/on	se (s')	lavera	he/she/it/one will wash
nous	nous	laverons	we will wash
vous	vous	laverez	you will wash
ils/elles	se (s')	laveront	they will wash

Irregular verbs in the future tense

There are some verbs that <u>do not</u> use their infinitives as the stem for the future tense, including **avoir**, **être**, **faire** and **aller**, which are shown in full in the **Verb Tables** at the back of the book.

Other irregular verbs include:

Verb	Meaning	je	tu	il/elle/on	nous	vous	ils/elles
devoir	*to have to, must*	devrai	devras	devra	devrons	devrez	devront
pouvoir	*to be able to, can*	pourrai	pourras	pourra	pourrons	pourrez	pourront
savoir	*to know*	saurai	sauras	saura	saurons	saurez	sauront
tenir	*to hold*	tiendrai	tiendras	tiendra	tiendrons	tiendrez	tiendront
venir	*to come*	viendrai	viendras	viendra	viendrons	viendrez	viendront
voir	*to see*	verrai	verras	verra	verrons	verrez	verront
vouloir	*to want*	voudrai	voudras	voudra	voudrons	voudrez	voudront

Viendras-tu me voir jouer demain soir?
Will you come to see me play tomorrow night?
Tu ne pourras pas entrer sans ticket.
You won't be admitted without a ticket.
Je te tiendrai au courant.   I'll keep you informed.
Nous verrons demain si j'ai raison.   We'll see tomorrow if I'm right.

il faut becomes il faudra (meaning *it will be necessary to*).

Il faudra que tu me donnes ton adresse.   You'll have to give me your address.

il pleut becomes il pleuvra (meaning *it will rain*).

Il pleuvra jusqu'à la fin du mois.   It'll rain until the end of the month.

For further explanation of grammatical terms, please see pages 8-11.

The conditional

Forming the conditional

To form the conditional in French, you have to use:

- the infinitive of -er and -ir verbs, for example, donner-, finir-
- the infinitive without the final e of -re verbs, for example, attendr-

Then add the correct ending to the stem, depending on whether you are talking about je, tu, il, elle, on, nous, vous, ils or elles. The endings are the same for all verbs.

Pronoun	Ending	Add to stem, e.g. donner-, finir-, attendr-	Meanings
je (j')	-ais	je donnerais je finirais j'attendrais	I would give I would finish I would wait
tu	-ais	tu donnerais tu finirais tu attendrais	you would give you would finish you would wait
il elle on	-ait	il/elle/on donnerait il/elle/on finirait il/elle/on attendrait	he/she/it/one would give he/she/it/one would finish he/she/it/one would wait
nous	-ions	nous donnerions nous finirions nous attendrions	we would give we would finish we would wait
vous	-iez	vous donneriez vous finiriez vous attendriez	you would give you would finish you would wait
ils elles	-aient	ils/elles donneraient ils/elles finiraient ils/elles attendraient	they would give they would finish they would wait

Note that you have to be careful not to mix up the future tense and the conditional. They look very similar.

Future	Conditional
je donnerai	je donnerais
je finirai	je finirais
j'attendrai	j'attendrais
j'aimerai	j'aimerais
je voudrai	je voudrais
je viendrai	je viendrais
je serai	je serais

J'aimerais qu'il neige à Noël.   I'd like it to snow at Christmas.

Je serais moins inquiet si je savais où elle est.

I wouldn't be so worried if I knew where she was.

Je finirais ce travail aujourd'hui s'il n'était pas si tard.

I'd finish this work today if it weren't so late.

Spelling changes in -er verbs

As with the future tense, a few -er verbs change their spellings slightly in the conditional. The forms with spelling changes have been underlined in the tables below.

With verbs such as **appeler** (meaning *to call*), which end in -eler, the l doubles throughout the conditional. The double consonant (ll) affects the pronunciation of the word. In **appeler**, the first e sounds like the vowel sound at the end of the English word *teacher*, but in **appellerais** the first e sounds like the one in the English word *pet*.

Pronoun	Example verb: appeler
j'	appellerais
tu	appellerais
il/elle/on	appellerait
nous	appellerions
vous	appelleriez
ils/elles	appelleraient

Je l'appellerais si j'avais son numéro de téléphone.
I'd call her if I had her phone number.
Nous appellerions une ambulance s'il était gravement blessé.
We'd call an ambulance if he were seriously injured.
Qui appelleriez-vous en cas de besoin?
Who would you phone if you needed help?

The exceptions to this rule are geler (meaning *to freeze*) and peler (meaning *to peel*), which change in the same way as lever.

With verbs such as jeter (meaning *to throw*), which end in -eter, the t doubles throughout the conditional. The double consonant (tt) affects the pronunciation of the word. In jeter, the first e sounds like the vowel sound at the end of the English word *teacher*, but in jetterais the first e sounds like the one in the English word *pet*.

Pronoun	Example verb: jeter
je	jetterais
tu	jetterais
il/elle/on	jetterait
nous	jetterions
vous	jetteriez
ils/elles	jetteraient

Je jetterais ces vieux vêtements si j'étais sûr qu'il ne serviront plus.
I'd throw these old clothes away if I were sure they were no longer any use.
Nous jetterions la balle plus fort s'ils pouvaient la rattraper.
We'd throw the ball harder if they could catch it.

The exceptions to this rule include acheter (meaning *to buy*), which changes in the same way as lever.

With verbs such as nettoyer (meaning *to clean*), that end in -yer, the y changes to i throughout the conditional.

Pronoun	Example verb: nettoyer
je	nettoierais
tu	nettoierais
il/elle/on	nettoierait
nous	nettoierions
vous	nettoieriez
ils/elles	nettoieraient

Il nettoierait le grenier s'il avait le courage.
He'd clean the attic if he had the heart.

Verbs ending in -ayer, such as payer (meaning *to pay*) and essayer (meaning *to try*), can be spelled with either a y or an i. So je paierais and je payerais, for example, are both correct.

With verbs such as lever (meaning *to raise*), peser (meaning *to weigh*) and acheter (meaning *to buy*), e changes to è throughout the conditional. In lever the first e sounds like the vowel sound at the end of the English word *teacher*, but in lèverais and so on the first e sounds like the one in the English word *pet*.

For further explanation of grammatical terms, please see pages 8-11.

Pronoun	Example verb: lever
je	lèverais
tu	lèverais
il/elle/on	lèverait
nous	lèverions
vous	lèveriez
ils/elles	lèveraient

Nous lèverions la main si nous n'étions pas si timides.
We'd put our hands up if we weren't so shy.
Je lèverais la vitre s'il ne faisait pas si chaud dans cette voiture.
I'd wind up the window if it weren't so hot in this car.

Reflexive verbs in the conditional

The conditional of reflexive verbs is formed in just the same way as for ordinary verbs, except that you have to remember to give the reflexive pronoun (me, te, se, nous, vous, se).

Subject pronoun	Reflexive pronoun	Example with laver	Meaning
je	me (m')	laverais	I would wash
tu	te (t')	laverais	you would wash
il/elle/on	se (s')	laverait	he/she/it would wash
nous	nous	laverions	we would wash
vous	vous	laveriez	you would wash
ils/elles	se (s')	laveraient	they would wash

Je me laverais si la douche fonctionnait.   I'd wash if the shower worked.

Irregular verbs in the conditional

The same verbs that are irregular in the future tense are irregular in the conditional, including: avoir, être, faire, aller, devoir, pouvoir, savoir, tenir, venir, voir, vouloir.

To form the conditional of an irregular verb, use the same stem as for the future tense, for example: avoir > aur, -être > ser-

Then add the usual endings for the conditional.

Infinitive	Future stem	Conditional endings	Conditional form
avoir	aur-	-ais, -ais, -ait, -ions, -iez, -aient	j'aurais, tu aurais, il/elle/on aurait, nous aurions, vous auriez, ils/elles auraient
être	ser-	-ais, -ais, -ait, -ions, -iez, -aient	je serais, tu serais, il/elle/on serait, nous serions, vous seriez, ils/elles seraient
faire	fer-	-ais, -ais, -ait, -ions, -iez, -aient	je ferais, tu ferais, il/elle/on ferait nous ferions, vous feriez, ils/elles feraient
aller	ir-	-ais, -ais, -ait, -ions, -iez, -aient	j'irais, tu irais, il/elle/on irait, nous irions, vous iriez, ils/elles iraient

J'irais si j'avais le temps.   I would go if I had time.
Je voudrais un kilo de poires, s'il vous plaît.   I'd like a kilo of pears, please.
Tu devrais t'excuser.   You should say you're sorry.

The most important irregular verbs are shown in full in the **Verb Tables** at the back of the book.

For further explanation of grammatical terms, please see pages 8-11.

The perfect tense

Forming the perfect tense

The imperfect, future and conditional tenses in French are made up of just <u>one</u> word, for example, **je donne**, **tu finissais** or **il attendra**. The perfect tense has <u>two</u> parts to it:

- the <u>present</u> tense of the verb **avoir** (meaning *to have*) or **être** (meaning *to be*)
- a part of the main verb called the <u>past participle</u>, like *given*, *finished* and *done* in English

In other words, the perfect tense in French is like the form *I have done* in English.

For more information on forming the present tense of avoir and être, look in the **Verb Tables** at the back of the book.

Forming the past participle

To form the past participle of regular verbs, you use the <u>infinitive</u> of the verb. For **-er** verbs, you replace the **-er** at the end of the infinitive with **é**.

Infinitive	Take off -er	Add -é
donner (*to give*)	donn-	donn<u>é</u>
tomber (*to fall*)	tomb-	tomb<u>é</u>

For **-ir** verbs, you replace the **-ir** at the end of the infinitive with **-i**.

Infinitive	Take off -ir	Add -i
finir (*to finish*)	fin-	fin<u>i</u>
partir (*to leave, to go*)	part-	part<u>i</u>

For -re verbs, you replace the -re at the end of the infinitive with -u.

Infinitive	Take off -re	Add -u
attendre (*to wait*)	attend-	attend<u>u</u>
descendre (*to go down, to come down, to get off*)	descend-	descend<u>u</u>

Verbs that form their perfect tense with avoir

Most verbs form their perfect tense with avoir, for example donner:

Pronoun	avoir	Past participle	Meaning
j'	ai	donné	I gave I have given
tu	as	donné	you gave you have given
il/elle/on	a	donné	he/she/it/one gave he/she/it/one has given
nous	avons	donné	we gave we have given
vous	avez	donné	you gave you have given
ils/elles	ont	donné	they gave they have given

Elle a donné son numéro de téléphone à Claude.
She gave Claude her phone number.
Il a acheté un ordinateur.   He's bought a computer.
Je n'ai pas regardé la télé hier.   I didn't watch TV yesterday.

For further explanation of grammatical terms, please see pages 8-11.

The perfect tense of -ir verbs like finir is formed in the same way, except for the past participle: j'ai fini, tu as fini and so on.

The perfect tense of -re verbs like attendre is formed in the same way, except for the past participle: j'ai attendu, tu as attendu and so on.

avoir or être?

MOST verbs form their perfect tense with avoir.

There are two main groups of verbs which form their perfect tense with être instead of avoir:

- all reflexive verbs
- a group of verbs that are mainly used to talk about movement or a change of some kind, including these ones:

aller   to go
Je suis allé au match de football hier.
I went to the football match yesterday.
venir   to come
arriver   to arrive, to happen
partir   to leave, to go
descendre   to go down, to come down, to get off
Vous êtes descendu à quelle station?   Which station did you get off at?
monter   to go up, to come up
entrer   to go in, to come in
sortir   to go out, to come out
Il est sorti acheter un journal.   He's gone out to buy a newspaper.
mourir   to die
naître   to be born
devenir   to become
rester   to stay
tomber   to fall

Some verbs take avoir when they are used with a direct object, for example:

> descendre quelque chose
> to get something down, to bring something down, to take something down
> Est-ce que tu as descendu les bagages? Did you bring the bags down?
> monter quelque chose to go up something, to come up something
> Elle a monté les escaliers. She went up the stairs.
> sortir quelque chose to take something out
> Elle a sorti son porte-monnaie de son sac.
> She took her purse out of her handbag.

Verbs that form their perfect tense with être

When a verb takes être, the past participle <u>ALWAYS</u> agrees with the subject of the verb; that is, the endings change in the feminine and plural forms.

	Masculine endings	Examples	Feminine endings	Examples
Singular	-	tombé parti descendu	-e	tombé<u>e</u> part<u>ie</u> descendu<u>e</u>
Plural	-s	tombé<u>s</u> parti<u>s</u> descendu<u>s</u>	-es	tombé<u>es</u> part<u>ies</u> descendu<u>es</u>

> Est-ce ton frère est <u>allé</u> à l'étranger? Did your brother go abroad?
> Elle est <u>venue</u> avec nous. She came with us.
> Ils sont <u>partis</u> à six heures. They left at six o'clock.
> Mes cousines sont <u>arrivées</u> hier.
> My cousins arrived yesterday. (*The cousins are female.*)

Here are the perfect tense forms of tomber in full:

Pronoun	avoir	Past participle	Meaning
je	suis	tombé (*masculine*) tombée (*feminine*)	I fell/I have fallen
tu	es	tombé (*masculine*) tombée (*feminine*)	you fell/you have fallen
il	est	tombé	he/it fell, he/it has fallen
elle	est	tombée	she/it fell, she/it has fallen
on	est	tombé (*singular*) tombés (*masculine plural*) tombées (*feminine plural*)	one fell/one has fallen, we fell/we have fallen
nous	sommes	tombés (*masculine*) tombées (*feminine*)	we fell/we have fallen
vous	êtes	tombé (*masculine singular*) tombée (*feminine singular*) tombés (*masculine plural*) tombées (*feminine plural*)	you fell/you have fallen
ils	sont	tombés	they fell/they have fallen
elles	sont	tombées	they fell/they have fallen

When on means *we*, the past participle can agree with the subject of the sentence, but it is optional.

> On est <u>arrivés</u> en retard.   We arrived late. (*masculine*)
> On est <u>rentrées</u> toutes les deux à la même heure.
> We both came in at the same time. (*feminine*)

The perfect tense of -ir verbs like partir is formed in the same way, except for the past participle: je suis parti(e), tu es parti(e) and so on.

The perfect tense of -re verbs like descendre is formed in the same way, except for the past participle: je suis descendu(e), tu es descendu(e) and so on.

When a verb takes avoir, the past participle usually stays in the masculine singular form, as shown in the table for donner, and does not change for the feminine or plural forms.

> Il a <u>fini</u> sa dissertation.   He's finished his essay.
> Elles ont <u>fini</u> leur dissertation.   They've finished their essay.

In one particular case, however, the past participle of verbs with avoir does change in the feminine and plural forms. In the sentences above, dissertation is the direct object of the verb finir. When the direct object comes <u>AFTER</u> the verb, as it does in the examples above, then the past participle doesn't change. If the direct object comes <u>BEFORE</u> the verb, however, the past participle has to change to agree with that direct object.

> la dissertation qu'il a fini<u>e</u> hier   the essay that he finished yesterday
> la dissertation qu'elles ont fini<u>e</u> hier   the essay that they finished yesterday

Since object pronouns usually come BEFORE the verb, the past participle changes to agree with the pronoun.

> Il a bu son thé? – Oui, il l'a <u>bu</u>.   Did he drink his tea? – Yes, he's drunk it.
> Il a bu sa limonade? – Oui, il l'a <u>bue</u>.
> Did he drink his lemonade? – Yes, he's drunk it.

Remember that with verbs taking être, it is the <u>subject</u> of the verb that tells you what ending to add to the past participle. Compare this with the rule for verbs taking avoir that have a direct object; in their case, it is the <u>direct object</u> coming before the verb that tells you what ending to add to the past participle.

The perfect tense of reflexive verbs

Here is the perfect tense of the reflexive verb se laver (meaning *to wash (oneself)*, *to have a wash, to get washed*) in full. Remember that all reflexive verbs take être, and so the past participle of reflexive verbs usually agrees with the subject of the sentence.

For further explanation of grammatical terms, please see pages 8-11.

Subject pronoun	Reflexive pronoun	Present tense of être	Past participle	Meaning
je	me	suis	lavé (*masculine*) lavée (*feminine*)	I washed myself
tu	t'	es	lavé (*masculine*) lavée (*feminine*)	you washed yourself
il	s'	est	lavé	he washed himself one washed oneself
elle	s'	est	lavée	she washed herself
on	s'	est	lavé (*singular*) lavés (*masculine plural*) lavées (*feminine plural*)	one washed oneself we washed ourselves
nous	nous	sommes	lavés (*masculine*) lavées (*feminine*)	we washed ourselves
vous	vous	êtes	lavé (*masculine singular*) lavée (*feminine singular*) lavés (*masculine plural*) lavées (*feminine plural*)	you washed yourself (*singular*) you washed yourselves (*plural*)
ils	se	sont	lavés	they washed themselves
elles	se	sont	lavées	they washed themselves

When on means *we*, the past participle can agree with the subject of the sentence, but it is optional.

> On s'est <u>lavées</u> l'une après l'autre.
> We washed ourselves one after the other. (*feminine*)

The past participle of reflexive verbs <u>DOES NOT</u> change if the direct object (la jambe in the example below) <u>FOLLOWS</u> the verb.

> Elle s'est cassé la jambe.   She's broken her leg.

Irregular verbs in the perfect tense

Some past participles are irregular. There aren't too many, so try to learn them.

avoir (meaning *to have*)	> eu
devoir (meaning *to have to, must*)	> dû
dire (meaning *to say, to tell*)	> dit
être (meaning *to be*)	> été
faire (meaning *to do, to make*)	> fait
mettre (meaning *to put*)	> mis
pouvoir (meaning *to be able to, can*)	> pu
prendre (meaning *to take*)	> pris
savoir (meaning *to know*)	> su
tenir (meaning *to hold*)	> tenu
venir (meaning *to come*)	> venu
voir (meaning *to see*)	> vu
vouloir (meaning *to want*)	> voulu

> J'ai pris le bus pour venir au travail.   I took the bus to get in to work.
> Elle ne l'a su qu'au dernier moment.   She only knew at the last moment.
> Tu as vu ce film quatre fois, tu ne veux pas changer?
> You've seen this movie four times, wouldn't you like to watch something else?
> As-tu fait bon voyage?   Did you have a safe journey?
> Nous sommes venus à pied.   We've come on foot.

il pleut becomes il a plu (*it rained*).
il faut becomes il a fallu (*it was necessary*).

The most important irregular verbs are shown in full in the **Verb Tables** at the back of the book.

For further explanation of grammatical terms, please see pages 8-11.

The pluperfect tense

Forming the pluperfect tense

Like the perfect tense, the pluperfect tense in French has <u>two</u> parts to it:

- the <u>imperfect</u> tense of the verb avoir (meaning *to have*) or être (meaning *to be*)
- the past participle

If a verb takes avoir in the perfect tense, then it will take avoir in the pluperfect too. If a verb takes être in the perfect, then it will take être in the pluperfect too.

Verbs taking avoir

Here are the pluperfect tense forms of donner (meaning *to give*) in full.

Pronoun	avoir	Past participle	Meaning
j'	avais	donné	I had given
tu	avais	donné	you had given
il/elle/on	avait	donné	he/she/it/one had given
nous	avions	donné	we had given
vous	aviez	donné	you had given
ils/elles	avaient	donné	they had given

J'avais donné ce collier à ma nièce. I'd given this necklace to my niece.

Elle avait porté le sac pendant trois heures et maintenant elle était fatiguée.
She'd carried the bag for three hours and now she was exhausted.

Nous avions oublié de leur donner un plan.
We'd forgotten to give them a map.

Je n'avais pas entendu ce qu'il avait dit. I hadn't heard what he had said.

The pluperfect tense of -ir verbs like finir (meaning *to finish*) is formed in the same way, except for the past participle: j'avais fini, tu avais fini and so on.

The pluperfect tense of -re verbs like attendre (meaning *to wait*) is formed in the same way, except for the past participle: j'avais attendu, tu avais attendu and so on.

Verbs taking être

Here are the pluperfect tense forms of tomber (meaning *to fall*) in full. When a verb takes être in the pluperfect tense, the past participle <u>always</u> agrees with the subject of the verb; that is, the endings change in the feminine and plural forms.

Pronoun	être	Past participle	Meaning
j'	étais	tombé (*masculine*) tombée (*feminine*)	I had fallen
tu	étais	tombé (*masculine*) tombée (*feminine*)	you had fallen
il	était	tombé	he/it had fallen
elle	était	tombée	she/it had fallen
on	était	tombé (*singular*) tombés (*masculine plural*) tombées (*feminine plural*)	one had fallen we had fallen
nous	étions	tombés (*masculine*) tombées (*feminine*)	we had fallen
vous	étiez	tombé (*masculine singular*) tombée (*feminine singular*) tombés (*masculine plural*) tombées (*feminine plural*)	you had fallen
ils	étaient	tombés	they had fallen
elles	étaient	tombées	they had fallen

Elle était tombée dans l'escalier.   She had fallen down the stairs.

Nous étions venus dire au revoir à la famille.

We had come to say goodbye to the family.

Elles étaient arrivées avec un jour de retard.   They had arrived a day late.

The pluperfect tense of -ir verbs like partir (meaning *to leave, to go*) is formed in the same way, except for the past participle: j'étais parti(e), tu étais parti(e) and so on.

The pluperfect tense of -re verbs like descendre (meaning *to come down, to go down, to get off*) is formed in the same way, except for the past participle: j'étais descendu(e), tu étais descendu(e) and so on.

Reflexive verbs in the pluperfect tense

Reflexive verbs in the pluperfect tense are formed in the same way as in the perfect tense, but with the imperfect tense of the verb être.

Nous nous étions levés deux heures plus tôt.

We'd got up two hours earlier.

Elle s'était regardée dans le miroir.   She had looked at herself in the mirror.

Elle s'était cassé le bras.   She'd broken her arm.

Je n'avais pas entendu ce qu'elles s'étaient dit.

I hadn't heard what they had said to each other.

Irregular verbs in the pluperfect tense

Irregular past participles are the same as for the perfect tense. The pluperfect tense of many irregular verbs is shown in the **Verb Tables** at the back of the book.

The past historic tense

Forming the past historic tense of -er verbs

To form the past historic tense of -er verbs, you use the same stem of the verb as for the present tense. Then you add the correct ending, depending on whether you are referring to je, tu, il, elle, on, nous, vous, ils or elles.

Pronoun	Ending	Add to stem, e.g. donn-	Meanings
je (j')	-ai	je donnai	I gave
tu	-as	tu donnas	you gave
il	-a	il donna	
elle		elle donna	
on		on donna	he/she/it/one gave
nous	-âmes	nous donnâmes	we gave
vous	-âtes	vous donnâtes	you gave
ils	-èrent	ils donnèrent	
elles		elles donnèrent	they gave

Nous donnâmes un peu d'argent aux mendiants.
We gave a little money to the beggars.
Il me regarda avec anxiété.   He looked at me anxiously.

Forming the past historic tense of -ir and -re verbs

To form the past historic tense of -ir and -re verbs, you use the same stem of the verb as for the present tense. Then you add the correct ending, depending on whether you are referring to je, tu, il, elle, on, nous, vous, ils or elles. The je, tu and il/elle/on forms of regular -ir verbs are the same in the past historic as in the present tense (je finis, tu finis, il/elle/on finit).

For further explanation of grammatical terms, please see pages 8-11.

Pronoun	Ending	Add to stem, e.g. fin-, attend-	Meanings
je (j')	-is	je fini<u>s</u>	I finished
		j'attendi<u>s</u>	I waited
tu	-is	tu fini<u>s</u>	you finished
		tu attendi<u>s</u>	you waited
il	-it	il/elle/on fini<u>t</u>	he/she/it/one finished
elle/on		il/elle/on attendi<u>t</u>	he/she/it/one waited
nous	-îmes	nous fin<u>î</u>mes	we finished
		nous attend<u>î</u>mes	we waited
vous	-îtes	vous fin<u>î</u>tes	you finished
		vous attend<u>î</u>tes	you waited
ils	-irent	ils/elles fini<u>rent</u>	they finished
elles		ils/elles attendi<u>rent</u>	they waited

Il <u>finit</u> son repas et <u>sortit</u> de la pièce.   He finished his meal and left the room.
Elles <u>attendirent</u> leurs parents devant la gare.
They waited for their parents outside the station.

Spelling changes in -er verbs

As with the present tense, a few -er verbs change their spellings slightly when they are used in the past historic. The forms with spelling changes have been <u>underlined</u> in the tables.

With verbs such as lancer (meaning *to throw*), which end in -cer, c becomes ç before an a or an o. This is so that the letter c is still pronounced as in the English word *ice*.

Pronoun	Example verb: lancer
je	lançai
tu	lanças
il/elle/on	lança
nous	lançâmes
vous	lançâtes
ils/elles	lancèrent

Il commença à pleuvoir.   It started to rain.

Il annonça son mariage ce jour-là.   He announced his wedding that day.

With verbs such as manger (meaning *to eat*), which end in -ger, g becomes ge before an a or an o. This is so that the letter g is still pronounced like the s in the English word *leisure*.

Pronoun	Example verb: manger
je	mangeai
tu	mangeas
il/elle/on	mangea
nous	mangeâmes
vous	mangeâtes
ils/elles	mangèrent

Il chargea les bagages dans le coffre.   He loaded the luggage into the boot.

Nous changeâmes d'avis au dernier moment.

We changed our minds at the last moment.

Elle mangea tant de chocolat qu'elle ne se sentit pas bien.

She ate so much chocolate that she didn't feel well.

Reflexive verbs in the past historic tense

The past historic tense of reflexive verbs is formed just as for ordinary verbs, except that you add the reflexive pronoun (me, te, se, nous, vous, se).

Subject pronoun	Reflexive pronoun	Example with laver	Meaning
je	me (m')	lavai	I washed
tu	te (t')	lavas	you washed
il/elle/on	se (s')	lava	he/she/it/one washed
nous	nous	lavâmes	we washed
vous	vous	lavâtes	you washed
ils/elles	se (s')	lavèrent	they washed

Irregular verbs in the past historic tense

There are some verbs that <u>do not</u> use their present tense stem as the stem for the past historic tense, including avoir, être and faire. These verbs are shown in full in the **Verb Tables** at the back of the book.

The present participle

Forming the present participle

To form the present participle of regular -er, -ir and -re verbs, you use the nous form of the present tense and replace the -ons ending with -ant.

nous form of present tense	Take off -ons	Add -ant
donnons	donn-	donnant
lançons	lanç-	lançant
mangeons	mange-	mangeant
finissons	finiss-	finissant
partons	part-	partant
attendons	attend-	attendant
descendons	descend-	descendant

Il s'est fait mal en lançant la balle.   He hurt himself throwing the ball.
J'ai décidé de lire en attendant.   I decided to read while I was waiting.
Nous chantions en finissant de ranger.   We sang while we finished tidying up.

Irregular verbs

Three verbs have an irregular present participle:

avoir (meaning *to have*)   > ayant
Ayant cinq ans de plus que nous, elle avait plus d'expérience.
Being five years older than we were, she had more experience.
être (meaning *to be*)   > étant
Il gagne sa vie en étant musicien.   He makes a living being a musician.
savoir (meaning *to know*)   > sachant
Ne sachant pas quoi faire, il décida de demander conseil.
Not knowing what to do, he decided to ask for advice.

For further explanation of grammatical terms, please see pages 8-11.

The subjunctive

Forming the present subjunctive of -er verbs

To form the stem of the present subjunctive you take the <u>infinitive</u> and chop off -er, just as for the present tense. Then you add the correct ending, depending on whether you are referring to je, tu, il, elle, on, nous, vous, ils or elles.

For -er verbs the endings are the same as for the ordinary present tense, apart from the nous and vous forms, which have an extra i, as in the imperfect tense.

Pronoun	Ending	Add to stem, e.g. donn-	Meanings
je (j')	-e	je donne	I give
tu	-es	tu donnes	you give
il elle on	-e	il donne elle donne on donne	he/she/it/one gives
nous	-ions	nous donnions	we give
vous	-iez	vous donniez	you give
ils elles	-ent	ils donnent elles donnent	they give

Il faudrait que nous donnions des renseignements précis.
We must give precise information.
J'attends que tu changes la roue.   I'm waiting for you to change the tyre.
J'aimerais que vous arrêtiez de faire du bruit.
I'd like you to stop making a noise.

Forming the present subjunctive of -ir verbs

To form the stem of the present subjunctive you take the <u>infinitive</u> and chop off -ir, just as for the present tense. Then you add the correct ending, depending on whether you are referring to to je, tu, il, elle, on, nous, vous, ils or elles.

Pronoun	Ending	Add to stem, e.g. fin-	Meanings
je (j')	-isse	je fin<u>isse</u>	I finish
tu	-isses	tu fin<u>isses</u>	you finish
il elle on	-isse	il fin<u>isse</u> elle fin<u>isse</u> on fin<u>isse</u>	he/she/it/one finishes
nous	-issions	nous fin<u>issions</u>	we finish
vous	-issiez	vous fin<u>issiez</u>	you finish
ils elles	-issent	ils fin<u>issent</u> elles fin<u>issent</u>	they finish

Ils refusent que vous finissiez plus tôt ce soir.
They refuse to let you finish earlier tonight.
Je voudrais qu'ils réfléchissent à ce problème.
I want them to give this problem some thought.
Nous voulons que tu choisisses ce qui te plaît.
We want you to choose what you like.

Forming the present subjunctive of -re verbs

To form the stem of the present subjunctive you take the <u>infinitive</u> and chop off
-re, just as for the present tense. Then you add the correct ending, depending on
whether you are referring to je, tu, il, elle, on, nous, vous, ils or elles.

Pronoun	Ending	Add to stem, e.g. attend-	Meanings
je (j')	-e	j'attend<u>e</u>	I wait
tu	-es	tu attend<u>es</u>	you wait
il	-e	il attend<u>e</u>	he/she/it/one waits
elle		elle attend<u>e</u>	
on		on attend<u>e</u>	
nous	-ions	nous attend<u>ions</u>	we wait
vous	-iez	vous attend<u>iez</u>	you wait
ils	-ent	ils attend<u>ent</u>	they wait
elles		elles attend<u>ent</u>	

Je ne veux pas que tu m'attendes dans le froid.

I don't want you to wait for me in the cold.

Il souhaite que nous vendions la maison.

He would like us to sell the house.

Il faut que nous descendions dans la cour pour les voir.

We have to go down to the playground to see them.

Verb Combinations

Verbs followed by an infinitive with no preposition

A number of verbs and groups of verbs can be followed by an infinitive with no preposition. The infinitive is the form of the verb that is found in the dictionary, such as donner (meaning *to give*), finir (meaning *to finish*) and attendre (meaning *to wait*). The following important group of verbs are all very irregular, but they crop up so frequently that they are worth learning in full:

devoir (*to have to, must, to be due to*)
Tu dois être fatiguée.   You must be tired.
Elle doit partir.   She has to leave.
Le nouveau centre commercial doit ouvrir en mai.
The new shopping centre is due to open in May.

pouvoir (*can, may*)
Je peux t'aider, si tu veux.   I can help you, if you like.
Puis-je venir vous voir samedi?   May I come and see you on Saturday?

savoir (*to know how to, can*)
Tu sais conduire?   Can you drive?
Je sais faire les omelettes.   I know how to make omelettes.

vouloir (*to want*)
Élise veut rester un jour de plus.   Élise wants to stay one more day.
Ma voiture ne veut pas démarrer.   My car won't start.
Voulez-vous boire quelque chose?   Would you like something to drink?
Je voudrais acheter un ordinateur.   I'd like to buy a computer.

falloir (meaning *to be necessary*) and valoir mieux (meaning *to be better*) are only used in the infinitive and with il.
Il faut prendre une décision.   We/you *etc*. have to make a decision.
Il vaut mieux téléphoner avant.   It's better to ring first.

For further explanation of grammatical terms, please see pages 8-11.

The following common verbs can also be followed by an infinitive <u>without</u> a preposition:

adorer (to love)
J'adore regarder la mer.   I love looking at the sea.

aimer (to like, to love)
Elle aimait jouer du piano.   She loved playing the piano.

aimer mieux (to prefer)
J'aimerais mieux aller à la montagne cette année.
I'd prefer to go to the mountains this year.

désirer (to want)
Il désire améliorer son espagnol.   He wants to improve his Spanish.

détester (to hate)
Elle déteste faire la vaisselle.   She hates doing the dishes.

envoyer (to send)
Il l'avait envoyée acheter du pain.   He'd sent her to buy some bread.

espérer (to hope)
J'espère te voir la semaine prochaine.   I hope to see you next week.

faire (to make, to have something done) that is, faire faire quelque chose
Ne me fais pas rire!   Don't make me laugh!
J'ai fait réparer mes chaussures.   I've had my shoes mended.

laisser (to let)
Il m'a laissé m'occuper des animaux tout seul.
He left me to look after the animals on my own.

préférer (*to prefer*)
Je préfère manger à la cantine.   I prefer to eat in the canteen.

sembler (*to seem*)
Elle semblait ne jamais s'inquiéter de rien.
She seemed never to worry about anything.

Some of these verbs combine with infinitives to make set phrases with a special meaning.

aller chercher quelque chose   to go and get something
Va chercher ton papa!   Go and get your dad!

laisser tomber quelque chose   to drop something
Paul a laissé tomber le vase.   Paul dropped the vase.

vouloir dire quelque chose   to mean something
Qu'est-ce que ça veut dire?   What does that mean?

Verbs that relate to seeing or hearing, such as voir (meaning *to see*), regarder (meaning *to watch*, *to look at*), écouter (meaning *to listen to*) and entendre (meaning *to hear*) can be followed by an infinitive.

Il nous a vus arriver.   He saw us arrive.
On entend chanter les oiseaux.   You can hear the birds singing.

Verbs that relate to movement of some kind and do not have a direct object, such as aller (meaning *to go*) and venir (meaning *to come*), can be followed by an infinitive.

Je vais voir Nicolas ce soir.   I'm going to see Nicolas tonight.
Viens voir!   Come and see!

Verbs followed by à + infinitive

There are some common verbs that can be followed by à and an infinitive.

s'amuser à faire quelque chose   to have fun doing something

Ils s'amusaient à jeter des cailloux dans la mare.
They had fun throwing stones in the pond.
Elles se sont amusées à repeindre sa voiture en rose.
They had fun painting his car pink.

apprendre à faire quelque chose   to learn to do something

J'apprends à skier.   I'm learning to ski.
Nous avons appris à faire un site internet.   We learned to make a website.
Elle apprendra à lire dans deux ans.   She'll learn how to read in two years.

commencer à faire quelque chose   to begin to do something

Il a commencé à pleuvoir.   It began to rain.
As-tu commencé à faire tes valises?   Have you begun packing yet?
J'ai commencé à lire le livre que tu m'as donné.
I have started reading the book that you've given to me.

continuer à faire quelque chose   to go on doing something

Il a continué à discuter.   He went on talking.
Il continuera à jouer du violon.   He'll keep on playing the violin.

s'habituer à faire quelque chose   to get used to doing something

Nous nous habituons à nous lever tôt.
We're getting used to getting up early.
Ils se sont habitués au froid.   They've got used to the cold.

Some verbs can be followed by a person's name or by a noun relating to a person, and then by à and an infinitive. Sometimes you need to put à in front of the person too.

aider quelqu'un <u>à</u> faire quelque chose   to help someone do something

Elle m'a aidé à fermer le magasin.   She helped me close up the shop.
Nous les avons aidées à pousser la voiture.   We helped them push the car.

apprendre <u>à</u> quelqu'un <u>à</u> faire quelque chose
to teach someone to do something

Il m'avait appris à pêcher.   He had taught me to fish.
Il a appris à sa fille à cuisiner.   He taught his daughter to cook.

inviter quelqu'un <u>à</u> faire quelque chose   to invite someone to do something

Elle l'a invité à prendre la parole.   She invited him to speak.
Il l'avait invitée à danser.   He'd invited her to dance.

Verbs followed by à + object

These are some common verbs that can be followed by à and an object: the person or thing that the verb 'happens' to. à is often the equivalent of the English word *to* when it is used with an indirect object after verbs like *send*, *give* and *say*.

dire quelque chose à quelqu'un to say something <u>to</u> someone

Elle m'a dit la vérité. She told me the truth.
Il dira son secret à ses petits-enfants.
He will tell his secret to his grandchildren.

donner quelque chose à quelqu'un to give something <u>to</u> someone

Elle a donné son adresse à ses cousins. She gave her address to her cousins.
Ça me donne faim. That makes me feel hungry.

écrire quelque chose à quelqu'un to write something <u>to</u> someone

Elle a écrit une lettre à son acteur préféré.
She wrote a letter to her favourite actor.
Nous nous écrivons régulièrement. We write to each other regularly.

envoyer quelque chose à quelqu'un to send something <u>to</u> someone

Il enverra un e-mail à ses parents. He'll send his parents an e-mail.
Ma tante m'a envoyé une carte pour mon anniversaire.
My aunt sent me a card for my birthday.

montrer quelque chose à quelqu'un to show something <u>to</u> someone

Elle montre ses dessins à sa mère. She shows her drawings to her mother.
Ils nous ont montré une vieille église. They showed us an old church.

Here are some verbs taking à in French that have a different construction in English.

croire **à** quelque chose   to believe _in_ something

Ils ne croient plus à la paix.   They no longer believe in peace.

s'intéresser **à** quelqu'un/quelque chose
to be interested _in_ someone/something

Est-ce que vous vous intéressez à la politique?
Are you interested in politics?
Elle s'intéresse de plus en plus à cet auteur.
She's more and more interested in this author.

jouer **à** quelque chose   to play something (_sports, games_)

Elle joue au tennis.   She plays tennis.
Ils jouent aux cartes depuis six heures.   They've been playing cards since six.

obéir **à** quelqu'un   to obey someone

Elle refuse d'obéir à ses parents.   She won't obey her parents.
Le cheval obéissait à tous les ordres de son maître.
The horse obeyed every single one of his master's commands.

penser **à** quelqu'un/quelque chose   to think _about_ someone/something

Il pense à elle chaque à chaque fois qu'il voit la mer.
He thinks about her every time he sees the sea.
Cette photo me fait penser à la Grèce.   This picture reminds me of Greece.
Je pense à mes vacances.   I'm thinking about my holidays.

répondre **à** quelqu'un   to answer someone

Elle a demandé à nouveau mais il ne voulait pas lui répondre.
She asked again but he wouldn't reply.
Tu ne m'as toujours pas répondu.   You still haven't answered me.

For further explanation of grammatical terms, please see pages 8-11.

téléphoner à quelqu'un   to phone someone

Je téléphonerai à Marie.   I'll phone Marie.

Nous avons des nouvelles de Marie, nous lui avons téléphoné hier.

We've got news from Marie, we phoned her yesterday.

plaire followed by à is a common way of saying you like something.

plaire à quelqu'un   to please someone (*literally*)

Ton cadeau me plaît beaucoup.   I like your present a lot.

Ce film plaît beaucoup aux jeunes.

This film is very popular with young people.

Cette région plaît beaucoup aux britanniques.

This area is very popular with the British.

Ce chapeau lui plaisait beaucoup.   He liked this hat very much.

Elle lui plaît.   He fancies her.

manquer à works quite differently from its English equivalent, *to miss*. The English object is the French subject, and the English subject is the French object.

manquer à quelqu'un   to be missed by someone (*literally*)

Tu (*subject*) me (*object*) manques.   I (*subject*) miss you (*object*).

Mon pays (*subject*) me (*object*) manque beaucoup.

I (*subject*) miss my country (*object*) very much.

Elle manque à sa famille.   Her family miss her.

Mes parents me manquent.   I miss my parents.

There are also some verbs where you can put a direct object before à. The verb demander is the most common.

demander quelque chose à quelqu'un

to ask someone something, to ask someone for something

Demandons l'addition au serveur.   Let's ask the waiter for the bill.

Verbs followed by de + infinitive

There are some common verbs that can be followed by de and an infinitive.

arrêter de faire quelque chose, s'arrêter de faire quelque chose
to stop doing something

Il voudrait arrêter de fumer.   He'd like to stop smoking.
Il n'a pas arrêté de parler.   He didn't stop talking.
Ils se sont arrêtés de jouer.   They stopped playing.

commencer de faire quelque chose   to start doing something

J'ai commencé de lire ce livre.   I've started reading this book.
As-tu commencé de réviser?   Have you started revising?

continuer de faire quelque chose   to go on doing something

Ils continuent de se voir.   They still see each other.
Continueras-tu de m'écrire?   Will you keep writing to me?

décider de faire quelque chose   to decide to do something

J'ai décidé de lui écrire.   I decided to write to her.
J'ai décidé de ne plus venir au cours.   I've decided to stop going to the class.

se dépêcher de faire quelque chose   to hurry to do something

Dépêche-toi de finir ton petit-déjeuner!
Hurry up and finish your breakfast!

essayer de faire quelque chose   to try to do something

J'ai essayé de t'appeler mais la ligne était occupée.
I tried to ring you but the line was engaged.
Essaie d'aller les voir à Noël.   Try to visit them at Christmas.

s'excuser d'avoir fait quelque chose   to apologize for doing something

Nous nous sommes excusés d'avoir fait tant de bruit.
We apologized for making so much noise.

finir de faire quelque chose   to finish doing something

Il a fini de ranger les assiettes mais il doit laver les verres.
He's finished putting away the plates but he still has to wash the glasses.
Elle finira de te lire cette histoire demain.
She'll finish reading you this story tomorrow.

oublier de faire quelque chose   to forget to do something

Elle a oublié de lui dire qu'elle ne viendra pas.
She forgot to tell him that she won't come.
Je n'oublierai plus jamais de lui souhaiter son anniversaire.
I'll never forget to wish her a happy birthday ever again.

proposer de faire quelque chose   to suggest doing something

Elle a proposé d'aller au restaurant.
She suggested going to the restaurant.
As-tu proposé un verre à nos invités?   Have you offered our guests a drink?

refuser de faire quelque chose   to refuse to do something

Il refuserait de venir s'il savait qui sera là.
He'd refuse to come if he knew who would be there.
Elle a refusé de jouer dans notre équipe.   She refused to play in our team.

suggérer de faire quelque chose   to suggest doing something

Je leur ai suggéré de partir de bonne heure.
I suggested that they set off early.
Comme il faisait beau, nous avons suggéré d'aller à la fête à pied.
As the weather was nice, we suggested going to the party on foot.
Beaucoup de gens étaient bloqués par la neige et ils ont suggéré de
remettre la réunion à demain.
Many people were snowbound and they suggested putting off the meeting
to the next day.

The following verbs meaning asking or telling are also followed by de and an infinitive. Sometimes you need to put à in front of the person you are asking or telling.

commander à quelqu'un de faire quelque chose
to order someone to do something

Malgré la tempête il a commandé à l'équipage de se rassembler sur le pont.
Despite the storm he ordered the crew to assemble on deck.

demander à quelqu'un de faire quelque chose
to ask someone to do something

J'ai demandé au plombier de venir à huit heures précises.
I asked the plumber to come at eight sharp.
Je te demanderai peut-être de m'aider à tailler la haie.
I might ask you to help me trim the hedge.

dire à quelqu'un de faire quelque chose   to tell someone to do something

Elle a dit à ses élèves de ne pas en parler.
She asked her students not to talk about it.
Il lui a dit de se lever.   He told him to get up.

empêcher quelqu'un de faire quelque chose
to prevent someone from doing something

Il m'empêchait d'aller au cinéma.   He wouldn't let me go to the cinema.
Le soleil l'empêchait de bien voir la route.
She couldn't see the road clearly because of the sunlight.

remercier quelqu'un de faire quelque chose
to thank someone for doing something

Elle a remercié ses amis d'être venus la voir à l'aéroport puis elle est
montée dans l'avion.
She thanked her friends for seeing her off at the airport and got on the plane.

Verbs followed by de + object

These are some common verbs that can be followed by de and an object:
the person or thing that the verb 'happens' to. Here are some verbs taking de in
French that have a different construction in English.

changer <u>de</u> quelque chose   to change something (*one's shoes and so on*)

Je change de chaussures et j'arrive!
I'll change my shoes and then I'll be ready!
Il a changé d'avis, il ne vient plus.
He's changed his mind, he's not coming anymore.

dépendre <u>de</u> quelqu'un/quelque chose   to depend <u>on</u> someone/something

Ça dépend du temps.   It depends on the weather.
Le goût du vin dépend aussi de son âge.
The taste of wine also depends on its age.

s'excuser <u>de</u> quelque chose   to apologize <u>for</u> something

Il s'est excusé de son retard.   He apologized for being late.
Elle s'excuse de son impolitesse.   She apologizes for her rudeness.

jouer <u>de</u> quelque chose   to play something

Il joue de la guitare et du piano.   He plays the guitar and the piano.

parler <u>de</u> quelque chose   to talk <u>about</u> something

Il a parlé de sa nouvelle voiture.   He talked about his new car.
Les choses dont elle parle ne m'intéressent pas.
I'm not interested in the things she talks about.

se servir <u>de</u> quelque chose   to use something

Je me suis servi de ta pelle.   I used your spade.
Elle s'est servie de sa voiture pour aller acheter du pain au village.
She used his car to go and buy some bread in the village.

se souvenir <u>de</u> quelqu'un/quelque chose
to remember someone/something

Je ne me souviens pas de son adresse.   I can't remember his address.
Ce professeur se souvient de toi.   This teacher remembers you.
Je ne m'en souviens plus.   I can't remember it any more.

Some common phrases using avoir also contain de.

<u>avoir</u> besoin <u>de</u> quelque chose   to need something

J'ai besoin de mon parapluie.   I need my umbrella.
Elle a besoin de lui.   She needs him.

<u>avoir</u> envie <u>de</u> quelque chose   to want something

J'ai envie de chocolat.   I want chocolate.

<u>avoir</u> peur <u>de</u> quelque chose   to be afraid of something

Il a peur du noir.   He's afraid of the dark.
Elle avait peur des serpents.   She was afraid of snakes.

There are also some verbs where you can put a direct object before de, remercier
is the most common.

remercier quelqu'un <u>de</u> quelque chose   to thank someone for something

Je l'ai remerciée de son aide.   I thanked her for her help.
Nous les avons remerciés de leur accueil.
We thanked them for their welcome.

Verbs taking a direct object in French but not in English

In English there are a few verbs that are followed by *for*, *on*, *in*, *to* or *at* which, in French, are not followed by a preposition such as à or de. Here are the most common:

attendre quelqu'un/quelque chose to wait <u>for</u> sb/sth

J'attends ce moment depuis longtemps.
I've been waiting a long time for this moment.
Je l'ai attendu dehors. I waited for him outside.

chercher quelqu'un/quelque chose to look <u>for</u> sb/sth

Je cherche mes clefs. I'm looking for my keys.
Je l'ai cherchée partout. I looked for her everywhere.

demander quelqu'un/quelque chose to ask <u>for</u> sb/sth

Pendant son premier jour à l'école, il ne cessait de demander sa mère.
Throughout his first day at school he kept asking for his mother.
J'ai demandé un crayon et du papier. I asked for a pen and some paper.

écouter quelqu'un/quelque chose to listen <u>to</u> sb/sth

Nous écoutions Serge chanter. We'd listen to Serge sing.
Ils écoutent le bruit de la pluie. They listen to the noise of the rain.

espérer quelque chose to hope <u>for</u> sth

Nous espérons un rétablissement rapide.
We're hoping for a prompt recovery.

payer quelque chose to pay <u>for</u> sth

Combien as-tu payé ta voiture? How much did you pay for your car?
Il a même payé le taxi. He even paid for the taxi.

regarder quelqu'un/quelque chose   to look at sb/sth

Il me regardait.   He was looking at me.
Elle regardait ses photos de vacances   She looked at his holiday pictures.

habiter can be used with or without a preposition.

habiter is mostly used <u>without a preposition</u> when you are talking about living in a house, a flat and so on.

Nous habitons un petit appartement en ville.
We live in a small flat in town.

Use habiter <u>with à</u> when you are talking about a town or city, and au (*singular*) or aux (*plural*) with the names of countries that are masculine in French.

Nous habitons <u>à</u> Liverpool.   We live in Liverpool.
Nous habitons <u>aux</u> États-Unis.   We live in the United States.
Il habite <u>à</u> Montpellier.   He lives in Montpellier.
Il habite <u>au</u> Canada.   He lives in Canada.

Use habiter <u>with en</u> when you are talking about feminine countries.

Nous habitons <u>en</u> Espagne.   We live in Spain.
Ils habitent <u>en</u> Nouvelle-Zélande.   They live in New Zealand.

VERB TABLES

Introduction

The **Verb Tables** in the following section contain 115 tables of French verbs (some regular and some irregular) in alphabetical order. Each table shows you the following forms: **Present, Present Subjunctive, Perfect, Imperfect Future, Conditional, Past Historic, Pluperfect, Imperative** and the **Present** and **Past Participles**. For more information on these tenses and how they are formed you should look at the section on Verb Formation in the main text on pages 12–65. If you want to find out in more detail how verbs are used in different contexts, the *Easy Learning French Grammar* will give you additional information.

In order to help you use the verbs shown in Verb Tables correctly, there are also a number of example phrases at the bottom of each page to show the verb as it is used in context.

In French there are both **regular** (their forms follow the normal rules) and **irregular** verbs (their forms do not follow the normal rules). The regular verbs in these tables are:

donner (regular **-er** verb, Verb Table 70)
finir (regular **-ir** verb, Verb Table 100)
attendre (regular **-re** verb, Verb Table 22)

The irregular verbs are shown in full.

The **Verb Index** at the end of this section contains over 2000 verbs, each of which is cross-referred to one of the verbs given in the Verb Tables. The table shows the patterns that the verb listed in the index follows.

acheter (to buy)

PRESENT

j'	**achète**
tu	**achètes**
il/elle/on	**achète**
nous	**achetons**
vous	**achetez**
ils/elles	**achètent**

PRESENT SUBJUNCTIVE

j'	**achète**
tu	**achètes**
il/elle/on	**achète**
nous	**achetions**
vous	**achetiez**
ils/elles	**achètent**

PERFECT

j'	**ai acheté**
tu	**as acheté**
il/elle/on	**a acheté**
nous	**avons acheté**
vous	**avez acheté**
ils/elles	**ont acheté**

IMPERFECT

j'	**achetais**
tu	**achetais**
il/elle/on	**achetait**
nous	**achetions**
vous	**achetiez**
ils/elles	**achetaient**

PRESENT PARTICIPLE

achetant

PAST PARTICIPLE

acheté

EXAMPLE PHRASES

Nous n'**achetons** jamais de chips. We never buy crisps.

Qu'est-ce que tu **as acheté**? What did you buy?

N'**achète** rien pour moi. Don't buy anything for me.

Il faut que j'**achète** un cadeau pour son anniversaire. I must buy a present for his birthday.

Ses parents lui **achetaient** des bonbons. His parents bought him sweets.

je/j' = I **tu** = you **il** = he/it **elle** = she/it **on** = we/one **nous** = we **vous** = you **ils/elles** = they

acheter

FUTURE

j'	**achèterai**
tU	**achèteras**
il/elle/on	**achètera**
nous	**achèterons**
vous	**achèterez**
ils/elles	**achèteront**

CONDITIONAL

j'	**achèterais**
tu	**achèterais**
il/elle/on	**achèterait**
nous	**achèterions**
vous	**achèteriez**
ils/elles	**achèteraient**

PAST HISTORIC

j'	**achetai**
tu	**achetas**
il/elle/on	**acheta**
nous	**achetâmes**
vous	**achetâtes**
ils/elles	**achetèrent**

PLUPERFECT

j'	**avais acheté**
tu	**avais acheté**
il/elle/on	**avait acheté**
nous	**avions acheté**
vous	**aviez acheté**
ils/elles	**avaient acheté**

IMPERATIVE

achète / achetons / achetez

EXAMPLE PHRASES

J'**achèterai** des gâteaux à la pâtisserie. I'll buy some cakes at the cake shop.

Elle **acheta** la robe rouge. She bought the red dress.

Si j'étais riche j'**achèterais** un voilier. If I were rich, I'd buy a yacht.

Il lui **avait acheté** une jolie robe, mais elle ne voulait pas la porter.
He'd bought her a nice dress, but she didn't want to wear it.

---

je/j' = I tu = you il = he/it elle = she/it on = we/one nous = we vous = you ils/elles = they

acquérir (to acquire)

PRESENT		**PRESENT SUBJUNCTIVE**	
j'	acquiers	j'	acquière
tu	acquiers	tu	acquières
il/elle/on	acquiert	il/elle/on	acquière
nous	acquérons	nous	acquérions
vous	acquérez	vous	acquériez
ils/elles	acquièrent	ils/elles	acquièrent

PERFECT		**IMPERFECT**	
j'	ai acquis	j'	acquérais
tu	as acquis	tu	acquérais
il/elle/on	a acquis	il/elle/on	acquérait
nous	avons acquis	nous	acquérions
vous	avez acquis	vous	acquériez
ils/elles	ont acquis	ils/elles	acquéraient

PRESENT PARTICIPLE
acquérant

PAST PARTICIPLE
acquis

EXAMPLE PHRASES

Nous **acquérons** de nouvelles connaissances tous les jours. We acquire new knowledge every day.

Les mauvaises habitudes s'**acquièrent** facilement. One easily acquires bad habits.

Elle **a acquis** la nationalité française en 2003. She acquired French nationality in 2003.

Il faut qu'il **acquière** de l'expérience avant que nous puissions lui offrir un travail. He has to gain some experience before we can offer him a job.

---

acquérir

FUTURE

j'	**acquerrai**
tu	**acquerras**
il/elle/on	**acquerra**
nous	**acquerrons**
vous	**acquerrez**
ils/elles	**acquerront**

CONDITIONAL

j'	**acquerrais**
tu	**acquerrais**
il/elle/on	**acquerrait**
nous	**acquerrions**
vous	**acquerriez**
ils/elles	**acquerraient**

PAST HISTORIC

j'	**acquis**
tu	**acquis**
il/elle/on	**acquit**
nous	**acquîmes**
vous	**acquîtes**
ils/elles	**acquirent**

PLUPERFECT

j'	**avais acquis**
tu	**avais acquis**
il/elle/on	**avait acquis**
nous	**avions acquis**
vous	**aviez acquis**
ils/elles	**avaient acquis**

IMPERATIVE

acquiers / acquérons / acquérez

EXAMPLE PHRASES

Elle **acquit** soudain la certitude qu'il lui avait toujours menti. She suddenly felt certain that he'd always lied to her.

Tu **acquerrais** un peu d'expérience si tu travaillais cet été. You'd gain some experience if you worked this summer.

Il **avait** mystérieusement **acquis** une superbe voiture de sport. He had mysteriously acquired a beautiful sportscar.

Le tableau **avait acquis** beaucoup de valeur. The painting had risen a lot in value.

je/j' = I **tu** = you **il** = he/it **elle** = she/it **on** = we/one **nous** = we **vous** = you **ils/elles** = they

aller (to go)

	PRESENT		PRESENT SUBJUNCTIVE
je	**vais**	j'	**aille**
tu	**vas**	tu	**ailles**
il/elle/on	**va**	il/elle/on	**aille**
nous	**allons**	nous	**allions**
vous	**allez**	vous	**alliez**
ils/elles	**vont**	ils/elles	**aillent**

	PERFECT		IMPERFECT
je	**suis allé(e)**	j'	**allais**
tu	**es allé(e)**	tu	**allais**
il/elle/on	**est allé(e)**	il/elle/on	**allait**
nous	**sommes allé(e)s**	nous	**allions**
vous	**êtes allé(e)(s)**	vous	**alliez**
ils/elles	**sont allé(e)s**	ils/elles	**allaient**

PRESENT PARTICIPLE	PAST PARTICIPLE
allant	allé

EXAMPLE PHRASES

Vous **allez** souvent au cinéma? Do you often go to the cinema?

Je **suis allé** à Londres. I went to London.

Est-ce que tu **es** déjà **allé** en Allemagne? Have you ever been to Germany?

Va voir s'ils sont arrivés. Go and see whether they have arrived.

Il faut que j'**aille** la chercher à la gare. I have to go and get her at the station.

J'**allais** tous les jours à l'école à pied. I would walk to school every day.

je/j' = I   **tu** = you   **il** = he/it   **elle** = she/it   **on** = we/one   **nous** = we   **vous** = you   **ils/elles** = they

aller

FUTURE

j'	**irai**
tu	**iras**
il/elle/on	**ira**
nous	**irons**
vous	**irez**
ils/elles	**iront**

CONDITIONAL

j'	**irais**
tu	**irais**
il/elle/on	**irait**
nous	**irions**
vous	**iriez**
ils/elles	**iraient**

PAST HISTORIC

j'	**allai**
tu	**allas**
il/elle/on	**alla**
nous	**allâmes**
vous	**allâtes**
ils/elles	**allèrent**

PLUPERFECT

j'	**étais allé(e)**
tu	**étais allé(e)**
il/elle/on	**était allé(e)**
nous	**étions allé(e)s**
vous	**étiez allé(e)(s)**
ils/elles	**étaient allé(e)s**

IMPERATIVE

va / allons / allez

EXAMPLE PHRASES

J'**irai** en ville demain. I'll go into town tomorrow.

Ils **allèrent** la voir à l'hôpital. They went to see her at the hospital.

J'**irais** au théâtre avec toi s'il restait des places. I'd go to the theatre with
you if there were any tickets left.

Nous **étions allés** à Paris en avion mais nous étions rentrés par le train.
We'd flown to Paris, but we'd come back by train.

s'amuser (to play; to enjoy oneself)

PRESENT		PRESENT SUBJUNCTIVE	
je	**m'amuse**	je	**m'amuse**
tu	**t'amuses**	tu	**t'amuses**
il/elle/on	**s'amuse**	il/elle/on	**s'amuse**
nous	**nous amusons**	nous	**nous amusions**
vous	**vous amusez**	vous	**vous amusiez**
ils/elles	**s'amusent**	ils/elles	**s'amusent**

PERFECT		IMPERFECT	
je	**me suis amusé(e)**	je	**m'amusais**
tu	**t'es amusé(e)**	tu	**t'amusais**
il/elle/on	**s'est amusé(e)**	il/elle/on	**s'amusait**
nous	**nous sommes amusé(e)s**	nous	**nous amusions**
vous	**vous êtes amusé(e)(s)**	vous	**vous amusiez**
ils/elles	**se sont amusé(e)s**	ils/elles	**s'amusaient**

PRESENT PARTICIPLE	PAST PARTICIPLE
s'amusant	amusé

EXAMPLE PHRASES

Les enfants **s'amusent** dehors. The children are playing outside.

On **s'est** bien **amusés** à cette soirée. We really enjoyed ourselves at that party.

Amuse-toi bien avec Florence. Have fun with Florence.

J'ai peur que personne ne **s'amuse** cet après-midi. I'm scared nobody enjoys themselves this afternoon.

Ils **s'amusaient** à sauter dans les flaques d'eau. They had fun jumping in the puddles.

je/j' = I   **tu** = you   **il** = he/it   **elle** = she/it   **on** = we/one   **nous** = we   **vous** = you   **ils/elles** = they

s'amuser

FUTURE

je	**m'amuserai**
tu	**t'amuseras**
il/elle/on	**s'amusera**
nous	**nous amuserons**
vous	**vous amuserez**
ils/elles	**s'amuseront**

CONDITIONAL

je	**m'amuserais**
tu	**t'amuserais**
il/elle/on	**s'amuserait**
nous	**nous amuserions**
vous	**vous amuseriez**
ils/elles	**s'amuseraient**

PAST HISTORIC

je	**m'amusai**
tu	**t'amusas**
il/elle/on	**s'amusa**
nous	**nous amusâmes**
vous	**vous amusâtes**
ils/elles	**s'amusèrent**

PLUPERFECT

je	**m'étais amusé(e)**
tu	**t'étais amusé(e)**
il/elle/on	**s'était amusé(e)**
nous	**nous étions amusé(e)s**
vous	**vous étiez amusé(e)(s)**
ils/elles	**s'étaient amusé(e)s**

IMPERATIVE

amuse-toi / amusons-nous / amusez-vous

EXAMPLE PHRASES

Je suis sûr qu'ils **s'amuseront** comme des fous. I'm sure they'll have a whale of a time.

Ils **s'amusèrent** à dessiner un monstre. They had fun drawing a monster.

Tu **t'amuserais** bien si tu venais avec nous. You'd have fun if you came with us.

Je **m'étais** bien **amusé** à leur mariage. I'd really enjoyed myself at their wedding.

je/j' = I **tu** = you **il** = he/it **elle** = she/it **on** = we/one **nous** = we **vous** = you **ils/elles** = they

apercevoir (to notice)

PRESENT

j'	aperçois
tu	aperçois
il/elle/on	aperçoit
nous	apercevons
vous	apercevez
ils/elles	aperçoivent

PRESENT SUBJUNCTIVE

j'	aperçoive
tu	aperçoives
il/elle/on	aperçoive
nous	apercevions
vous	aperceviez
ils/elles	aperçoivent

PERFECT

j'	ai aperçu
tu	as aperçu
il/elle/on	a aperçu
nous	avons aperçu
vous	avez aperçu
ils/elles	ont aperçu

IMPERFECT

j'	apercevais
tu	apercevais
il/elle/on	apercevait
nous	apercevions
vous	aperceviez
ils/elles	apercevaient

PRESENT PARTICIPLE
apercevant

PAST PARTICIPLE
aperçu

EXAMPLE PHRASES

J'**aperçois** une lumière là-bas. I can see a light over there.

Je l'**ai aperçue** hier au marché. I saw her yesterday at the market.

Ils ont marché longtemps, jusqu'à ce qu'ils **aperçoivent** une maison.
  They walked for a long time, until they saw a house.

Je les **apercevais** de temps en temps en allant travailler. I saw them from
  time to time on my way to work.

---

je/j' = I   **tu** = you   **il** = he/it   **elle** = she/it   **on** = we/one   **nous** = we   **vous** = you   **ils/elles** = they

apercevoir

FUTURE

j'	apercevrai
tu	apercevras
il/elle/on	apercevra
nous	apercevrons
vous	apercevrez
ils/elles	apercevront

CONDITIONAL

j'	apercevrais
tu	apercevrais
il/elle/on	apercevrait
nous	apercevrions
vous	apercevriez
ils/elles	apercevraient

PAST HISTORIC

j'	aperçus
tu	aperçus
il/elle/on	aperçut
nous	aperçûmes
vous	aperçûtes
ils/elles	aperçurent

PLUPERFECT

j'	avais aperçu
tu	avais aperçu
il/elle/on	avait aperçu
nous	avions aperçu
vous	aviez aperçu
ils/elles	avaient aperçu

IMPERATIVE

not used

EXAMPLE PHRASES

Va jusqu'à l'arrêt du bus et tu **apercevras** le magasin au coin de la rue.
  Go up to the bus stop and you'll see the shop on the street corner.
Ils **aperçurent** une silhouette au loin. They saw a shadow in the distance.
Il l'**avait aperçue** une ou deux fois chez les Duval il y avait très longtemps.
  He'd seen her once or twice at the Duvals' a long time before.
Je ne me souvenais pas de l'endroit où je l'**avais aperçu**. I couldn't remember
  where I'd seen him.

je/j' = I **tu** = you **il** = he/it **elle** = she/it **on** = we/one **nous** = we **vous** = you **ils/elles** = they

appeler (to call)

PRESENT

j'	appelle
tu	appelles
il/elle/on	appelle
nous	appelons
vous	appelez
ils/elles	appellent

PRESENT SUBJUNCTIVE

j'	appelle
tu	appelles
il/elle/on	appelle
nous	appelions
vous	appeliez
ils/elles	appellent

PERFECT

j'	ai appelé
tu	as appelé
il/elle/on	a appelé
nous	avons appelé
vous	avez appelé
ils/elles	ont appelé

IMPERFECT

j'	appelais
tu	appelais
il/elle/on	appelait
nous	appelions
vous	appeliez
ils/elles	appelaient

PRESENT PARTICIPLE

appelant

PAST PARTICIPLE

appelé

EXAMPLE PHRASES

Louise! Descends: maman t'**appelle**. Louise! Go downstairs – mum's calling you.

Comment tu t'**appelles**? What's your name?

Elle **a appelé** le médecin. She called the doctor.

Appelle-moi sur mon portable. Ring me on my mobile.

Il faut que je l'**appelle** après dîner. I must ring her after dinner.

Elle **appelait** souvent le soir. She often rang in the evening.

---

je/j' = I   **tu** = you   **il** = he/it   **elle** = she/it   **on** = we/one   **nous** = we   **vous** = you   **ils/elles** = they

appeler

FUTURE

j'	appellerai
tu	appelleras
il/elle/on	appellera
nous	appellerons
vous	appellerez
ils/elles	appelleront

CONDITIONAL

j'	appellerais
tu	appellerais
il/elle/on	appellerait
nous	appellerions
vous	appelleriez
ils/elles	appelleraient

PAST HISTORIC

j'	appelai
tu	appelas
il/elle/on	appela
nous	appelâmes
vous	appelâtes
ils/elles	appelèrent

PLUPERFECT

j'	avais appelé
tu	avais appelé
il/elle/on	avait appelé
nous	avions appelé
vous	aviez appelé
ils/elles	avaient appelé

IMPERATIVE

appelle / appelons / appelez

EXAMPLE PHRASES

Je t'**appellerai** demain. I'll ring you tomorrow.

On **appela** mon nom et je me levai. My name was called and I stood up.

Je l'**appellerais** si j'étais sûr de ne pas le déranger. I'd ring him if I was sure
not to disturb him.

Elle m'**avait appelé** mais je ne l'avais pas entendue. She had called me but
I hadn't heard her.

---

je/j' = I   tu = you   il = he/it   elle = she/it   on = we/one   nous = we   vous = you   ils/elles = they

appuyer (to lean/press)

PRESENT

j'	appuie
tu	appuies
il/elle/on	appuie
nous	appuyons
vous	appuyez
ils/elles	appuient

PRESENT SUBJUNCTIVE

j'	appuie
tu	appuies
il/elle/on	appuie
nous	appuyions
vous	appuyiez
ils/elles	appuient

PERFECT

j'	ai appuyé
tu	as appuyé
il/elle/on	a appuyé
nous	avons appuyé
vous	avez appuyé
ils/elles	ont appuyé

IMPERFECT

j'	appuyais
tu	appuyais
il/elle/on	appuyait
nous	appuyions
vous	appuyiez
ils/elles	appuyaient

PRESENT PARTICIPLE

appuyant

PAST PARTICIPLE

appuyé

EXAMPLE PHRASES

Elle **a appuyé** son vélo contre le mur. She leaned her bike against the wall.

Appuie sur le bouton rouge. Press the red button.

N'**appuie** pas trop fort. Don't press too hard.

Appuyez bien sur le couvercle. Press well on the lid.

Il faut que tu **appuies** fort. You have to press hard.

je/j' = I   **tu** = you   **il** = he/it   **elle** = she/it   **on** = we/one   **nous** = we   **vous** = you   **ils/elles** = they

appuyer

FUTURE

j'	appuierai
tu	appuieras
il/elle/on	appuiera
nous	appuierons
vous	appuierez
ils/elles	appuieront

CONDITIONAL

j'	appuierais
tu	appuierais
il/elle/on	appuierait
nous	appuierions
vous	appuieriez
ils/elles	appuieraient

PAST HISTORIC

j'	appuyai
tu	appuyas
il/elle/on	appuya
nous	appuyâmes
vous	appuyâtes
ils/elles	appuyèrent

PLUPERFECT

j'	avais appuyé
tu	avais appuyé
il/elle/on	avait appuyé
nous	avions appuyé
vous	aviez appuyé
ils/elles	avaient appuyé

IMPERATIVE

appuie / appuyons / appuyez

EXAMPLE PHRASES

J'**appuierai** trois fois sur la sonnette. I'll press the bell three times.

Il **appuya** longtemps mais la colle ne tenait pas. He pressed for a long time but the glue didn't hold.

Il n'**appuierait** pas si fort si tu le laissais faire. He wouldn't press so hard if you'd let him do it.

Elle n'**avait** pas **appuyé** assez fort et la cloche n'avait pas sonné. She hadn't pressed hard enough and the bell hadn't rung.

---

je/j' = I **tu** = you **il** = he/it **elle** = she/it **on** = we/one **nous** = we **vous** = you **ils/elles** = they

arriver (to arrive)

PRESENT

j'	arrive
tu	arrives
il/elle/on	arrive
nous	arrivons
vous	arrivez
ils/elles	arrivent

PRESENT SUBJUNCTIVE

j'	arrive
tu	arrives
il/elle/on	arrive
nous	arrivions
vous	arriviez
ils/elles	arrivent

PERFECT

je	suis arrivé(e)
tu	es arrivé(e)
il/elle/on	est arrivé(e)
nous	sommes arrivé(e)s
vous	êtes arrivé(e)(s)
ils/elles	sont arrivé(e)s

IMPERFECT

j'	arrivais
tu	arrivais
il/elle/on	arrivait
nous	arrivions
vous	arriviez
ils/elles	arrivaient

PRESENT PARTICIPLE
arrivant

PAST PARTICIPLE
arrivé

EXAMPLE PHRASES

J'**arrive** à l'école à huit heures. I arrive at school at 8 o'clock.

Qu'est-ce qui **est arrivé** à Aurélie? What happened to Aurélie?

N'**arrivez** pas en retard demain. Don't arrive late tomorrow.

Il faut que j'**arrive** à jouer cet air pour la leçon de demain. I'll have to be able to play this tune for tomorrow's lesson.

Il m'**arrivait** de dormir jusqu'à midi. I sometimes slept till midday.

je/j' = I   **tu** = you   **il** = he/it   **elle** = she/it   **on** = we/one   **nous** = we   **vous** = you   **ils/elles** = they

arriver

FUTURE

j'	**arriverai**
tu	**arriveras**
il/elle/on	**arrivera**
nous	**arriverons**
vous	**arriverez**
ils/elles	**arriveront**

CONDITIONAL

j'	**arriverais**
tu	**arriverais**
il/elle/on	**arriverait**
nous	**arriverions**
vous	**arriveriez**
ils/elles	**arriveraient**

PAST HISTORIC

j'	**arrivai**
tu	**arrivas**
il/elle/on	**arriva**
nous	**arrivâmes**
vous	**arrivâtes**
ils/elles	**arrivèrent**

PLUPERFECT

j'	**étais arrivé(e)**
tu	**étais arrivé(e)**
il/elle/on	**était arrivé(e)**
nous	**étions arrivé(e)s**
vous	**étiez arrivé(e)(s)**
ils/elles	**étaient arrivé(e)s**

IMPERATIVE

arrive / arrivons / arrivez

EXAMPLE PHRASES

Arriveras-tu à l'heure pour ton rendez-vous? Will you be on time for your appointment?

La réunion était finie depuis longtemps quand il **arriva**. The meeting had finished long before he arrived.

Je n'**arriverais** jamais à faire tout ce travail sans ton aide. I would never be able to get all this work done without your help.

Le prof n'**était** pas encore **arrivé**. The teacher hadn't arrived yet.

je/j' = I **tu** = you **il** = he/it **elle** = she/it **on** = we/one **nous** = we **vous** = you **ils/elles** = they

s'asseoir (to sit down)

<table>
<tr><td colspan="2">

PRESENT

</td><td colspan="2">

PRESENT SUBJUNCTIVE

</td></tr>
<tr><td>je</td><td>**m'assieds/m'assois**</td><td>je</td><td>**m'asseye**</td></tr>
<tr><td>tu</td><td>**t'assieds/t'assois**</td><td>tu</td><td>**t'asseyes**</td></tr>
<tr><td>il/elle/on</td><td>**s'assied/s'assoit**</td><td>il/elle/on</td><td>**s'asseye**</td></tr>
<tr><td>nous</td><td>**nous asseyons/nous assoyons**</td><td>nous</td><td>**nous asseyions**</td></tr>
<tr><td>vous</td><td>**vous asseyez/vous assoyez**</td><td>vous</td><td>**vous asseyiez**</td></tr>
<tr><td>ils/elles</td><td>**s'asseyent/s'assoient**</td><td>ils/elles</td><td>**s'asseyent**</td></tr>
</table>

<table>
<tr><td colspan="2">

PERFECT

</td><td colspan="2">

IMPERFECT

</td></tr>
<tr><td>je</td><td>**me suis assis(e)**</td><td>je</td><td>**m'asseyais**</td></tr>
<tr><td>tu</td><td>**t'es assis(e)**</td><td>tu</td><td>**t'asseyais**</td></tr>
<tr><td>il/elle/on</td><td>**s'est assis(e)**</td><td>il/elle/on</td><td>**s'asseyait**</td></tr>
<tr><td>nous</td><td>**nous sommes assis(es)**</td><td>nous</td><td>**nous asseyions**</td></tr>
<tr><td>vous</td><td>**vous êtes assis(e(s))**</td><td>vous</td><td>**vous asseyiez**</td></tr>
<tr><td>ils/elles</td><td>**se sont assis(es)**</td><td>ils/elles</td><td>**s'asseyaient**</td></tr>
</table>

PRESENT PARTICIPLE

s'asseyant

PAST PARTICIPLE

assis

EXAMPLE PHRASES

Je peux **m'asseoir**? May I sit down?

Je **me suis assise** sur un chewing-gum! I've sat on chewing-gum!

Assieds-toi, Nicole. Sit down Nicole.

Asseyez-vous, les enfants. Sit down children.

On **s'asseyait** toujours l'un à côté de l'autre. We would always sit next to each other.

---

je/j' = I   **tu** = you   **il** = he/it   **elle** = she/it   **on** = we/one   **nous** = we   **vous** = you   **ils/elles** = they

s'asseoir

FUTURE

je	**m'assiérai**
tu	**t'assiéras**
il/elle/on	**s'assiéra**
nous	**nous assiérons**
vous	**vous assiérez**
ils/elles	**s'assiéront**

CONDITIONAL

je	**m'assiérais**
tu	**t'assiérais**
il/elle/on	**s'assiérait**
nous	**nous assiérons**
vous	**vous assiérez**
ils/elles	**s'assiéraient**

PAST HISTORIC

je	**m'assis**
tu	**t'assis**
il/elle/on	**s'assit**
nous	**nous assîmes**
vous	**vous assîtes**
ils/elles	**s'assirent**

PLUPERFECT

je	**m'étais assis(e)**
tu	**t'étais assis(e)**
il/elle/on	**s'était assis(e)**
nous	**nous étions assis(es)**
vous	**vous étiez assis(e(s))**
ils/elles	**s'étaient assis(es)**

IMPERATIVE

assieds-toi / asseyons-nous / asseyez-vous

EXAMPLE PHRASES

Je **m'assiérai** à côté de toi. I'll sit next to you.

Il **s'assit** en face de moi. He sat down opposite me.

Je ne **m'assiérais** pas là si j'étais toi. I wouldn't sit there if I were you.

Elle ne **s'était** pas encore **assise** quand la fillette l'appela à nouveau.
    She hadn't even sat down when the little girl called her once again.

je/j' = I **tu** = you **il** = he/it **elle** = she/it **on** = we/one **nous** = we **vous** = you **ils/elles** = they

atteindre (to reach)

PRESENT		PRESENT SUBJUNCTIVE	
j'	**atteins**	j'	**atteigne**
tu	**atteins**	tu	**atteignes**
il/elle/on	**atteint**	il/elle/on	**atteigne**
nous	**atteignons**	nous	**atteignions**
vous	**atteignez**	vous	**atteigniez**
ils/elles	**atteignent**	ils/elles	**atteignent**

PERFECT		IMPERFECT	
j'	**ai atteint**	j'	**atteignais**
tu	**as atteint**	tu	**atteignais**
il/elle/on	**a atteint**	il/elle/on	**atteignait**
nous	**avons atteint**	nous	**atteignions**
vous	**avez atteint**	vous	**atteigniez**
ils/elles	**ont atteint**	ils/elles	**atteignaient**

PRESENT PARTICIPLE
atteignant

PAST PARTICIPLE
atteint

EXAMPLE PHRASES

Je n'arrive pas à **atteindre** ma valise. I can't reach my suitcase.

Cette Ferrari **atteint** une vitesse de 245 km/h. This Ferrari reaches a speed of 245km/h.

Ils **ont atteint** le sommet en quatre heures et demie. They reached the summit in four and a half hours.

Ils **atteignaient** Paris quand l'accident se produisit. They were nearing Paris when the accident happened.

---

je/j' = I   **tu** = you   **il** = he/it   **elle** = she/it   **on** = we/one   **nous** = we   **vous** = you   **ils/elles** = they

atteindre

FUTURE

j'	**atteindrai**
tu	**atteindras**
il/elle/on	**atteindra**
nous	**atteindrons**
vous	**atteindrez**
ils/elles	**atteindront**

CONDITIONAL

j'	**atteindrais**
tu	**atteindrais**
il/elle/on	**atteindrait**
nous	**atteindrions**
vous	**atteindriez**
ils/elles	**atteindraient**

PAST HISTORIC

j'	**atteignis**
tu	**atteignis**
il/elle/on	**atteignit**
nous	**atteignîmes**
vous	**atteignîtes**
ils/elles	**atteignirent**

PLUPERFECT

j'	**avais atteint**
tu	**avais atteint**
il/elle/on	**avait atteint**
nous	**avions atteint**
vous	**aviez atteint**
ils/elles	**avaient atteint**

IMPERATIVE

atteins / atteignons / atteignez

EXAMPLE PHRASES

Nous **atteindrons** Rouen dans dix minutes. We'll reach Rouen in ten minutes.

Il **atteignit** sa destination en trois semaines. He reached his destination in three weeks.

Il se rendit compte qu'il n'**atteindrait** jamais son but. He realized that he would never reach his goal.

Le tableau **avait atteint** un prix exorbitant. The painting had reached a prohibitive price.

je/j' = I **tu** = you **il** = he/it **elle** = she/it **on** = we/one **nous** = we **vous** = you **ils/elles** = they

attendre (to wait)

PRESENT		PRESENT SUBJUNCTIVE	
j'	**attends**	j'	**attende**
tu	**attends**	tu	**attendes**
il/elle/on	**attend**	il/elle/on	**attende**
nous	**attendons**	nous	**attendions**
vous	**attendez**	vous	**attendiez**
ils/elles	**attendent**	ils/elles	**attendent**

PERFECT		IMPERFECT	
j'	**ai attendu**	j'	**attendais**
tu	**as attendu**	tu	**attendais**
il/elle/on	**a attendu**	il/elle/on	**attendait**
nous	**avons attendu**	nous	**attendions**
vous	**avez attendu**	vous	**attendiez**
ils/elles	**ont attendu**	ils/elles	**attendaient**

PRESENT PARTICIPLE
attendant

PAST PARTICIPLE
attendu

EXAMPLE PHRASES

Tu **attends** depuis longtemps? Have you been waiting long?

Je l'**ai attendu** à la poste. I waited for him at the post office.

Attends-moi! Wait for me!

Elle veut que je l'**attende** dans le hall. She wants me to wait for her in the hall.

Elle **attendait** un bébé. She was expecting a baby.

je/j' = I   **tu** = you   **il** = he/it   **elle** = she/it   **on** = we/one   **nous** = we   **vous** = you   **ils/elles** = they

attendre

FUTURE

j'	**attendrai**
tu	**attendras**
il/elle/on	**attendra**
nous	**attendrons**
vous	**attendrez**
ils/elles	**attendront**

CONDITIONAL

j'	**attendrais**
tu	**attendrais**
il/elle/on	**attendrait**
nous	**attendrions**
vous	**attendriez**
ils/elles	**attendraient**

PAST HISTORIC

j'	**attendis**
tu	**attendis**
il/elle/on	**attendit**
nous	**attendîmes**
vous	**attendîtes**
ils/elles	**attendirent**

PLUPERFECT

j'	**avais attendu**
tu	**avais attendu**
il/elle/on	**avait attendu**
nous	**avions attendu**
vous	**aviez attendu**
ils/elles	**avaient attendu**

IMPERATIVE

attends / attendons / attendez

EXAMPLE PHRASES

J'**attendrai** qu'il ne pleuve plus. I'll wait until it's stopped raining.

Nous **attendîmes** en silence. We waited in silence.

Je t'**attendrais** si tu n'étais pas si lente. I'd wait for you if you weren't so slow.

Elle m'**avait attendu** patiemment devant la poste. She had patiently waited for me in front of the post office.

je/j' = I **tu** = you **il** = he/it **elle** = she/it **on** = we/one **nous** = we **vous** = you **ils/elles** = they

avoir (to have)

PRESENT

j'	**ai**
tu	**as**
il/elle/on	**a**
nous	**avons**
vous	**avez**
ils/elles	**ont**

PRESENT SUBJUNCTIVE

j'	**aie**
tu	**aies**
il/elle/on	**ait**
nous	**ayons**
vous	**ayez**
ils/elles	**aient**

PERFECT

j'	**ai eu**
tu	**as eu**
il/elle/on	**a eu**
nous	**avons eu**
vous	**avez eu**
ils/elles	**ont eu**

IMPERFECT

j'	**avais**
tu	**avais**
il/elle/on	**avait**
nous	**avions**
vous	**aviez**
ils/elles	**avaient**

PRESENT PARTICIPLE

ayant

PAST PARTICIPLE

eu

EXAMPLE PHRASES

Il **a** les yeux bleus. He's got blue eyes.

Quel âge **as**-tu? How old are you?

Il y **a** beaucoup de monde. There are lots of people.

Il **a eu** un accident. He's had an accident.

J'**avais** faim. I was hungry.

avoir

FUTURE

j'	**aurai**
tu	**auras**
il/elle/on	**aura**
nous	**aurons**
vous	**aurez**
ils/elles	**auront**

CONDITIONAL

j'	**aurais**
tu	**aurais**
il/elle/on	**aurait**
nous	**aurions**
vous	**auriez**
ils/elles	**auraient**

PAST HISTORIC

j'	**eus**
tu	**eus**
il/elle/on	**eut**
nous	**eûmes**
vous	**eûtes**
ils/elles	**eurent**

PLUPERFECT

j'	**avais eu**
tu	**avais eu**
il/elle/on	**avait eu**
nous	**avions eu**
vous	**aviez eu**
ils/elles	**avaient eu**

IMPERATIVE

aie / ayons / ayez

EXAMPLE PHRASES

Cloé **aura** cinq ans au mois d'août. Cloé will be five in August.

J'**eus** soudain l'idée de lui rendre visite. I suddenly thought of paying him a visit.

Je n'**aurais** pas tant mangé si j'avais su qu'il y avait un dessert. I wouldn't have eaten so much if I'd known that there was a pudding.

Paul **avait eu** mal au ventre toute la nuit. Paul had had a sore stomach all night.

---

je/j' = I   **tu** = you   **il** = he/it   **elle** = she/it   **on** = we/one   **nous** = we   **vous** = you   **ils/elles** = they

battre (to beat)

PRESENT		PRESENT SUBJUNCTIVE	
je	**bats**	je	**batte**
tu	**bats**	tu	**battes**
il/elle/on	**bat**	il/elle/on	**batte**
nous	**battons**	nous	**battions**
vous	**battez**	vous	**battiez**
ils/elles	**battent**	ils/elles	**battent**

PERFECT		IMPERFECT	
j'	**ai battu**	je	**battais**
tu	**as battu**	tu	**battais**
il/elle/on	**a battu**	il/elle/on	**battait**
nous	**avons battu**	nous	**battions**
vous	**avez battu**	vous	**battiez**
ils/elles	**ont battu**	ils/elles	**battaient**

PRESENT PARTICIPLE
battant

PAST PARTICIPLE
battu

EXAMPLE PHRASES

J'ai le cœur qui **bat vite**! My heart's beating fast!

Arrêtez de vous **battre**! Stop fighting!

On les **a battus** deux à un. We beat them two-one.

Bats les cartes s'il te plaît. Shuffle the cards please.

Elle le **battait** toujours au poker. She'd always beat him at poker.

---

je/j' = I   **tu** = you   **il** = he/it   **elle** = she/it   **on** = we/one   **nous** = we   **vous** = you   **ils/elles** = they

battre

FUTURE		**CONDITIONAL**	
je	**battrai**	je	**battrais**
tu	**battras**	tu	**battrais**
il/elle/on	**battra**	il/elle/on	**battrait**
nous	**battrons**	nous	**battrions**
vous	**battrez**	vous	**battriez**
ils/elles	**battront**	ils/elles	**battraient**

PAST HISTORIC		**PLUPERFECT**	
je	**battis**	j'	**avais battu**
tu	**battis**	tu	**avais battu**
il/elle/on	**battit**	il/elle/on	**avait battu**
nous	**battîmes**	nous	**avions battu**
vous	**battîtes**	vous	**aviez battu**
ils/elles	**battirent**	ils/elles	**avaient battu**

IMPERATIVE

bats / battons / battez

EXAMPLE PHRASES

Tu ne me **battras** jamais à la course. You'll never beat me at running.

Elle le **battit** au Scrabble®. She beat him at Scrabble®.

Ils se **battraient** tout le temps si je les laissais faire. They'd fight all the time if I let them.

Elle **avait battu** le record du monde du saut à la perche. She'd beaten the world record for the pole vault.

je/j' = I **tu** = you **il** = he/it **elle** = she/it **on** = we/one **nous** = we **vous** = you **ils/elles** = they

boire (to drink)

PRESENT

je	**bois**
tu	**bois**
il/elle/on	**boit**
nous	**buvons**
vous	**buvez**
ils/elles	**boivent**

PRESENT SUBJUNCTIVE

je	**boive**
tu	**boives**
il/elle/on	**boive**
nous	**buvions**
vous	**buviez**
ils/elles	**boivent**

PERFECT

j'	**ai bu**
tu	**as bu**
il/elle/on	**a bu**
nous	**avons bu**
vous	**avez bu**
ils/elles	**ont bu**

IMPERFECT

je	**buvais**
tu	**buvais**
il/elle/on	**buvait**
nous	**buvions**
vous	**buviez**
ils/elles	**buvaient**

PRESENT PARTICIPLE

buvant

PAST PARTICIPLE

bu

EXAMPLE PHRASES

Qu'est-ce que tu veux **boire**? What would you like to drink?

Il ne **boit** jamais d'alcool. He never drinks alcohol.

J'**ai bu** un litre d'eau. I drank a litre of water.

Bois ton café avant de partir. Drink your coffee before we leave.

Elle **buvait** un whisky tous les soirs. She had a whisky every night.

---

je/j' = I   **tu** = you   **il** = he/it   **elle** = she/it   **on** = we/one   **nous** = we   **vous** = you   **ils/elles** = they

boire

FUTURE

je	**boirai**
tu	**boiras**
il/elle/on	**boira**
nous	**boirons**
vous	**boirez**
ils/elles	**boiront**

CONDITIONAL

je	**boirais**
tu	**boirais**
il/elle/on	**boirait**
nous	**boirions**
vous	**boiriez**
ils/elles	**boiraient**

PAST HISTORIC

je	**bus**
tu	**bus**
il/elle/on	**but**
nous	**bûmes**
vous	**bûtes**
ils/elles	**burent**

PLUPERFECT

j'	**avais bu**
tu	**avais bu**
il/elle/on	**avait bu**
nous	**avions bu**
vous	**aviez bu**
ils/elles	**avaient bu**

IMPERATIVE

bois / buvons / buvez

EXAMPLE PHRASES

Que **boirez**-vous? What will you have to drink?

Il **but** son jus d'orange d'un trait. He drank his orange juice in one gulp.

Je **boirais** bien un cognac. I'd quite like a brandy.

On voyait qu'il **avait bu**. He was obviously drunk.

je/j' = I **tu** = you **il** = he/it **elle** = she/it **on** = we/one **nous** = we **vous** = you **ils/elles** = they

bouillir (to boil)

PRESENT

je	**bous**
tu	**bous**
il/elle/on	**bout**
nous	**bouillons**
vous	**bouillez**
ils/elles	**bouillent**

PRESENT SUBJUNCTIVE

je	**bouille**
tu	**bouilles**
il/elle/on	**bouille**
nous	**bouillions**
vous	**bouilliez**
ils/elles	**bouillent**

PERFECT

j'	**ai bouilli**
tu	**as bouilli**
il/elle/on	**a bouilli**
nous	**avons bouilli**
vous	**avez bouilli**
ils/elles	**ont bouilli**

IMPERFECT

je	**bouillais**
tu	**bouillais**
il/elle/on	**bouillait**
nous	**bouillions**
vous	**bouilliez**
ils/elles	**bouillaient**

PRESENT PARTICIPLE
bouillant

PAST PARTICIPLE
bouilli

EXAMPLE PHRASES

Tu peux mettre de l'eau à **bouillir**? Can you boil some water?

Faites **bouillir** pendant quelques minutes. Boil for a few minutes.

L'eau **bout**. The water's boiling.

La soupe **a bouilli** trop longtemps. The soup had boiled for too long.

Je **bouillais** d'impatience. I was bursting with impatience.

---

je/j' = I   tu = you   il = he/it   elle = she/it   on = we/one   **nous** = we   **vous** = you   **ils/elles** = they

bouillir

FUTURE

je	**bouillirai**
tu	**bouilliras**
il/elle/on	**bouillira**
nous	**bouillirons**
vous	**bouillirez**
ils/elles	**bouilliront**

CONDITIONAL

je	**bouillirais**
tu	**bouillirais**
il/elle/on	**bouillirait**
nous	**bouillirions**
vous	**bouilliriez**
ils/elles	**bouilliraient**

PAST HISTORIC

je	**bouillis**
tu	**bouillis**
il/elle/on	**bouillit**
nous	**bouillîmes**
vous	**bouillîtes**
ils/elles	**bouillirent**

PLUPERFECT

j'	**avais bouilli**
tu	**avais bouilli**
il/elle/on	**avait bouilli**
nous	**avions bouilli**
vous	**aviez bouilli**
ils/elles	**avaient bouilli**

IMPERATIVE

bous / bouillons / bouillez

EXAMPLE PHRASES

Quand l'eau **bouillira,** la bouilloire sifflera. When the water boils, the kettle will whistle.

Le lait **bouillit** et déborda. The milk boiled over.

L'eau n'**avait** pas encore **bouilli**. The water hadn't boiled yet.

je/j' = I **tu** = you **il** = he/it **elle** = she/it **on** = we/one **nous** = we **vous** = you **ils/elles** = they

commencer (to start; to begin)

PRESENT		PRESENT SUBJUNCTIVE	
je	commence	je	commence
tu	commences	tu	commences
il/elle/on	commence	il/elle/on	commence
nous	commençons	nous	commencions
vous	commencez	vous	commenciez
ils/elles	commencent	ils/elles	commencent

PERFECT		IMPERFECT	
j'	ai commencé	je	commençais
tu	as commencé	tu	commençais
il/elle/on	a commencé	il/elle/on	commençait
nous	avons commencé	nous	commencions
vous	avez commencé	vous	commenciez
ils/elles	ont commencé	ils/elles	commençaient

PRESENT PARTICIPLE
commençant

PAST PARTICIPLE
commencé

EXAMPLE PHRASES

Les cours **commencent** à neuf heures. Lessons start at nine o'clock.

Tu **as** déjà **commencé** de réviser pour tes examens? Have you started revising for your exams?

Ne **commence** pas à m'embêter. Don't start annoying me.

J'aimerais que tu **commences** à faire les valises. I'd like you to start packing the suitcases.

Son attitude **commençait** à m'énerver. Her attitude had started to annoy me.

---

je/j' = I   **tu** = you   **il** = he/it   **elle** = she/it   **on** = we/one   **nous** = we   **vous** = you   **ils/elles** = they

commencer

FUTURE

je	**commencerai**
tu	**commenceras**
il/elle/on	**commencera**
nous	**commencerons**
vous	**commencerez**
ils/elles	**commenceront**

CONDITIONAL

je	**commencerais**
tu	**commencerais**
il/elle/on	**commencerait**
nous	**commencerions**
vous	**commenceriez**
ils/elles	**commenceraient**

PAST HISTORIC

je	**commençai**
tu	**commenças**
il/elle/on	**commença**
nous	**commençâmes**
vous	**commençâtes**
ils/elles	**commencèrent**

PLUPERFECT

j'	**avais commencé**
tu	**avais commencé**
il/elle/on	**avait commencé**
nous	**avions commencé**
vous	**aviez commencé**
ils/elles	**avaient commencé**

IMPERATIVE

commence / commençons / commencez

EXAMPLE PHRASES

Nous ne **commencerons** pas sans toi. We won't start without you.

C'est quand les nouveaux voisins arrivèrent que les ennuis **commencèrent**.
  It's when the new neighbours arrived that the problems started.

Nous **commencerions** une partie de cartes si nous étions sûrs d'avoir le
  temps de la finir. We'd start a game of cards if we were sure we'd have time
  to finish it.

Il **avait commencé** à pleuvoir. It had started to rain.

---

je/j' = I   tu = you   il = he/it   elle = she/it   on = we/one   nous = we   vous = you   ils/elles = they

conclure (to conclude)

PRESENT		PRESENT SUBJUNCTIVE	
je	**conclus**	je	**conclue**
tu	**conclus**	tu	**conclues**
il/elle/on	**conclut**	il/elle/on	**conclue**
nous	**concluons**	nous	**concluions**
vous	**concluez**	vous	**concluiez**
ils/elles	**concluent**	ils/elles	**concluent**

PERFECT		IMPERFECT	
j'	**ai conclu**	je	**concluais**
tu	**as conclu**	tu	**concluais**
il/elle/on	**a conclu**	il/elle/on	**concluait**
nous	**avons conclu**	nous	**concluions**
vous	**avez conclu**	vous	**concluiez**
ils/elles	**ont conclu**	ils/elles	**concluaient**

PRESENT PARTICIPLE
concluant

PAST PARTICIPLE
conclu

EXAMPLE PHRASES

J'en **conclus** qu'il ne m'a pas dit la vérité. I conclude from this that he didn't
   tell me the truth.

Ils **ont conclu** un marché. They concluded a deal.

Il en **a conclu** qu'il s'était trompé. He concluded that he had got it wrong.

Il faut que je **conclue** le marché aujourd'hui. I must conclude the deal today.

conclure

FUTURE

je	**conclurai**
tu	**concluras**
il/elle/on	**conclura**
nous	**conclurons**
vous	**conclurez**
ils/elles	**concluront**

CONDITIONAL

je	**conclurais**
tu	**conclurais**
il/elle/on	**conclurait**
nous	**conclurions**
vous	**concluriez**
ils/elles	**concluraient**

PAST HISTORIC

je	**conclus**
tu	**conclus**
il/elle/on	**conclut**
nous	**conclûmes**
vous	**conclûtes**
ils/elles	**conclurent**

PLUPERFECT

j'	**avais conclu**
tu	**avais conclu**
il/elle/on	**avait conclu**
nous	**avions conclu**
vous	**aviez conclu**
ils/elles	**avaient conclu**

IMPERATIVE
conclus / concluons / concluez

EXAMPLE PHRASES

Je **conclurai** par ces mots... I will conclude with these words...

Elle en **conclut** qu'il était parti. She concluded that he had gone.

Nous n'**avions** encore rien **conclu** quand il est arrivé. We hadn't concluded anything when he arrived.

Ils **avaient conclu** la soirée par une partie de cartes. They had concluded the evening with a game of cards.

je/j' = I **tu** = you **il** = he/it **elle** = she/it **on** = we/one **nous** = we **vous** = you **ils/elles** = they

conduire (to drive)

PRESENT

je	conduis
tu	conduis
il/elle/on	conduit
nous	conduisons
vous	conduisez
ils/elles	conduisent

PRESENT SUBJUNCTIVE

je	conduise
tu	conduises
il/elle/on	conduise
nous	conduisions
vous	conduisiez
ils/elles	conduisent

PERFECT

j'	ai conduit
tu	as conduit
il/elle/on	a conduit
nous	avons conduit
vous	avez conduit
ils/elles	ont conduit

IMPERFECT

je	conduisais
tu	conduisais
il/elle/on	conduisait
nous	conduisions
vous	conduisiez
ils/elles	conduisaient

PRESENT PARTICIPLE

conduisant

PAST PARTICIPLE

conduit

EXAMPLE PHRASES

Elle **conduit** sa fille à l'école tous les matins. She drives her daughter to school every morning.

Cela fait longtemps que je n'**ai** pas **conduit**. I haven't driven for a long time.

Conduis prudemment. Drive carefully.

J'aimerais que tu me **conduises** à la gare. I'd like you to drive me to the station.

Il **conduisait** lentement quand l'accident est arrivé. He was driving slowly when the accident happened.

conduire

FUTURE

je	**conduirai**
tu	**conduiras**
il/elle/on	**conduira**
nous	**conduirons**
vous	**conduirez**
ils/elles	**conduiront**

CONDITIONAL

je	**conduirais**
tu	**conduirais**
il/elle/on	**conduirait**
nous	**conduirions**
vous	**conduiriez**
ils/elles	**conduiraient**

PAST HISTORIC

je	**conduisis**
tu	**conduisis**
il/elle/on	**conduisit**
nous	**conduisîmes**
vous	**conduisîtes**
ils/elles	**conduisirent**

PLUPERFECT

j'	**avais conduit**
tu	**avais conduit**
il/elle/on	**avait conduit**
nous	**avions conduit**
vous	**aviez conduit**
ils/elles	**avaient conduit**

IMPERATIVE
conduis / conduisons / conduisez

EXAMPLE PHRASES

Je te **conduirai** chez le docteur. I'll drive you to the doctor's.

Elle **conduisit** sans dire un mot. She drove without saying a word.

Je te **conduirais** en ville si j'avais le temps. I'd drive you into town if I had time.

Elle **avait conduit** toute la nuit et elle était épuisée. She'd driven all night and she was exhausted.

---

je/j' = I **tu** = you **il** = he/it **elle** = she/it **on** = we/one **nous** = we **vous** = you **ils/elles** = they

connaître (to know)

PRESENT

je	**connais**
tu	**connais**
il/elle/on	**connaît**
nous	**connaissons**
vous	**connaissez**
ils/elles	**connaissent**

PRESENT SUBJUNCTIVE

je	**connaisse**
tu	**connaisses**
il/elle/on	**connaisse**
nous	**connaissions**
vous	**connaissiez**
ils/elles	**connaissent**

PERFECT

j'	**ai connu**
tu	**as connu**
il/elle/on	**a connu**
nous	**avons connu**
vous	**avez connu**
ils/elles	**ont connu**

IMPERFECT

je	**connaissais**
tu	**connaissais**
il/elle/on	**connaissait**
nous	**connaissions**
vous	**connaissiez**
ils/elles	**connaissaient**

PRESENT PARTICIPLE

connaissant

PAST PARTICIPLE

connu

EXAMPLE PHRASES

Je ne **connais** pas du tout cette région. I don't know the area at all.

Vous **connaissez** M. Amiot? Do you know Mr Amiot?

Il n'**a** pas **connu** son grand-père. He never knew his granddad.

Je **connaissais** bien sa mère. I knew his mother well.

je/j' = I **tu** = you **il** = he/it **elle** = she/it **on** = we/one **nous** = we **vous** = you **ils/elles** = they

connaître

FUTURE

je	**connaîtrai**
tu	**connaîtras**
il/elle/on	**connaîtra**
nous	**connaîtrons**
vous	**connaîtrez**
ils/elles	**connaîtront**

CONDITIONAL

je	**connaîtrais**
tu	**connaîtrais**
il/elle/on	**connaîtrait**
nous	**connaîtrions**
vous	**connaîtriez**
ils/elles	**connaîtraient**

PAST HISTORIC

je	**connus**
tu	**connus**
il/elle/on	**connut**
nous	**connûmes**
vous	**connûtes**
ils/elles	**connurent**

PLUPERFECT

j'	**avais connu**
tu	**avais connu**
il/elle/on	**avait connu**
nous	**avions connu**
vous	**aviez connu**
ils/elles	**avaient connu**

IMPERATIVE

connais / connaissons / connaissez

EXAMPLE PHRASES

Je ne la **connaîtrai** jamais bien. I'll never know her well.

Il **connut** d'abord Laura puis il rencontra Claire. First he got to know Laura and then he met Claire.

Nous ne nous **connaîtrions** pas s'il ne nous avait pas présentés. We wouldn't know each other if he hadn't introduced us.

J'aurais gagné si j'**avais connu** la réponse à la dernière question. I would have won if I had known the answer to the last question.

Ils s'**étaient connus** à Rouen. They'd first met in Rouen.

je/j' = I **tu** = you **il** = he/it **elle** = she/it **on** = we/one **nous** = we **vous** = you **ils/elles** = they

continuer (to continue; to go on)

PRESENT

je	**continue**
tu	**continues**
il/elle/on	**continue**
nous	**continuons**
vous	**continuez**
ils/elles	**continuent**

PRESENT SUBJUNCTIVE

je	**continue**
tu	**continues**
il/elle/on	**continue**
nous	**continuions**
vous	**continuiez**
ils/elles	**continuent**

PERFECT

j'	**ai continué**
tu	**as continué**
il/elle/on	**a continué**
nous	**avons continué**
vous	**avez continué**
ils/elles	**ont continué**

IMPERFECT

je	**continuais**
tu	**continuais**
il/elle/on	**continuait**
nous	**continuions**
vous	**continuiez**
ils/elles	**continuaient**

PRESENT PARTICIPLE
continuant

PAST PARTICIPLE
continué

EXAMPLE PHRASES

Il **continue** de fumer malgré son asthme. He keeps on smoking despite his asthma.

Ils **ont continué** à regarder la télé sans me dire bonjour. They went on watching TV without saying hello to me.

Il faut que tu **continues** à réviser si tu veux réussir à ton examen. You'll have to carry on revising if you want to do well in your exam.

La phrase **continuait** sur la page suivante. The sentence continued on the next page.

je/j' = I   **tu** = you   **il** = he/it   **elle** = she/it   **on** = we/one   **nous** = we   **vous** = you   **ils/elles** = they

continuer

FUTURE

je	**continuerai**
tu	**continueras**
il/elle/on	**continuera**
nous	**continuerons**
vous	**continuerez**
ils/elles	**continueront**

CONDITIONAL

je	**continuerais**
tu	**continuerais**
il/elle/on	**continuerait**
nous	**continuerions**
vous	**continueriez**
ils/elles	**continueraient**

PAST HISTORIC

je	**continuai**
tu	**continuas**
il/elle/on	**continua**
nous	**continuâmes**
vous	**continuâtes**
ils/elles	**continuèrent**

PLUPERFECT

j'	**avais continué**
tu	**avais continué**
il/elle/on	**avait continué**
nous	**avions continué**
vous	**aviez continué**
ils/elles	**avaient continué**

IMPERATIVE

continue / continuons / continuez

EXAMPLE PHRASES

Nous **continuerons** l'histoire demain. We'll continue the story tomorrow.

Ils **continuèrent** à la harceler toute la soirée. They went on harassing her all evening.

Je **continuerais** à regarder ce film si j'avais le temps. I'd carry on watching this film if I had time.

Ils **avaient continué** à lui rendre visite même après leur déménagement. They had carried on visiting her even after they had moved house.

je/j' = I   **tu** = you   **il** = he/it   **elle** = she/it   **on** = we/one   **nous** = we   **vous** = you   **ils/elles** = they

coudre (to sew)

PRESENT

je	**couds**
tu	**couds**
il/elle/on	**coud**
nous	**cousons**
vous	**cousez**
ils/elles	**cousent**

PRESENT SUBJUNCTIVE

je	**couse**
tu	**couses**
il/elle/on	**couse**
nous	**cousions**
vous	**cousiez**
ils/elles	**cousent**

PERFECT

j'	**ai cousu**
tu	**as cousu**
il/elle/on	**a cousu**
nous	**avons cousu**
vous	**avez cousu**
ils/elles	**ont cousu**

IMPERFECT

je	**cousais**
tu	**cousais**
il/elle/on	**cousait**
nous	**cousions**
vous	**cousiez**
ils/elles	**cousaient**

PRESENT PARTICIPLE

cousant

PAST PARTICIPLE

cousu

EXAMPLE PHRASES

Tu sais **coudre**? Can you sew?

Ma mère **coud** beaucoup. My mum sews a lot.

J'**ai cousu** toute la soirée hier. I spent all evening yesterday sewing.

Elle **cousait** tous les soirs après dîner. She would sew every night after dinner.

coudre

FUTURE

je	coudrai
tu	coudras
il/elle/on	coudra
nous	coudrons
vous	coudrez
ils/elles	coudront

CONDITIONAL

je	coudrais
tu	coudrais
il/elle/on	coudrait
nous	coudrions
vous	coudriez
ils/elles	coudraient

PAST HISTORIC

je	cousus
tu	cousus
il/elle/on	cousut
nous	cousûmes
vous	cousûtes
ils/elles	cousurent

PLUPERFECT

j'	avais cousu
tu	avais cousu
il/elle/on	avait cousu
nous	avions cousu
vous	aviez cousu
ils/elles	avaient cousu

IMPERATIVE

couds / cousons / cousez

EXAMPLE PHRASES

Demain, je **coudrai** l'écusson sur ton sweat. Tomorrow, I'll sew the badge on your sweatshirt.

Elle **cousut** rapidement le bouton. She quickly sewed the button on.

Je **coudrais** l'ourlet si j'étais sûr de ce que je faisais. I'd sew the hem if I knew what I was doing.

Je n'**avais** pas bien **cousu** le bouton et je l'avais perdu. I hadn't sewn the button on properly and I'd lost it.

je/j' = I **tu** = you **il** = he/it **elle** = she/it **on** = we/one **nous** = we **vous** = you **ils/elles** = they

courir (to run)

PRESENT

je	**cours**
tu	**cours**
il/elle/on	**court**
nous	**courons**
vous	**courez**
ils/elles	**courent**

PRESENT SUBJUNCTIVE

je	**coure**
tu	**coures**
il/elle/on	**coure**
nous	**courions**
vous	**couriez**
ils/elles	**courent**

PERFECT

j'	**ai couru**
tu	**as couru**
il/elle/on	**a couru**
nous	**avons couru**
vous	**avez couru**
ils/elles	**ont couru**

IMPERFECT

je	**courais**
tu	**courais**
il/elle/on	**courait**
nous	**courions**
vous	**couriez**
ils/elles	**couraient**

PRESENT PARTICIPLE

courant

PAST PARTICIPLE

couru

EXAMPLE PHRASES

Je ne **cours** pas très vite. I can't run very fast.

J'**ai couru** jusqu'à l'école. I ran all the way to school.

Ne **courez** pas dans le couloir. Don't run in the corridor.

Elle est sortie en **courant**. She ran out.

je/j' = I   **tu** = you   **il** = he/it   **elle** = she/it   **on** = we/one   **nous** = we   **vous** = you   **ils/elles** = they

courir

FUTURE

je	**courrai**
tu	**courras**
il/elle/on	**courra**
nous	**courrons**
vous	**courrez**
ils/elles	**courront**

CONDITIONAL

je	**courrais**
tu	**courrais**
il/elle/on	**courrait**
nous	**courrions**
vous	**courriez**
ils/elles	**courraient**

PAST HISTORIC

je	**courus**
tu	**courus**
il/elle/on	**courut**
nous	**courûmes**
vous	**courûtes**
ils/elles	**coururent**

PLUPERFECT

j'	**avais couru**
tu	**avais couru**
il/elle/on	**avait couru**
nous	**avions couru**
vous	**aviez couru**
ils/elles	**avaient couru**

IMPERATIVE

cours / courons / courez

EXAMPLE PHRASES

L' été prochain, nous **courrons** le marathon de Londres. Next summer, we'll run the London marathon.

Il **courut** après elle, mais elle était trop rapide. He ran after her, but she was too fast.

Je **courrais** bien plus vite si je n'étais pas fatigué. I'd run much faster if I wasn't tired.

J'étais essoufflé parce que j'**avais couru**. I was out of breath because I'd been running.

je/j' = I **tu** = you **il** = he/it **elle** = she/it **on** = we/one **nous** = we **vous** = you **ils/elles** = they

craindre (to fear)

PRESENT

je	**crains**
tu	**crains**
il/elle/on	**craint**
nous	**craignons**
vous	**craignez**
ils/elles	**craignent**

PRESENT SUBJUNCTIVE

je	**craigne**
tu	**craignes**
il/elle/on	**craigne**
nous	**craignions**
vous	**craigniez**
ils/elles	**craignent**

PERFECT

j'	**ai craint**
tu	**as craint**
il/elle/on	**a craint**
nous	**avons craint**
vous	**avez craint**
ils/elles	**ont craint**

IMPERFECT

je	**craignais**
tu	**craignais**
il/elle/on	**craignait**
nous	**craignions**
vous	**craigniez**
ils/elles	**craignaient**

PRESENT PARTICIPLE

craignant

PAST PARTICIPLE

craint

EXAMPLE PHRASES

Tu n'as rien à **craindre**. You've got nothing to fear.

Je **crains** le pire. I fear the worst.

Ne **craignez** rien, ce chien n'est pas méchant. Don't be scared, this dog is harmless.

Il **craignait** qu'elle ne soit partie. He feared that she had gone.

craindre

FUTURE

je	**craindrai**
tu	**craindras**
il/elle/on	**craindra**
nous	**craindrons**
vous	**craindrez**
ils/elles	**craindront**

CONDITIONAL

je	**craindrais**
tu	**craindrais**
il/elle/on	**craindrait**
nous	**craindrions**
vous	**craindriez**
ils/elles	**craindraient**

PAST HISTORIC

je	**craignis**
tu	**craignis**
il/elle/on	**craignit**
nous	**craignîmes**
vous	**craignîtes**
ils/elles	**craignirent**

PLUPERFECT

j'	**avais craint**
tu	**avais craint**
il/elle/on	**avait craint**
nous	**avions craint**
vous	**aviez craint**
ils/elles	**avaient craint**

IMPERATIVE

crains / craignons / craignez

EXAMPLE PHRASES

Je **craignis** qu'il ne se vexe. I feared he might get upset.

Je ne le **craindrais** pas tant s'il n'était pas si irritable. I wouldn't fear him so much if he wasn't so irritable.

Si j'étais toi, je **craindrais** sa colère. If I were you, I'd fear his anger.

Elle **avait craint** sa colère, mais il n'avait rien dit. She had feared his anger, but he didn't say anything.

je/j' = I   **tu** = you   **il** = he/it   **elle** = she/it   **on** = we/one   **nous** = we   **vous** = you   **ils/elles** = they

créer (to create)

PRESENT

je	**crée**
tu	**crées**
il/elle/on	**crée**
nous	**créons**
vous	**créez**
ils/elles	**créent**

PRESENT SUBJUNCTIVE

je	**crée**
tu	**crées**
il/elle/on	**crée**
nous	**créions**
vous	**créiez**
ils/elles	**créent**

PERFECT

j'	**ai créé**
tu	**as créé**
il/elle/on	**a créé**
nous	**avons créé**
vous	**avez créé**
ils/elles	**ont créé**

IMPERFECT

je	**créais**
tu	**créais**
il/elle/on	**créait**
nous	**créions**
vous	**créiez**
ils/elles	**créaient**

PRESENT PARTICIPLE

créant

PAST PARTICIPLE

créé

EXAMPLE PHRASES

Ce virus **crée** des difficultés dans le monde entier. This virus is causing
   problems all over the world.

Il **a créé** une nouvelle recette. He's created a new recipe.

Nous avons **créé** ce parfum spécialement pour cette occasion. We've created
   this perfume specially for this occasion.

Elle **créait** souvent des disputes entre nous. She would often cause
   arguments between us.

je/j' = I **tu** = you **il** = he/it **elle** = she/it **on** = we/one **nous** = we **vous** = you **ils/elles** = they

créer

FUTURE

je	**créerai**
tu	**créeras**
il/elle/on	**créera**
nous	**créerons**
vous	**créerez**
ils/elles	**créeront**

CONDITIONAL

je	**créerais**
tu	**créerais**
il/elle/on	**créerait**
nous	**créerions**
vous	**créeriez**
ils/elles	**créeraient**

PAST HISTORIC

je	**créai**
tu	**créas**
il/elle/on	**créa**
nous	**créâmes**
vous	**créâtes**
ils/elles	**créèrent**

PLUPERFECT

j'	**avais créé**
tu	**avais créé**
il/elle/on	**avait créé**
nous	**avions créé**
vous	**aviez créé**
ils/elles	**avaient créé**

IMPERATIVE
crée / créons / créez

EXAMPLE PHRASES

Le gouvernement **créera** deux mille emplois supplémentaires. The government will create an extra two thousand jobs.

Les licenciements créèrent des tensions dans l'entreprise. The redundancies created tensions in the firm.

Elle **avait créé** une crème qui allait révolutionner l'industrie des produits cosmétiques. She had created a cream which was to revolutionize the cosmetics industry.

je/j' = I **tu** = you **il** = he/it **elle** = she/it **on** = we/one **nous** = we **vous** = you **ils/elles** = they

crier (to shout)

PRESENT

je	**crie**
tu	**cries**
il/elle/on	**crie**
nous	**crions**
vous	**criez**
ils/elles	**crient**

PRESENT SUBJUNCTIVE

je	**crie**
tu	**cries**
il/elle/on	**crie**
nous	**criions**
vous	**criiez**
ils/elles	**crient**

PERFECT

j'	**ai crié**
tu	**as crié**
il/elle/on	**a crié**
nous	**avons crié**
vous	**avez crié**
ils/elles	**ont crié**

IMPERFECT

je	**criais**
tu	**criais**
il/elle/on	**criait**
nous	**criions**
vous	**criiez**
ils/elles	**criaient**

PRESENT PARTICIPLE

criant

PAST PARTICIPLE

crié

EXAMPLE PHRASES

La maîtresse **crie** tout le temps après nous. The teacher's always shouting after us.

Elle **a crié** au secours. She cried for help.

Ne **crie** pas comme ça! Don't shout!

Je ne veux pas que tu **cries** devant mes copines. I don't want you to shout in front of my friends.

Il **criait** toujours plus fort que moi. He would always shout louder than me.

je/j' = I **tu** = you **il** = he/it **elle** = she/it **on** = we/one **nous** = we **vous** = you **ils/elles** = they

crier

FUTURE

je	**crierai**
tu	**crieras**
il/elle/on	**criera**
nous	**crierons**
vous	**crierez**
ils/elles	**crieront**

CONDITIONAL

je	**crierais**
tu	**crierais**
il/elle/on	**crierait**
nous	**crierions**
vous	**crieriez**
ils/elles	**crieraient**

PAST HISTORIC

je	**criai**
tu	**crias**
il/elle/on	**cria**
nous	**criâmes**
vous	**criâtes**
ils/elles	**crièrent**

PLUPERFECT

j'	**avais crié**
tu	**avais crié**
il/elle/on	**avait crié**
nous	**avions crié**
vous	**aviez crié**
ils/elles	**avaient crié**

IMPERATIVE

crie / crions / criez

EXAMPLE PHRASES

Ton père ne **criera** pas si tu lui expliques ce qui s'est passé. Your dad won't shout if you explain to him what happened.

"Attention!", **cria**-t-il. "Watch out!" he shouted.

Elle **crierait** drôlement si tu lui tachais sa robe. She would really shout if you stained her dress.

Il n'**avait** pas **crié** comme ça depuis longtemps. He hadn't shouted like that for a long time.

je/j' = I **tu** = you **il** = he/it **elle** = she/it **on** = we/one **nous** = we **vous** = you **ils/elles** = they

croire (to believe)

PRESENT		PRESENT SUBJUNCTIVE	
je	**crois**	je	**croie**
tu	**crois**	tu	**croies**
il/elle/on	**croit**	il/elle/on	**croie**
nous	**croyons**	nous	**croyions**
vous	**croyez**	vous	**croyiez**
ils/elles	**croient**	ils/elles	**croient**

PERFECT		IMPERFECT	
j'	**ai cru**	je	**croyais**
tu	**as cru**	tu	**croyais**
il/elle/on	**a cru**	il/elle/on	**croyait**
nous	**avons cru**	nous	**croyions**
vous	**avez cru**	vous	**croyiez**
ils/elles	**ont cru**	ils/elles	**croyaient**

PRESENT PARTICIPLE	PAST PARTICIPLE
croyant	cru

EXAMPLE PHRASES

Je ne te **crois** pas. I don't believe you.

J'**ai cru** que tu n'allais pas venir. I thought you weren't going to come.

Crois-moi, Mme Leblond est très stricte. Believe me, Mrs Leblond is very strict.

Il faut que tu me **croies**. You have to believe me.

Elle **croyait** encore au père Noël. She still believed in Father Christmas.

---

je/j' = I   **tu** = you   **il** = he/it   **elle** = she/it   **on** = we/one   **nous** = we   **vous** = you   **ils/elles** = they

croire

FUTURE

je	**croirai**
tu	**croiras**
il/elle/on	**croira**
nous	**croirons**
vous	**croirez**
ils/elles	**croiront**

CONDITIONAL

je	**croirais**
tu	**croirais**
il/elle/on	**croirait**
nous	**croirions**
vous	**croiriez**
ils/elles	**croiraient**

PAST HISTORIC

je	**crus**
tu	**crus**
il/elle/on	**crut**
nous	**crûmes**
vous	**crûtes**
ils/elles	**crurent**

PLUPERFECT

j'	**avais cru**
tu	**avais cru**
il/elle/on	**avait cru**
nous	**avions cru**
vous	**aviez cru**
ils/elles	**avaient cru**

IMPERATIVE

crois / croyons / croyez

EXAMPLE PHRASES

Elle ne me **croira** pas si je lui dis que j'ai gagné. She won't believe me if I tell her that I won.

Il **crut** que je me moquais de lui. He thought that I was making fun of him.

Elle te **croirait** peut-être si tu lui disais que tu as oublié ton maillot de bain. She might believe you if you tell her that you forgot your swimming costume.

Au début, il ne m'**avait** pas **cru**, mais plus tard il s'était rendu compte que c'était vrai. Initially he hadn't believed me, but later he had realized that it was true.

je/j' = I **tu** = you **il** = he/it **elle** = she/it **on** = we/one **nous** = we **vous** = you **ils/elles** = they

croître (to grow; to increase)

PRESENT

je	**croîs**
tu	**croîs**
il/elle/on	**croît**
nous	**croissons**
vous	**croissez**
ils/elles	**croissent**

PRESENT SUBJUNCTIVE

je	**croisse**
tu	**croisses**
il/elle/on	**croisse**
nous	**croissions**
vous	**croissiez**
ils/elles	**croissent**

PERFECT

j'	**ai crû**
tu	**as crû**
il/elle/on	**a crû**
nous	**avons crû**
vous	**avez crû**
ils/elles	**ont crû**

IMPERFECT

je	**croissais**
tu	**croissais**
il/elle/on	**croissait**
nous	**croissions**
vous	**croissiez**
ils/elles	**croissaient**

PRESENT PARTICIPLE

croissant

PAST PARTICIPLE

crû (*NB*: **crue, crus, crues**)

EXAMPLE PHRASES

Les ventes **croissent** de 6% par an. Sales are growing by 6% per year.

C'est une plante qui **croît** dans les pays chauds. This plant grows in hot countries.

Le nombre de gens qui partent travailler à l'étranger va **croissant**.
An increasing number of people go and work abroad.

---

je/j' = I **tu** = you **il** = he/it **elle** = she/it **on** = we/one **nous** = we **vous** = you **ils/elles** = they

croître

FUTURE

je	**croîtrai**
tu	**croîtras**
il/elle/on	**croîtra**
nous	**croîtrons**
vous	**croîtrez**
ils/elles	**croîtront**

CONDITIONAL

je	**croîtrais**
tu	**croîtrais**
il/elle/on	**croîtrait**
nous	**croîtrions**
vous	**croîtriez**
ils/elles	**croîtraient**

PAST HISTORIC

je	**crûs**
tu	**crûs**
il/elle/on	**crût**
nous	**crûmes**
vous	**crûtes**
ils/elles	**crûrent**

PLUPERFECT

j'	**avais crû**
tu	**avais crû**
il/elle/on	**avait crû**
nous	**avions crû**
vous	**aviez crû**
ils/elles	**avaient crû**

IMPERATIVE

croîs/ croissons / croissez

EXAMPLE PHRASES

Les problèmes **crûrent** de jour en jour. Problems increased day after day.

Les dépenses **croîtraient** rapidement si on ne faisait pas attention.

Spending would increase rapidly if we weren't careful.

cueillir (to pick)

PRESENT

je	**cueille**
tu	**cueilles**
il/elle/on	**cueille**
nous	**cueillons**
vous	**cueillez**
ils/elles	**cueillent**

PRESENT SUBJUNCTIVE

je	**cueille**
tu	**cueilles**
il/elle/on	**cueille**
nous	**cueillions**
vous	**cueilliez**
ils/elles	**cueillent**

PERFECT

j'	**ai cueilli**
tu	**as cueilli**
il/elle/on	**a cueilli**
nous	**avons cueilli**
vous	**avez cueilli**
ils/elles	**ont cueilli**

IMPERFECT

je	**cueillais**
tu	**cueillais**
il/elle/on	**cueillait**
nous	**cueillions**
vous	**cueilliez**
ils/elles	**cueillaient**

PRESENT PARTICIPLE
cueillant

PAST PARTICIPLE
cueilli

EXAMPLE PHRASES

Il est interdit de **cueillir** des fleurs sauvages dans la montagne. It's forbidden to pick wild flowers in the mountains.

J'**ai cueilli** quelques fraises dans le jardin. I picked a few strawberries in the garden.

Ne **cueille** pas les fleurs dans le parc. Don't pick the flowers in the park.

J'aimerais que tu me **cueilles** des mûres pour faire de la confiture. I'd like you to pick some blackberries for me to make jam.

cueillir

FUTURE

je	**cueillerai**
tu	**cueilleras**
il/elle/on	**cueillera**
nous	**cueillerons**
vous	**cueillerez**
ils/elles	**cueilleront**

CONDITIONAL

je	**cueillerais**
tu	**cueillerais**
il/elle/on	**cueillerait**
nous	**cueillerions**
vous	**cueilleriez**
ils/elles	**cueilleraient**

PAST HISTORIC

je	**cueillis**
tu	**cueillis**
il/elle/on	**cueillit**
nous	**cueillîmes**
vous	**cueillîtes**
ils/elles	**cueillirent**

PLUPERFECT

j'	**avais cueilli**
tu	**avais cueilli**
il/elle/on	**avait cueilli**
nous	**avions cueilli**
vous	**aviez cueilli**
ils/elles	**avaient cueilli**

IMPERATIVE

cueille / cueillons / cueillez

EXAMPLE PHRASES

Je **cueillerai** des framboises à la ferme. I'll pick some raspberries at the farm.

Elle **cueillit** des fraises des bois. She picked some wild strawberries.

Je **cueillerais** toutes les fleurs de la terre entière pour toi. I'd pick all the flowers in the whole wide world for you.

Il lui **avait cueilli** un beau bouquet de fleurs. He'd picked a beautiful bunch of flowers for her.

je/j' = I **tu** = you **il** = he/it **elle** = she/it **on** = we/one **nous** = we **vous** = you **ils/elles** = they

cuire (to cook)

PRESENT		PRESENT SUBJUNCTIVE	
je	**cuis**	je	**cuise**
tu	**cuis**	tu	**cuises**
il/elle/on	**cuit**	il/elle/on	**cuise**
nous	**cuisons**	nous	**cuisions**
vous	**cuisez**	vous	**cuisiez**
ils/elles	**cuisent**	ils/elles	**cuisent**

PERFECT		IMPERFECT	
j'	**ai cuit**	je	**cuisais**
tu	**as cuit**	tu	**cuisais**
il/elle/on	**a cuit**	il/elle/on	**cuisait**
nous	**avons cuit**	nous	**cuisions**
vous	**avez cuit**	vous	**cuisiez**
ils/elles	**ont cuit**	ils/elles	**cuisaient**

PRESENT PARTICIPLE	PAST PARTICIPLE
cuisant	cuit

EXAMPLE PHRASES

Ce gâteau prend environ une heure à **cuire**. This cake takes about an hour to bake.

En général, je **cuis** les légumes à la vapeur. I usually steam vegetables.

Je les **ai cuits** au beurre. I cooked them in butter.

Mon père **cuisait** toujours la viande au barbecue. My dad always barbecued meat.

cuire

FUTURE

je	**cuirai**
tu	**cuiras**
il/elle/on	**cuira**
nous	**cuirons**
vous	**cuirez**
ils/elles	**cuiront**

CONDITIONAL

je	**cuirais**
tu	**cuirais**
il/elle/on	**cuirait**
nous	**cuirions**
vous	**cuiriez**
ils/elles	**cuiraient**

PAST HISTORIC

je	**cuisis**
tu	**cuisis**
il/elle/on	**cuisit**
nous	**cuisîmes**
vous	**cuisîtes**
ils/elles	**cuisirent**

PLUPERFECT

j'	**avais cuit**
tu	**avais cuit**
il/elle/on	**avait cuit**
nous	**avions cuit**
vous	**aviez cuit**
ils/elles	**avaient cuit**

IMPERATIVE

cuis / cuisons / cuisez

EXAMPLE PHRASES

Nous **cuirons** les côtelettes sur le gril. We'll grill the chops.

Elle **cuisit** l'omelette et la servit. She cooked the omelette and served it.

Je **cuirais** les crêpes plus longtemps si je n'avais pas peur de les faire brûler.
    I'd cook the pancakes longer if I wasn't scared of burning them.

Elle **avait cuit** le poisson au four. She'd baked the fish in the oven.

---

je/j' = I **tu** = you **il** = he/it **elle** = she/it **on** = we/one **nous** = we **vous** = you **ils/elles** = they

se débrouiller (to manage)

PRESENT

je	**me débrouille**
tu	**te débrouilles**
il/elle/on	**se débrouille**
nous	**nous débrouillons**
vous	**vous débrouillez**
ils/elles	**se débrouillent**

PRESENT SUBJUNCTIVE

je	**me débrouille**
tu	**te débrouilles**
il/elle/on	**se débrouille**
nous	**nous débrouillions**
vous	**vous débrouilliez**
ils/elles	**se débrouillent**

PERFECT

je	**me suis débrouillé(e)**
tu	**t'es débrouillé(e)**
il/elle/on	**s'est débrouillé(e)**
nous	**nous sommes débrouillé(e)s**
vous	**vous êtes débrouillé(e)(s)**
ils/elles	**se sont débrouillé(e)s**

IMPERFECT

je	**me débrouillais**
tu	**te débrouillais**
il/elle/on	**se débrouillait**
nous	**nous débrouillions**
vous	**vous débrouilliez**
ils/elles	**se débrouillaient**

PRESENT PARTICIPLE
se débrouillant

PAST PARTICIPLE
débrouillé

EXAMPLE PHRASES

Elle **se débrouille** bien à l'école. She gets on well at school.

C'était difficile, mais je ne **me suis** pas trop mal **débrouillé**. It was difficult, but I managed OK.

Débrouille-toi tout seul. Sort things out for yourself.

Débrouillez-vous pour arriver à l'heure. Make sure you're on time.

Je **me débrouillais** mieux en français qu'en maths. I got on better in French than in maths.

---

je/j' = I **tu** = you **il** = he/it **elle** = she/it **on** = we/one **nous** = we **vous** = you **ils/elles** = they

se débrouiller

FUTURE

je	**me débrouillerai**
tu	**te débrouilleras**
il/elle/on	**se débrouillera**
nous	**nous débrouillerons**
vous	**vous débrouillerez**
ils/elles	**se débrouilleront**

CONDITIONAL

je	**me débrouillerais**
tu	**te débrouillerais**
il/elle/on	**se débrouillerait**
nous	**nous débrouillerions**
vous	**vous débrouilleriez**
ils/elles	**se débrouilleraient**

PAST HISTORIC

je	**me débrouillai**
tu	**te débrouillas**
il/elle/on	**se débrouilla**
nous	**nous débrouillâmes**
vous	**vous débrouillâtes**
ils/elles	**se débrouillèrent**

PLUPERFECT

je	**m'étais débrouillé(e)**
tu	**t'étais débrouillé(e)**
il/elle/on	**s'était débrouillé(e)**
nous	**nous étions débrouillé(e)s**
vous	**vous étiez débrouillé(e)(s)**
ils/elles	**s'étaient débrouillé(e)s**

IMPERATIVE

débrouille-toi / débrouillons-nous / débrouillez-vous

EXAMPLE PHRASES

Nous **nous débrouillerons** bien sans toi. We'll manage fine without you.

Il **se débrouilla** tant bien que mal pour préparer le dîner. He just about managed to prepare dinner.

Il **se débrouillerait** bien tout seul s'il était obligé. He would manage fine by himself if he had to.

Comme mes parents étaient partis, je **m'étais débrouillée** toute seule. As my parents were away, I had managed by myself.

je/j' = I **tu** = you **il** = he/it **elle** = she/it **on** = we/one **nous** = we **vous** = you **ils/elles** = they

descendre (to go down)

PRESENT

je	**descends**
tu	**descends**
il/elle/on	**descend**
nous	**descendons**
vous	**descendez**
ils/elles	**descendent**

PRESENT SUBJUNCTIVE

je	**descende**
tu	**descendes**
il/elle/on	**descende**
nous	**descendions**
vous	**descendiez**
ils/elles	**descendent**

PERFECT

je	**suis descendu(e)**
tu	**es descendu(e)**
il/elle/on	**est descendu(e)**
nous	**sommes descendu(e)s**
vous	**êtes descendu(e)(s)**
ils/elles	**sont descendu(e)s**

IMPERFECT

je	**descendais**
tu	**descendais**
il/elle/on	**descendait**
nous	**descendions**
vous	**descendiez**
ils/elles	**descendaient**

PRESENT PARTICIPLE

descendant

PAST PARTICIPLE

descendu

EXAMPLE PHRASES

Vous pouvez **descendre** ma valise, s'il vous plaît? Could you get my suitcase down, please?

Reste en bas: je **descends**! Stay downstairs – I'm coming down!

Nous **sommes descendus** à la station Trocadéro. We got off at Trocadéro.

Descendez la rue jusqu'au rond-point. Go down the street to the roundabout.

Il faut que je **descende** chercher quelque chose à la cave. I have to go down to the cellar to get something.

---

je/j' = I **tu** = you **il** = he/it **elle** = she/it **on** = we/one **nous** = we **vous** = you **ils/elles** = they

descendre

FUTURE

je	**descendrai**
tu	**descendras**
il/elle/on	**descendra**
nous	**descendrons**
vous	**descendrez**
ils/elles	**descendront**

CONDITIONAL

je	**descendrais**
tu	**descendrais**
il/elle/on	**descendrait**
nous	**descendrions**
vous	**descendriez**
ils/elles	**descendraient**

PAST HISTORIC

je	**descendis**
tu	**descendis**
il/elle/on	**descendit**
nous	**descendîmes**
vous	**descendîtes**
ils/elles	**descendirent**

PLUPERFECT

j'	**étais descendu(e)**
tu	**étais descendu(e)**
il/elle/on	**était descendu(e)**
nous	**étions descendu(e)s**
vous	**étiez descendu(e)(s)**
ils/elles	**étaient descendu(e)s**

IMPERATIVE

descends / descendons / descendez

EXAMPLE PHRASES

Nous **descendrons** dans le Midi au mois de juillet. We'll go down to the south of France in July.

Il **descendit** les escaliers en courant. He ran down the stairs.

Si j'étais toi, je ne **descendrais** pas l'escalier si vite. I wouldn't rush down the stairs if I were you.

Ils **étaient descendus** regarder la télé quand les plombs ont sauté. They had gone down to watch TV when the fuses blew.

je/j' = I **tu** = you **il** = he/it **elle** = she/it **on** = we/one **nous** = we **vous** = you **ils/elles** = they

devenir (to become)

PRESENT

je	deviens
tu	deviens
il/elle/on	devient
nous	devenons
vous	devenez
ils/elles	deviennent

PRESENT SUBJUNCTIVE

je	devienne
tu	deviennes
il/elle/on	devienne
nous	devenions
vous	deveniez
ils/elles	deviennent

PERFECT

je	suis devenu(e)
tu	es devenu(e)
il/elle/on	est devenu(e)
nous	sommes devenu(e)s
vous	êtes devenu(e)(s)
ils/elles	sont devenu(e)s

IMPERFECT

je	devenais
tu	devenais
il/elle/on	devenait
nous	devenions
vous	deveniez
ils/elles	devenaient

PRESENT PARTICIPLE

devenant

PAST PARTICIPLE

devenu

EXAMPLE PHRASES

Ça **devient** de plus en plus difficile. It's becoming more and more difficult.

Il **est devenu** médecin. He became a doctor.

Qu'est-ce qu'elle **est devenue**? What has become of her?

Il ne faut pas que ça **devienne** une corvée. It mustn't become a chore.

Elle **devenait** de plus en plus exigeante. She was becoming more and more demanding.

---

devenir

FUTURE

je	**deviendrai**
tu	**deviendras**
il/elle/on	**deviendra**
nous	**deviendrons**
vous	**deviendrez**
ils/elles	**deviendront**

CONDITIONAL

je	**deviendrais**
tu	**deviendrais**
il/elle/on	**deviendrait**
nous	**deviendrions**
vous	**deviendriez**
ils/elles	**deviendraient**

PAST HISTORIC

je	**devins**
tu	**devins**
il/elle/on	**devint**
nous	**devînmes**
vous	**devîntes**
ils/elles	**devinrent**

PLUPERFECT

j'	**étais devenu(e)**
tu	**étais devenu(e)**
il/elle/on	**était devenu(e)**
nous	**étions devenu(e)s**
vous	**étiez devenu(e)(s)**
ils/elles	**étaient devenu(e)s**

IMPERATIVE

deviens / devenons / devenez

EXAMPLE PHRASES

J'espère qu'elle ne **deviendra** pas comme sa mère. I hope that she won't become like her mother.

Elle **devint** la première femme à traverser l'Atlantique en avion. She became the first woman to fly across the Atlantic.

Si on les nourrissait trop, les poissons rouges **deviendraient** énormes. If we overfed them, the goldfish would become enormous.

Je me demandais ce qu'ils **étaient devenus**. I wondered what had become of them.

je/j' = I **tu** = you **il** = he/it **elle** = she/it **on** = we/one **nous** = we **vous** = you **ils/elles** = they

devoir (to have to; to owe)

PRESENT

je	**dois**
tu	**dois**
il/elle/on	**doit**
nous	**devons**
vous	**devez**
ils/elles	**doivent**

PRESENT SUBJUNCTIVE

je	**doive**
tu	**doives**
il/elle/on	**doive**
nous	**devions**
vous	**deviez**
ils/elles	**doivent**

PERFECT

j'	**ai dû**
tu	**as dû**
il/elle/on	**a dû**
nous	**avons dû**
vous	**avez dû**
ils/elles	**ont dû**

IMPERFECT

je	**devais**
tu	**devais**
il/elle/on	**devait**
nous	**devions**
vous	**deviez**
ils/elles	**devaient**

PRESENT PARTICIPLE

devant

PAST PARTICIPLE

dû (*NB*: **due, dus, dues**)

EXAMPLE PHRASES

Je **dois** aller faire les courses ce matin. I have to do the shopping this morning.

À quelle heure est-ce que tu **dois** partir? What time do you have to leave?

J'**ai dû** partir avant la fin du film. I had to leave before the end of the film.

Il **a dû** changer d'avis. He must have changed his mind.

Il **devait** prendre le train pour aller travailler. He had to go to work by train.

---

je/j' = I   **tu** = you   **il** = he/it   **elle** = she/it   **on** = we/one   **nous** = we   **vous** = you   **ils/elles** = they

devoir

FUTURE

je	**devrai**
tu	**devras**
il/elle/on	**devra**
nous	**devrons**
vous	**devrez**
ils/elles	**devront**

CONDITIONAL

je	**devrais**
tu	**devrais**
il/elle/on	**devrait**
nous	**devrions**
vous	**devriez**
ils/elles	**devraient**

PAST HISTORIC

je	**dus**
tu	**dus**
il/elle/on	**dut**
nous	**dûmes**
vous	**dûtes**
ils/elles	**durent**

PLUPERFECT

j'	**avais dû**
tu	**avais dû**
il/elle/on	**avait dû**
nous	**avions dû**
vous	**aviez dû**
ils/elles	**avaient dû**

IMPERATIVE

dois / devons / devez

EXAMPLE PHRASES

Ils **devront** finir leurs devoirs avant de venir. They'll have to finish their homework before they come.

Elle **dut** lui annoncer elle-même la mauvaise nouvelle. She had to tell him the bad news herself.

Tu ne **devrais** pas les déranger tout le temps comme ça. You shouldn't disturb them all the time like that.

Comme il était malade, il **avait dû** arrêter de fumer. As he were ill, he'd had to stop smoking.

je/j' = I **tu** = you **il** = he/it **elle** = she/it **on** = we/one **nous** = we **vous** = you **ils/elles** = they

dire (to say; to tell)

PRESENT

je **dis**

tu **dis**

il/elle/on **dit**

nous **disons**

vous **dites**

ils/elles **disent**

PRESENT SUBJUNCTIVE

je **dise**

tu **dises**

il/elle/on **dise**

nous **disions**

vous **disiez**

ils/elles **disent**

PERFECT

j' **ai dit**

tu **as dit**

il/elle/on **a dit**

nous **avons dit**

vous **avez dit**

ils/elles **ont dit**

IMPERFECT

je **disais**

tu **disais**

il/elle/on **disait**

nous **disions**

vous **disiez**

ils/elles **disaient**

PRESENT PARTICIPLE

disant

PAST PARTICIPLE

dit

EXAMPLE PHRASES

Qu'est-ce qu'elle **dit**? What is she saying?

Comment ça se **dit** en anglais? How do you say that in English?

"Bonjour!", **a-t-il dit**. "Hello!" he said.

Ne **dis** pas de bêtises. Don't talk nonsense.

Ils m'**ont dit** que le film était nul. They told me that the film was rubbish.

je/j' = I **tu** = you **il** = he/it **elle** = she/it **on** = we/one **nous** = we **vous** = you **ils/elles** = they

dire

FUTURE

je	**dirai**
tu	**diras**
il/elle/on	**dira**
nous	**dirons**
vous	**direz**
ils/elles	**diront**

CONDITIONAL

je	**dirais**
tu	**dirais**
il/elle/on	**dirait**
nous	**dirions**
vous	**diriez**
ils/elles	**diraient**

PAST HISTORIC

je	**dis**
tu	**dis**
il/elle/on	**dit**
nous	**dîmes**
vous	**dîtes**
ils/elles	**dirent**

PLUPERFECT

j'	**avais dit**
tu	**avais dit**
il/elle/on	**avait dit**
nous	**avions dit**
vous	**aviez dit**
ils/elles	**avaient dit**

IMPERATIVE

dis / disons / dites

EXAMPLE PHRASES

Je lui **dirai** de venir à midi. I'll tell him to come at midday.

"Viens ici!" **dit**-il. Mais le chien refusait de bouger. "Come here!" he said.
   But the dog refused to move.

On **dirait** qu'il va neiger. It looks like snow.

On ne m'**avait** pas **dit** que tu serais là. I hadn't been told that you'd be there.

donner (to give)

PRESENT

je	**donne**
tu	**donnes**
il/elle/on	**donne**
nous	**donnons**
vous	**donnez**
ils/elles	**donnent**

PRESENT SUBJUNCTIVE

je	**donne**
tu	**donnes**
il/elle/on	**donne**
nous	**donnions**
vous	**donniez**
ils/elles	**donnent**

PERFECT

j'	**ai donné**
tu	**as donné**
il/elle/on	**a donné**
nous	**avons donné**
vous	**avez donné**
ils/elles	**ont donné**

IMPERFECT

je	**donnais**
tu	**donnais**
il/elle/on	**donnait**
nous	**donnions**
vous	**donniez**
ils/elles	**donnaient**

PRESENT PARTICIPLE

donnant

PAST PARTICIPLE

donné

EXAMPLE PHRASES

L'appartement **donne** sur la place. The flat overlooks the square.

Est-ce que je t'**ai donné** mon adresse? Did I give you my address?

Donne-moi la main. Give me your hand.

Il faut que tu me **donnes** plus de détails. You must give me more details.

Je **donnais** des sucres aux chevaux. I'd give sugar lumps to the horses.

donner

FUTURE

je	**donnerai**
tu	**donneras**
il/elle/on	**donnera**
nous	**donnerons**
vous	**donnerez**
ils/elles	**donneront**

CONDITIONAL

je	**donnerais**
tu	**donnerais**
il/elle/on	**donnerait**
nous	**donnerions**
vous	**donneriez**
ils/elles	**donneraient**

PAST HISTORIC

je	**donnai**
tu	**donnas**
il/elle/on	**donna**
nous	**donnâmes**
vous	**donnâtes**
ils/elles	**donnèrent**

PLUPERFECT

j'	**avais donné**
tu	**avais donné**
il/elle/on	**avait donné**
nous	**avions donné**
vous	**aviez donné**
ils/elles	**avaient donné**

IMPERATIVE

donne / donnons / donnez

EXAMPLE PHRASES

Je te **donnerai** un ticket de métro. I'll give you a tube ticket.

Il lui **donna** un vieux livre. He gave him an old book.

Je lui **donnerais** des nouvelles si j'avais son adresse. I'd give her some news
if I had her address.

Je lui **avais donné** mon numéro de téléphone mais il a dû le perdre.
I had given him my phone number but he must have lost it.

dormir (to sleep)

PRESENT		PRESENT SUBJUNCTIVE	
je	**dors**	je	**dorme**
tu	**dors**	tu	**dormes**
il/elle/on	**dort**	il/elle/on	**dorme**
nous	**dormons**	nous	**dormions**
vous	**dormez**	vous	**dormiez**
ils/elles	**dorment**	ils/elles	**dorment**

PERFECT		IMPERFECT	
j'	**ai dormi**	je	**dormais**
tu	**as dormi**	tu	**dormais**
il/elle/on	**a dormi**	il/elle/on	**dormait**
nous	**avons dormi**	nous	**dormions**
vous	**avez dormi**	vous	**dormiez**
ils/elles	**ont dormi**	ils/elles	**dormaient**

PRESENT PARTICIPLE
dormant

PAST PARTICIPLE
dormi

EXAMPLE PHRASES

Nous **dormons** dans la même chambre. We sleep in the same bedroom.

Tu **as** bien **dormi**? Did you sleep well?

Dors bien. Sleep well.

Elle m'a fait une tisane pour que je **dorme** bien. She made me a herbal tea so that I got a good sleep.

À 9 heures, il **dormait** déjà. He was already asleep by nine.

dormir

FUTURE

je	**dormirai**
tu	**dormiras**
il/elle/on	**dormira**
nous	**dormirons**
vous	**dormirez**
ils/elles	**dormiront**

CONDITIONAL

je	**dormirais**
tu	**dormirais**
il/elle/on	**dormirait**
nous	**dormirions**
vous	**dormiriez**
ils/elles	**dormiraient**

PAST HISTORIC

je	**dormis**
tu	**dormis**
il/elle/on	**dormit**
nous	**dormîmes**
vous	**dormîtes**
ils/elles	**dormirent**

PLUPERFECT

j'	**avais dormi**
tu	**avais dormi**
il/elle/on	**avait dormi**
nous	**avions dormi**
vous	**aviez dormi**
ils/elles	**avaient dormi**

IMPERATIVE

dors / dormons / dormez

EXAMPLE PHRASES

Ce soir, nous **dormirons** sous la tente. Tonight we'll sleep in the tent.

Il était si fatigué qu'il **dormit** toute la journée. He was so tired that he slept all day.

Il **dormirait** mieux s'il buvait moins de café. He'd sleep better if he didn't drink so much coffee.

J'étais épuisé car je n'**avais** pas **dormi** de la nuit. I was exhausted as I hadn't slept all night.

je/j' = I **tu** = you **il** = he/it **elle** = she/it **on** = we/one **nous** = we **vous** = you **ils/elles** = they

écrire (to write)

PRESENT

j'	**écris**
tu	**écris**
il/elle/on	**écrit**
nous	**écrivons**
vous	**écrivez**
ils/elles	**écrivent**

PRESENT SUBJUNCTIVE

j'	**écrive**
tu	**écrives**
il/elle/on	**écrive**
nous	**écrivions**
vous	**écriviez**
ils/elles	**écrivent**

PERFECT

j'	**ai écrit**
tu	**as écrit**
il/elle/on	**a écrit**
nous	**avons écrit**
vous	**avez écrit**
ils/elles	**ont écrit**

IMPERFECT

j'	**écrivais**
tu	**écrivais**
il/elle/on	**écrivait**
nous	**écrivions**
vous	**écriviez**
ils/elles	**écrivaient**

PRESENT PARTICIPLE
écrivant

PAST PARTICIPLE
écrit

EXAMPLE PHRASES

Elle **écrit** des romans. She writes novels.

Tu **as écrit** à ta correspondante récemment? Have you written to your penfriend recently?

Écrivez votre nom en haut de la feuille. Write your name at the top of the page.

Elle aimerait que tu **écrives** plus souvent. She'd like you to write more often.

Il ne nous **écrivait** jamais quand il était en France. He never wrote to us when he was in France.

je/j' = I **tu** = you **il** = he/it **elle** = she/it **on** = we/one **nous** = we **vous** = you **ils/elles** = they

écrire

FUTURE

j'	**écrirai**
tu	**écriras**
il/elle/on	**écrira**
nous	**écrirons**
vous	**écrirez**
ils/elles	**écriront**

CONDITIONAL

j'	**écrirais**
tu	**écrirais**
il/elle/on	**écrirait**
nous	**écririons**
vous	**écririez**
ils/elles	**écriraient**

PAST HISTORIC

j'	**écrivis**
tu	**écrivis**
il/elle/on	**écrivit**
nous	**écrivîmes**
vous	**écrivîtes**
ils/elles	**écrivirent**

PLUPERFECT

j'	**avais écrit**
tu	**avais écrit**
il/elle/on	**avait écrit**
nous	**avions écrit**
vous	**aviez écrit**
ils/elles	**avaient écrit**

IMPERATIVE
écris / écrivons / écrivez

EXAMPLE PHRASES

Demain, j'**écrirai** une lettre au directeur. Tomorrow, I'll write a letter to the headmaster.

Il **écrivit** un poème à la lueur de la bougie. He wrote a poem by candlelight.

J'**écrirais** plus souvent si j'avais le temps. I'd write more often if I had the time.

Comme il n'**avait** encore rien **écrit** sur sa feuille, il se fit disputer par la maîtresse. As he hadn't written anything on his sheet yet, he was told off by the teacher.

---

je/j' = I **tu** = you **il** = he/it **elle** = she/it **on** = we/one **nous** = we **vous** = you **ils/elles** = they

émouvoir (to move)

PRESENT		PRESENT SUBJUNCTIVE	
j'	**émeus**	j'	**émeuve**
tu	**émeus**	tu	**émeuves**
il/elle/on	**émeut**	il/elle/on	**émeuve**
nous	**émouvons**	nous	**émeuvions**
vous	**émouvez**	vous	**émeuviez**
ils/elles	**émeuvent**	ils/elles	**émeuvent**

PERFECT		IMPERFECT	
j'	**ai ému**	j'	**émouvais**
tu	**as ému**	tu	**émouvais**
il/elle/on	**a ému**	il/elle/on	**émouvait**
nous	**avons ému**	nous	**émouvions**
vous	**avez ému**	vous	**émouviez**
ils/elles	**ont ému**	ils/elles	**émouvaient**

PRESENT PARTICIPLE
émouvant

PAST PARTICIPLE
ému

EXAMPLE PHRASES

Cette histoire m'**émeut** toujours beaucoup. This story always moves me to tears.

Sa fausse gentillesse ne m'**émeut** pas. I won't be moved by his fake kindness.

Ce film nous **a ému**. This film moved us.

Cela m'**émouvait** toujours de les voir se quitter à la fin de l'été. It always moved me to see them part at the end of the summer.

---

je/j' = I   tu = you   il = he/it   elle = she/it   on = we/one   **nous** = we   **vous** = you   **ils/elles** = they

émouvoir

FUTURE

j'	**émouvrai**
tu	**émouvras**
il/elle/on	**émouvra**
nous	**émouvrons**
vous	**émouvrez**
ils/elles	**émouvront**

CONDITIONAL

j'	**émouvrais**
tu	**émouvrais**
il/elle/on	**émouvrait**
nous	**émouvrions**
vous	**émouvriez**
ils/elles	**émouvraient**

PAST HISTORIC

j'	**émus**
tu	**émus**
il/elle/on	**émut**
nous	**émûmes**
vous	**émûtes**
ils/elles	**émurent**

PLUPERFECT

j'	**avais ému**
tu	**avais ému**
il/elle/on	**avait ému**
nous	**avions ému**
vous	**aviez ému**
ils/elles	**avaient ému**

IMPERATIVE

émeus / émouvons / émouvez

EXAMPLE PHRASES

Sa franchise l'**émut** vraiment. His frankness really moved her.
Sa lettre l'**avait** beaucoup **émue**. She had been deeply moved by his letter.

s'ennuyer (to be bored)

PRESENT

je	**m'ennuie**
tu	**t'ennuies**
il/elle/on	**s'ennuie**
nous	**nous ennuyons**
vous	**vous ennuyez**
ils/elles	**s'ennuient**

PRESENT SUBJUNCTIVE

je	**m'ennuie**
tu	**t'ennuies**
il/elle/on	**s'ennuie**
nous	**nous ennuyions**
vous	**vous ennuyiez**
ils/elles	**s'ennuient**

PERFECT

je	**me suis ennuyé(e)**
tu	**t'es ennuyé(e)**
il/elle/on	**s'est ennuyé(e)**
nous	**nous sommes ennuyé(e)s**
vous	**vous êtes ennuyé(e)(s)**
ils/elles	**se sont ennuyé(e)s**

IMPERFECT

je	**m'ennuyais**
tu	**t'ennuyais**
il/elle/on	**s'ennuyait**
nous	**nous ennuyions**
vous	**vous ennuyiez**
ils/elles	**s'ennuyaient**

PRESENT PARTICIPLE
s'ennuyant

PAST PARTICIPLE
ennuyé

EXAMPLE PHRASES

Elle **s'ennuie** un peu à l'école. She's a little bored at school.

Je **me suis ennuyé** quand tu étais partie. I got bored when you were away.

Ne **t'ennuie** pas trop cet après-midi. Don't get too bored this afternoon.

Je ne voudrais pas qu'elle **s'ennuie** avec moi. I wouldn't want her to get bored with me.

On ne **s'ennuyait** jamais avec lui. We never got bored with him.

---

je/j' = I   **tu** = you   **il** = he/it   **elle** = she/it   **on** = we/one   **nous** = we   **vous** = you   **ils/elles** = they

s'ennuyer

FUTURE

je	**m'ennuierai**
tu	**t'ennuieras**
il/elle/on	**s'ennuiera**
nous	**nous ennuierons**
vous	**vous ennuierez**
ils/elles	**s'ennuieront**

CONDITIONAL

je	**m'ennuierais**
tu	**t'ennuierais**
il/elle/on	**s'ennuierait**
nous	**nous ennuierions**
vous	**vous ennuieriez**
ils/elles	**s'ennuieraient**

PAST HISTORIC

je	**m'ennuyai**
tu	**t'ennuyas**
il/elle/on	**s'ennuya**
nous	**nous ennuyâmes**
vous	**vous ennuyâtes**
ils/elles	**s'ennuyèrent**

PLUPERFECT

je	**m'étais ennuyé(e)**
tu	**t'étais ennuyé(e)**
il/elle/on	**s'était ennuyé(e)**
nous	**nous étions ennuyé(e)s**
vous	**vous étiez ennuyé(e)(s)**
ils/elles	**s'étaient ennuyé(e)s**

IMPERATIVE

ennuie-toi / ennuyons-nous / ennuyez-vous

EXAMPLE PHRASES

Il **s'ennuiera** sûrement quand ses copains seront partis. He'll probably be bored when his friends are away.

Elle **s'ennuya** un peu. She got a little bored.

Tu ne **t'ennuierais** pas tant si tu allais jouer avec les autres. You wouldn't be so bored if you went to play with the others.

Il **s'était ennuyé** pendant les vacances et il était content de retrouver ses copains. He'd got bored during the holidays and he was happy to be with his friends again.

je/j' = I **tu** = you **il** = he/it **elle** = she/it **on** = we/one **nous** = we **vous** = you **ils/elles** = they

entendre (to hear)

PRESENT

j'	**entends**
tu	**entends**
il/elle/on	**entend**
nous	**entendons**
vous	**entendez**
ils/elles	**entendent**

PRESENT SUBJUNCTIVE

j'	**entende**
tu	**entendes**
il/elle/on	**entende**
nous	**entendions**
vous	**entendiez**
ils/elles	**entendent**

PERFECT

j'	**ai entendu**
tu	**as entendu**
il/elle/on	**a entendu**
nous	**avons entendu**
vous	**avez entendu**
ils/elles	**ont entendu**

IMPERFECT

j'	**entendais**
tu	**entendais**
il/elle/on	**entendait**
nous	**entendions**
vous	**entendiez**
ils/elles	**entendaient**

PRESENT PARTICIPLE
entendant

PAST PARTICIPLE
entendu

EXAMPLE PHRASES

Il n'**entend** pas bien. He can't hear very well.

Tu **as entendu** ce que je t'ai dit? Did you hear what I said to you?

Il ne faut pas qu'elle nous **entende**. She mustn't hear us.

Elle n'**entendait** jamais le réveil sonner. She never heard the alarm clock ring.

je/j' = I **tu** = you **il** = he/it **elle** = she/it **on** = we/one **nous** = we **vous** = you **ils/elles** = they

entendre

FUTURE

j'	**entendrai**
tu	**entendras**
il/elle/on	**entendra**
nous	**entendrons**
vous	**entendrez**
ils/elles	**entendront**

CONDITIONAL

j'	**entendrais**
tu	**entendrais**
il/elle/on	**entendrait**
nous	**entendrions**
vous	**entendriez**
ils/elles	**entendraient**

PAST HISTORIC

j'	**entendis**
tu	**entendis**
il/elle/on	**entendit**
nous	**entendîmes**
vous	**entendîtes**
ils/elles	**entendirent**

PLUPERFECT

j'	**avais entendu**
tu	**avais entendu**
il/elle/on	**avait entendu**
nous	**avions entendu**
vous	**aviez entendu**
ils/elles	**avaient entendu**

IMPERATIVE

entends / entendons / entendez

EXAMPLE PHRASES

Tu les **entendras** sûrement rentrer. You'll probably hear them come back.

Elle **entendit** les oiseaux chanter. She heard the birds singing.

On **entendrait** moins les voisins si les murs étaient plus épais. We'd hear the neighbours less if the walls were thicker.

Il ne les **avait** pas **entendus** arriver. He hadn't heard them arrive.

je/j' = I **tu** = you **il** = he/it **elle** = she/it **on** = we/one **nous** = we **vous** = you **ils/elles** = they

entrer (to come in; to go in)

PRESENT		PRESENT SUBJUNCTIVE	
j'	entre	j'	entre
tu	entres	tu	entres
il/elle/on	entre	il/elle/on	entre
nous	entrons	nous	entrions
vous	entrez	vous	entriez
ils/elles	entrent	ils/elles	entrent

PERFECT		IMPERFECT	
je	suis entré(e)	j'	entrais
tu	es entré(e)	tu	entrais
il/elle/on	est entré(e)	il/elle/on	entrait
nous	sommes entré(e)s	nous	entrions
vous	êtes entré(e)(s)	vous	entriez
ils/elles	sont entré(e)s	ils/elles	entraient

PRESENT PARTICIPLE
entrant

PAST PARTICIPLE
entré

EXAMPLE PHRASES

Je peux **entrer**? Can I come in?

Ils **sont** tous **entrés** dans la maison. They all went inside the house.

Entrez par la porte de derrière. Come in by the back door.

Essuie-toi les pieds en **entrant**. Wipe your feet as you come in.

entrer

FUTURE

j'	**entrerai**
tu	**entreras**
il/elle/on	**entrera**
nous	**entrerons**
vous	**entrerez**
ils/elles	**entreront**

CONDITIONAL

j'	**entrerais**
tu	**entrerais**
il/elle/on	**entrerait**
nous	**entrerions**
vous	**entreriez**
ils/elles	**entreraient**

PAST HISTORIC

j'	**entrai**
tu	**entras**
il/elle/on	**entra**
nous	**entrâmes**
vous	**entrâtes**
ils/elles	**entrèrent**

PLUPERFECT

j'	**étais entré(e)**
tu	**étais entré(e)**
il/elle/on	**était entré(e)**
nous	**étions entré(e)s**
vous	**étiez entré(e)(s)**
ils/elles	**étaient entré(e)s**

IMPERATIVE

entre / entrons / entrez

EXAMPLE PHRASES

Elle **entrera** en sixième à la rentrée. She'll go into first year of high school after the summer.

Comme personne ne répondit, il poussa la porte et **entra**. As nobody answered, he pushed the door and went in.

Je n'**entrerais** pas sans frapper si j'étais toi. I wouldn't go in without knocking if I were you.

Comme j'avais perdu les clés, j'**étais entré** par la fenêtre. As I'd lost the keys, I'd gone in through the window.

je/j' = I **tu** = you **il** = he/it **elle** = she/it **on** = we/one **nous** = we **vous** = you **ils/elles** = they

envoyer (to send)

PRESENT		PRESENT SUBJUNCTIVE	
j'	envoie	j'	envoie
tu	envoies	tu	envoies
il/elle/on	envoie	il/elle/on	envoie
nous	envoyons	nous	envoyions
vous	envoyez	vous	envoyiez
ils/elles	envoient	ils/elles	envoient

PERFECT		IMPERFECT	
j'	ai envoyé	j'	envoyais
tu	as envoyé	tu	envoyais
il/elle/on	a envoyé	il/elle/on	envoyait
nous	avons envoyé	nous	envoyions
vous	avez envoyé	vous	envoyiez
ils/elles	ont envoyé	ils/elles	envoyaient

PRESENT PARTICIPLE	PAST PARTICIPLE
envoyant	envoyé

EXAMPLE PHRASES

Ma cousine nous **envoie** toujours des cadeaux pour Noël. My cousin always sends us presents for Christmas.

J'**ai envoyé** une carte postale à ma tante. I sent my aunt a postcard.

Envoie-moi un e-mail. Send me an e-mail.

Il faut que j'**envoie** ce paquet demain. I must send this parcel away tomorrow.

Elle m'**envoyait** toujours une carte pour mon anniversaire. She would always send me a card for my birthday.

je/j' = I   **tu** = you   **il** = he/it   **elle** = she/it   **on** = we/one   **nous** = we   **vous** = you   **ils/elles** = they

envoyer

FUTURE

j'	**enverrai**
tu	**enverras**
il/elle/on	**enverra**
nous	**enverrons**
vous	**enverrez**
ils/elles	**enverront**

CONDITIONAL

j'	**enverrais**
tu	**enverrais**
il/elle/on	**enverrait**
nous	**enverrions**
vous	**enverriez**
ils/elles	**enverraient**

PAST HISTORIC

j'	**envoyai**
tu	**envoyas**
il/elle/on	**envoya**
nous	**envoyâmes**
vous	**envoyâtes**
ils/elles	**envoyèrent**

PLUPERFECT

j'	**avais envoyé**
tu	**avais envoyé**
il/elle/on	**avait envoyé**
nous	**avions envoyé**
vous	**aviez envoyé**
ils/elles	**avaient envoyé**

IMPERATIVE

envoie / envoyons / envoyez

EXAMPLE PHRASES

J'**enverrai** Julie te chercher à l'aéroport. I'll send Julie to fetch you at the airport.

Sa mère l'**envoya** chercher du pain. His mother sent him to get some bread.

Je lui **enverrais** un cadeau si j'étais sûr de lui faire plaisir. I'd send her a present if I thought it would make her happy.

Je ne lui **avais** pas **envoyé** mes vœux et elle était très vexée. I hadn't sent her a Christmas card and she was very upset.

je/j' = I **tu** = you **il** = he/it **elle** = she/it **on** = we/one **nous** = we **vous** = you **ils/elles** = they

espérer (to hope)

PRESENT		PRESENT SUBJUNCTIVE	
j'	**espère**	j'	**espère**
tu	**espères**	tu	**espères**
il/elle/on	**espère**	il/elle/on	**espère**
nous	**espérons**	nous	**espérions**
vous	**espérez**	vous	**espériez**
ils/elles	**espèrent**	ils/elles	**espèrent**

PERFECT		IMPERFECT	
j'	**ai espéré**	j'	**espérais**
tu	**as espéré**	tu	**espérais**
il/elle/on	**a espéré**	il/elle/on	**espérait**
nous	**avons espéré**	nous	**espérions**
vous	**avez espéré**	vous	**espériez**
ils/elles	**ont espéré**	ils/elles	**espéraient**

PRESENT PARTICIPLE
espérant

PAST PARTICIPLE
espéré

EXAMPLE PHRASES

J'**espère** que tu vas bien. I hope you're well.

Tu penses réussir tes examens? – J'**espère** bien! Do you think you'll pass your exams? – I hope so!

Il **espérait** pouvoir venir. He was hoping he'd be able to come.

Elle **espérait** qu'il n'était pas déjà parti. She was hoping that he hadn't already left.

---

je/j' = I tu = you il = he/it elle = she/it on = we/one nous = we vous = you ils/elles = they

espérer

FUTURE

j'	**espérerai**
tu	**espéreras**
il/elle/on	**espérera**
nous	**espérerons**
vous	**espérerez**
ils/elles	**espéreront**

CONDITIONAL

j'	**espérerais**
tu	**espérerais**
il/elle/on	**espérerait**
nous	**espérerions**
vous	**espéreriez**
ils/elles	**espéreraient**

PAST HISTORIC

j'	**espérai**
tu	**espéras**
il/elle/on	**espéra**
nous	**espérâmes**
vous	**espérâtes**
ils/elles	**espérèrent**

PLUPERFECT

j'	**avais espéré**
tu	**avais espéré**
il/elle/on	**avait espéré**
nous	**avions espéré**
vous	**aviez espéré**
ils/elles	**avaient espéré**

IMPERATIVE

espère / espérons / espérez

EXAMPLE PHRASES

Il **espéra** qu'ils se reverraient bientôt. He hoped that they would see each other again soon.

Si j'étais toi, je n'**espérerais** pas trop qu'il vienne: tu risques d'être déçu.
If I were you, I wouldn't put too much hope in him coming – you could be disappointed.

J'**avais espéré** que tu pourrais venir. I had hoped that you would be able to come.

je/j' = I **tu** = you **il** = he/it **elle** = she/it **on** = we/one **nous** = we **vous** = you **ils/elles** = they

essayer (to try)

PRESENT		PRESENT SUBJUNCTIVE	
j'	essaie	j'	essaie
tu	essaies	tu	essaies
il/elle/on	essaie	il/elle/on	essaie
nous	essayons	nous	essayions
vous	essayez	vous	essayiez
ils/elles	essaient	ils/elles	essaient

PERFECT		IMPERFECT	
j'	ai essayé	j'	essayais
tu	as essayé	tu	essayais
il/elle/on	a essayé	il/elle/on	essayait
nous	avons essayé	nous	essayions
vous	avez essayé	vous	essayiez
ils/elles	ont essayé	ils/elles	essayaient

PRESENT PARTICIPLE
essayant

PAST PARTICIPLE
essayé

EXAMPLE PHRASES

Elle adorait **essayer** mes vêtements. She loved trying on my clothes.

J'**ai essayé** de t'appeler hier soir. I tried to ring you last night.

Essaie de ne pas t'énerver. Try not to get all worked up.

Il faut que j'**essaie** cette nouvelle recette. I must try this new recipe.

Il **essayait** de la comprendre, mais il n'y arrivait pas. He tried to understand her, but he couldn't.

---

je/j' = I   **tu** = you   **il** = he/it   **elle** = she/it   **on** = we/one   **nous** = we   **vous** = you   **ils/elles** = they

essayer

FUTURE

j'	**essaierai**
tu	**essaieras**
il/elle/on	**essaiera**
nous	**essaierons**
vous	**essaierez**
ils/elles	**essaieront**

CONDITIONAL

j'	**essaierais**
tu	**essaierais**
il/elle/on	**essaierait**
nous	**essaierions**
vous	**essaieriez**
ils/elles	**essaieraient**

PAST HISTORIC

j'	**essayai**
tu	**essayas**
il/elle/on	**essaya**
nous	**essayâmes**
vous	**essayâtes**
ils/elles	**essayèrent**

PLUPERFECT

j'	**avais essayé**
tu	**avais essayé**
il/elle/on	**avait essayé**
nous	**avions essayé**
vous	**aviez essayé**
ils/elles	**avaient essayé**

IMPERATIVE

essaie / essayons / essayez

EXAMPLE PHRASES

J'**essaierai** d'aller le voir après le travail demain. I'll try to go and see him after work tomorrow.

Ils **essayèrent** de la rattraper. They tried to catch up with her.

Je n'**essaierais** pas de lui parler tout de suite si j'étais toi. I wouldn't try to speak to her right now if I were you.

Elle **avait essayé** la robe, mais elle ne lui allait pas. She'd tried on the dress, but it didn't fit her.

---

je/j' = I **tu** = you **il** = he/it **elle** = she/it **on** = we/one **nous** = we **vous** = you **ils/elles** = they

éteindre (to switch off)

PRESENT

j'	**éteins**
tu	**éteins**
il/elle/on	**éteint**
nous	**éteignons**
vous	**éteignez**
ils/elles	**éteignent**

PRESENT SUBJUNCTIVE

j'	**éteigne**
tu	**éteignes**
il/elle/on	**éteigne**
nous	**éteignions**
vous	**éteigniez**
ils/elles	**éteignent**

PERFECT

j'	**ai éteint**
tu	**as éteint**
il/elle/on	**a éteint**
nous	**avons éteint**
vous	**avez éteint**
ils/elles	**ont éteint**

IMPERFECT

j'	**éteignais**
tu	**éteignais**
il/elle/on	**éteignait**
nous	**éteignions**
vous	**éteigniez**
ils/elles	**éteignaient**

PRESENT PARTICIPLE
éteignant

PAST PARTICIPLE
éteint

EXAMPLE PHRASES

N'oubliez pas d'**éteindre** la lumière en sortant. Don't forget to switch off the light when you leave.

Elle n'**éteint** jamais la lumière dans sa chambre. She never switches off her bedroom light.

Tu **as éteint** la lumière dans la salle de bain? Have you switched off the bathroom light?

Karine, **éteins** la télé s'il te plaît. Switch off the TV please, Karine.

---

je/j' = I   tu = you   il = he/it   elle = she/it   on = we/one   **nous** = we   **vous** = you   **ils/elles** = they

éteindre

FUTURE

j'	**éteindrai**
tu	**éteindras**
il/elle/on	**éteindra**
nous	**éteindrons**
vous	**éteindrez**
ils/elles	**éteindront**

CONDITIONAL

j'	**éteindrais**
tu	**éteindrais**
il/elle/on	**éteindrait**
nous	**éteindrions**
vous	**éteindriez**
ils/elles	**éteindraient**

PAST HISTORIC

j'	**éteignis**
tu	**éteignis**
il/elle/on	**éteignit**
nous	**éteignîmes**
vous	**éteignîtes**
ils/elles	**éteignirent**

PLUPERFECT

j'	**avais éteint**
tu	**avais éteint**
il/elle/on	**avait éteint**
nous	**avions éteint**
vous	**aviez éteint**
ils/elles	**avaient éteint**

IMPERATIVE

éteins / éteignons / éteignez

EXAMPLE PHRASES

J'**éteindrai** tout avant de partir. I'll switch everything off before I leave.

Elle **éteignit** la lumière et s'endormit. She switched off the light and fell asleep.

Il **éteindrait** sa cigarette s'il savait que la fumée te dérange. He'd put out his cigarette if he knew that the smoke bothers you.

Il **avait éteint** son portable en entrant dans le cinéma. He'd switched off his mobile on the way in to the cinema.

je/j' = I **tu** = you **il** = he/it **elle** = she/it **on** = we/one **nous** = we **vous** = you **ils/elles** = they

être (to be)

PRESENT	
je	**suis**
tu	**es**
il/elle/on	**est**
nous	**sommes**
vous	**êtes**
ils/elles	**sont**

PRESENT SUBJUNCTIVE	
je	**sois**
tu	**sois**
il/elle/on	**soit**
nous	**soyons**
vous	**soyez**
ils/elles	**soient**

PERFECT	
j'	**ai été**
tu	**as été**
il/elle/on	**a été**
nous	**avons été**
vous	**avez été**
ils/elles	**ont été**

IMPERFECT	
j'	**étais**
tu	**étais**
il/elle/on	**était**
nous	**étions**
vous	**étiez**
ils/elles	**étaient**

PRESENT PARTICIPLE
étant

PAST PARTICIPLE
été

EXAMPLE PHRASES

Quelle heure **est**-il? – Il **est** dix heures. What time is it? – It's ten o'clock.

Ils ne **sont** pas encore **arrivés**. They haven't arrived yet.

Sois courageux. Be brave.

Je veux que vous **soyez** particulièrement sages aujourd'hui. I want you to behave particularly well today.

Il **était** professeur de maths dans mon lycée. He was a maths teacher in my school.

---

je/j' = I   **tu** = you   **il** = he/it   **elle** = she/it   **on** = we/one   **nous** = we   **vous** = you   **ils/elles** = they

être

FUTURE

je	**serai**
tu	**seras**
il/elle/on	**sera**
nous	**serons**
vous	**serez**
ils/elles	**seront**

CONDITIONAL

je	**serais**
tu	**serais**
il/elle/on	**serait**
nous	**serions**
vous	**seriez**
ils/elles	**seraient**

PAST HISTORIC

je	**fus**
tu	**fus**
il/elle/on	**fut**
nous	**fûmes**
vous	**fûtes**
ils/elles	**furent**

PLUPERFECT

j'	**avais été**
tu	**avais été**
il/elle/on	**avait été**
nous	**avions été**
vous	**aviez été**
ils/elles	**avaient été**

IMPERATIVE

sois / soyons / soyez

EXAMPLE PHRASES

Je **serai** chez moi à partir de midi. I'll be at home from midday onwards.

Il **fut** tellement vexé qu'il ne lui parla pas de la soirée. He was so upset that he didn't speak to her all evening.

Nous **serions** contents de vous voir si vous aviez le temps de passer. We'd be happy to see you if you had time to drop by.

Nous étions punis parce que nous n'**avions** pas **été** sages. We were punished because we hadn't been good.

---

je/j' = I   tu = you   il = he/it   elle = she/it   on = we/one   nous = we   vous = you   ils/elles = they

faillir (faire qch to almost do sth)

PRESENT

je	**faillis**
tu	**faillis**
il/elle/on	**faillit**
nous	**faillissons**
vous	**faillissez**
ils/elles	**faillissent**

PRESENT SUBJUNCTIVE

je	**faillisse**
tu	**faillisses**
il/elle/on	**faillisse**
nous	**faillissions**
vous	**faillissiez**
ils/elles	**faillissent**

PERFECT

j'	**ai failli**
tu	**as failli**
il/elle/on	**a failli**
nous	**avons failli**
vous	**avez failli**
ils/elles	**ont failli**

IMPERFECT

je	**faillissais**
tu	**faillissais**
il/elle/on	**faillissait**
nous	**faillissions**
vous	**faillissiez**
ils/elles	**faillissaient**

PRESENT PARTICIPLE

faillissant

PAST PARTICIPLE

failli

EXAMPLE PHRASES

J'**ai failli** tomber. I nearly fell.

Il **a failli** s'énerver. He nearly got angry.

Nous **avons failli** rater notre train. We nearly missed our train.

Ils **ont failli** ne pas venir. They nearly didn't come.

faillir

FUTURE

je	**faillirai**
tu	**failliras**
il/elle/on	**faillira**
nous	**faillirons**
vous	**faillirez**
ils/elles	**failliront**

CONDITIONAL

je	**faillirais**
tu	**faillirais**
il/elle/on	**faillirait**
nous	**faillirions**
vous	**failliriez**
ils/elles	**failliraient**

PAST HISTORIC

je	**faillis**
tu	**faillis**
il/elle/on	**faillit**
nous	**faillîmes**
vous	**faillîtes**
ils/elles	**faillirent**

PLUPERFECT

j'	**avais failli**
tu	**avais failli**
il/elle/on	**avait failli**
nous	**avions failli**
vous	**aviez failli**
ils/elles	**avaient failli**

IMPERATIVE

not used

EXAMPLE PHRASES

Il **faillit** s'en aller sans dire au revoir. He nearly left without saying goodbye.

Elle **faillit** pleurer quand ils lui annoncèrent la nouvelle. She nearly cried when they told her the news.

Nous **avions failli** nous perdre en venant vous voir ce jour-là. We had nearly got lost on our way to see you that day.

Ils **avaient failli** se battre, mais la cloche avait sonné au bon moment. They had nearly had a fight, but the bell had rang at the right time.

je/j' = I **tu** = you **il** = he/it **elle** = she/it **on** = we/one **nous** = we **vous** = you **ils/elles** = they

faire (to do; to make)

PRESENT		**PRESENT SUBJUNCTIVE**	
je	**fais**	je	**fasse**
tu	**fais**	tu	**fasses**
il/elle/on	**fait**	il/elle/on	**fasse**
nous	**faisons**	nous	**fassions**
vous	**faites**	vous	**fassiez**
ils/elles	**font**	ils/elles	**fassent**

PERFECT		**IMPERFECT**	
j'	**ai fait**	je	**faisais**
tu	**as fait**	tu	**faisais**
il/elle/on	**a fait**	il/elle/on	**faisait**
nous	**avons fait**	nous	**faisions**
vous	**avez fait**	vous	**faisiez**
ils/elles	**ont fait**	ils/elles	**faisaient**

PRESENT PARTICIPLE
faisant

PAST PARTICIPLE
fait

EXAMPLE PHRASES

Qu'est-ce que tu **fais**? What are you doing?

Qu'est-ce qu'il **a fait**? What has he done?

Il s'**est fait** couper les cheveux. He's had his haircut.

Ne **fais** pas l'idiot. Don't behave like an idiot.

J'aimerais que tu **fasses** la vaisselle plus souvent. I'd like you to wash the dishes more often.

Il ne **faisait** jamais son lit. He would never make his bed.

je/j' = I   **tu** = you   **il** = he/it   **elle** = she/it   **on** = we/one   **nous** = we   **vous** = you   **ils/elles** = they

faire

FUTURE

je	**ferai**
tu	**feras**
il/elle/on	**fera**
nous	**ferons**
vous	**ferez**
ils/elles	**feront**

CONDITIONAL

je	**ferais**
tu	**ferais**
il/elle/on	**ferait**
nous	**ferions**
vous	**feriez**
ils/elles	**feraient**

PAST HISTORIC

je	**fis**
tu	**fis**
il/elle/on	**fit**
nous	**fîmes**
vous	**fîtes**
ils/elles	**firent**

PLUPERFECT

j'	**avais fait**
tu	**avais fait**
il/elle/on	**avait fait**
nous	**avions fait**
vous	**aviez fait**
ils/elles	**avaient fait**

IMPERATIVE

fais / faisons / faites

EXAMPLE PHRASES

Demain, nous **ferons** une promenade sur la plage. Tomorrow, we'll go for a walk on the beach.

Il **fit** semblant de ne pas comprendre. He pretended not to understand.

Si je gagnais à la loterie, je **ferais** le tour du monde. If I won the lottery, I would take a trip round the world.

Elle **avait fait** un gâteau. She'd made a cake.

je/j' = I   **tu** = you   **il** = he/it   **elle** = she/it   **on** = we/one   **nous** = we   **vous** = you   **ils/elles** = they

falloir (to be necessary)

PRESENT
   il **faut**

PRESENT SUBJUNCTIVE
   il **faille**

PERFECT
   il **a fallu**

IMPERFECT
   il **fallait**

PRESENT PARTICIPLE
not used

PAST PARTICIPLE
fallu

EXAMPLE PHRASES

Il **faut** se dépêcher! We have to hurry up!

Il ne **faut** pas paniquer. Let's not panic.

Il **a fallu** que je lui prête ma voiture. I had to lend her my car.

Il me **fallait** de l'argent. I needed money.

falloir

FUTURE
il **faudra**

CONDITIONAL
il **faudrait**

PAST HISTORIC
il **fallut**

PLUPERFECT
il **avait fallu**

IMPERATIVE
not used

EXAMPLE PHRASES

Il **faudra** que tu sois là à 8 heures. You'll have to be there at 8.

Il **fallut** qu'ils partent de très bonne heure. They had to leave very early.

Il **faudrait** t'arrêter de fumer. You should stop smoking.

Il **avait fallu** nettoyer toute la maison. We'd had to clean the whole house.

je/j' = I **tu** = you **il** = he/it **elle** = she/it **on** = we/one **nous** = we **vous** = you **ils/elles** = they

finir (to finish)

PRESENT		PRESENT SUBJUNCTIVE	
je	**finis**	je	**finisse**
tu	**finis**	tu	**finisses**
il/elle/on	**finit**	il/elle/on	**finisse**
nous	**finissons**	nous	**finissions**
vous	**finissez**	vous	**finissiez**
ils/elles	**finissent**	ils/elles	**finissent**

PERFECT		IMPERFECT	
j'	**ai fini**	je	**finissais**
tu	**as fini**	tu	**finissais**
il/elle/on	**a fini**	il/elle/on	**finissait**
nous	**avons fini**	nous	**finissions**
vous	**avez fini**	vous	**finissiez**
ils/elles	**ont fini**	ils/elles	**finissaient**

PRESENT PARTICIPLE
finissant

PAST PARTICIPLE
fini

EXAMPLE PHRASES

Je **finis** mes cours à 17h. I finish my lessons at 5pm.

J'**ai fini**! I've finished!

Finis ta soupe! Finish your soup!

Il faut que je **finisse** mon livre avant de commencer celui-là. I have to finish my book before I start this one.

Elle **finissait** toujours en retard. She'd always finish late.

je/j' = I   **tu** = you   **il** = he/it   **elle** = she/it   **on** = we/one   **nous** = we   **vous** = you   **ils/elles** = they

finir

FUTURE

je	**finirai**
tu	**finiras**
il/elle/on	**finira**
nous	**finirons**
vous	**finirez**
ils/elles	**finiront**

CONDITIONAL

je	**finirais**
tu	**finirais**
il/elle/on	**finirait**
nous	**finirions**
vous	**finiriez**
ils/elles	**finiraient**

PAST HISTORIC

je	**finis**
tu	**finis**
il/elle/on	**finit**
nous	**finîmes**
vous	**finîtes**
ils/elles	**finirent**

PLUPERFECT

j'	**avais fini**
tu	**avais fini**
il/elle/on	**avait fini**
nous	**avions fini**
vous	**aviez fini**
ils/elles	**avaient fini**

IMPERATIVE
finis / finissons / finissez

EXAMPLE PHRASES

Je **finirai** mes devoirs demain. I'll finish my homework tomorrow.

Il **finit** son dîner et alla se coucher. He finished his dinner and went to bed.

Si on l'ignorait, elle **finirait** par comprendre. If we ignored her, she'd eventually understand.

Elle n'**avait** pas **fini** de manger quand nous sommes arrivés. She hadn't finished her lunch when we arrived.

je/j' = I   **tu** = you   **il** = he/it   **elle** = she/it   **on** = we/one   **nous** = we   **vous** = you   **ils/elles** = they

fuir (to flee)

PRESENT		**PRESENT SUBJUNCTIVE**	
je	**fuis**	je	**fuie**
tu	**fuis**	tu	**fuies**
il/elle/on	**fuit**	il/elle/on	**fuie**
nous	**fuyons**	nous	**fuyions**
vous	**fuyez**	vous	**fuyiez**
ils/elles	**fuient**	ils/elles	**fuient**

PERFECT		**IMPERFECT**	
j'	**ai fui**	je	**fuyais**
tu	**as fui**	tu	**fuyais**
il/elle/on	**a fui**	il/elle/on	**fuyait**
nous	**avons fui**	nous	**fuyions**
vous	**avez fui**	vous	**fuyiez**
ils/elles	**ont fui**	ils/elles	**fuyaient**

PRESENT PARTICIPLE
fuyant

PAST PARTICIPLE
fui

EXAMPLE PHRASES

J'ai un stylo qui **fuit**. My pen leaks.

Ils **ont fui** leur pays. They fled their country.

Il ne faut pas que tu le **fuies** comme ça. You mustn't run away from him like that.

Le robinet **fuyait**. The tap was dripping.

---

je/j' = I **tu** = you **il** = he/it **elle** = she/it **on** = we/one **nous** = we **vous** = you **ils/elles** = they

fuir

FUTURE

je	**fuirai**
tu	**fuiras**
il/elle/on	**fuira**
nous	**fuirons**
vous	**fuirez**
ils/elles	**fuiront**

CONDITIONAL

je	**fuirais**
tu	**fuirais**
il/elle/on	**fuirait**
nous	**fuirions**
vous	**fuiriez**
ils/elles	**fuiraient**

PAST HISTORIC

je	**fuis**
tu	**fuis**
il/elle/on	**fuit**
nous	**fuîmes**
vous	**fuîtes**
ils/elles	**fuirent**

PLUPERFECT

j'	**avais fui**
tu	**avais fui**
il/elle/on	**avait fui**
nous	**avions fui**
vous	**aviez fui**
ils/elles	**avaient fui**

IMPERATIVE

fuis / fuyons / fuyez

EXAMPLE PHRASES

Il **fuira** toujours les responsabilités. He will always run away from responsibilities.

Beaucoup de gens **fuirent** vers le sud. A lot of people fled south.

La machine à laver **fuirait** si on la remplissait trop. The washing machine would leak if we overloaded it.

Ils **avaient fui** leur village et s'étaient réfugiés dans les montagnes. They had fled from their village and had taken refuge in the mountains.

---

je/j' = I   tu = you   il = he/it   elle = she/it   on = we/one   nous = we   vous = you   ils/elles = they

haïr (to hate)

PRESENT

je	**hais**
tu	**hais**
il/elle/on	**hait**
nous	**haïssons**
vous	**haïssez**
ils/elles	**haïssent**

PRESENT SUBJUNCTIVE

je	**haïsse**
tu	**haïsses**
il/elle/on	**haïsse**
nous	**haïssions**
vous	**haïssiez**
ils/elles	**haïssent**

PERFECT

j'	**ai haï**
tu	**as haï**
il/elle/on	**a haï**
nous	**avons haï**
vous	**avez haï**
ils/elles	**ont haï**

IMPERFECT

je	**haïssais**
tu	**haïssais**
il/elle/on	**haïssait**
nous	**haïssions**
vous	**haïssiez**
ils/elles	**haïssaient**

PRESENT PARTICIPLE

haïssant

PAST PARTICIPLE

haï

EXAMPLE PHRASES

Je te **hais**! I hate you!

Ils se **haïssent**. They hate each other.

Il ne faut pas que tu le **haïsses** pour ça. You mustn't hate him for that.

Elle **haïssait** tout le monde. She hated everyone.

---

je/j' = I **tu** = you **il** = he/it **elle** = she/it **on** = we/one **nous** = we **vous** = you **ils/elles** = they

haïr

FUTURE

je	**haïrai**
tu	**haïras**
il/elle/on	**haïra**
nous	**haïrons**
vous	**haïrez**
ils/elles	**haïront**

CONDITIONAL

je	**haïrais**
tu	**haïrais**
il/elle/on	**haïrait**
nous	**haïrions**
vous	**haïriez**
ils/elles	**haïraient**

PAST HISTORIC

je	**haïs**
tu	**haïs**
il/elle/on	**haït**
nous	**haïmes**
vous	**haïtes**
ils/elles	**haïrent**

PLUPERFECT

j'	**avais haï**
tu	**avais haï**
il/elle/on	**avait haï**
nous	**avions haï**
vous	**aviez haï**
ils/elles	**avaient haï**

IMPERATIVE

hais / haïssons / haïssez

EXAMPLE PHRASES

Je la **haïrai** toujours. I'll always hate her.

Elle le **haït** pour ce qu'il venait de dire. She hated him for what he'd just said.

Elle me **haïrait** si je n'allais pas voir ses parents avec elle. She'd hate me if I didn't go and see her parents with her.

Elle m'**avait haï** durant toutes ces années et maintenant nous étions les meilleures amies du monde. She had hated me all these years and now we were the best of friends.

je/j' = I **tu** = you **il** = he/it **elle** = she/it **on** = we/one **nous** = we **vous** = you **ils/elles** = they

s'inquiéter (to worry)

PRESENT

je	**m'inquiète**
tu	**t'inquiètes**
il/elle/on	**s'inquiète**
nous	**nous inquiétons**
vous	**vous inquiétez**
ils/elles	**s'inquiètent**

PRESENT SUBJUNCTIVE

je	**m'inquiète**
tu	**t'inquiètes**
il/elle/on	**s'inquiète**
nous	**nous inquiétions**
vous	**vous inquiétiez**
ils/elles	**s'inquiètent**

PERFECT

je	**me suis inquiété(e)**
tu	**t'es inquiété(e)**
il/elle/on	**s'est inquiété(e)**
nous	**nous sommes inquiété(e)s**
vous	**vous êtes inquiété(e)(s)**
ils/elles	**se sont inquiété(e)s**

IMPERFECT

je	**m'inquiétais**
tu	**t'inquiétais**
il/elle/on	**s'inquiétait**
nous	**nous inquiétions**
vous	**vous inquiétiez**
ils/elles	**s'inquiétaient**

PRESENT PARTICIPLE
s'inquiétant

PAST PARTICIPLE
inquiété

EXAMPLE PHRASES

Elle **s'inquiète** toujours si je suis en retard. She always worries if I'm late.

Comme je savais où tu étais, je ne **me suis** pas **inquiétée**. As I knew where you were, I didn't worry.

Ne **t'inquiète** pas, je ne rentrerai pas tard. Don't worry, I'll not be late coming home.

Je ne veux pas qu'ils **s'inquiètent**. I don't want them to worry.

Ça **m'inquiétait** un peu que tu ne nous aies pas téléphoné. I was a little worried that you hadn't phoned us.

s'inquiéter

FUTURE

je	**m'inquiéterai**
tu	**t'inquiéteras**
il/elle/on	**s'inquiétera**
nous	**nous inquiéterons**
vous	**vous inquiéterez**
ils/elles	**s'inquiéteront**

CONDITIONAL

je	**m'inquiéterais**
tu	**t'inquiéterais**
il/elle/on	**s'inquiéterait**
nous	**nous inquiéterions**
vous	**vous inquiéteriez**
ils/elles	**s'inquiéteraient**

PAST HISTORIC

je	**m'inquiétai**
tu	**t'inquiétas**
il/elle/on	**s'inquiéta**
nous	**nous inquiétâmes**
vous	**vous inquiétâtes**
ils/elles	**s'inquiétèrent**

PLUPERFECT

je	**m'étais inquiété(e)**
tu	**t'étais inquiété(e)**
il/elle/on	**s'était inquiété(e)**
nous	**nous étions inquiété(e)s**
vous	**vous étiez inquiété(e)(s)**
ils/elles	**s'étaient inquiété(e)s**

IMPERATIVE

inquiète-toi / inquiétons-nous / inquiétez-vous

EXAMPLE PHRASES

Mes parents **s'inquiéteront** si j'y vais toute seule. My parents will worry if
  I go there on my own.

Il **s'inquiéta** pour elle. He worried about her.

Je **m'inquiéterais** moins si tu n'étais pas si loin. I'd worry less if you weren't
  so far away.

Comme ils savaient qu'elle était avec Vincent, ils ne **s'étaient** pas **inquiétés**.
  As they knew that she was with Vincent, they hadn't worried.

je/j' = I **tu** = you **il** = he/it **elle** = she/it **on** = we/one **nous** = we **vous** = you **ils/elles** = they

interdire (to forbid)

PRESENT

j'	interdis
tu	interdis
il/elle/on	interdit
nous	interdisons
vous	interdisez
ils/elles	interdisent

PRESENT SUBJUNCTIVE

j'	interdise
tu	interdises
il/elle/on	interdise
nous	interdisions
vous	interdisiez
ils/elles	interdisent

PERFECT

j'	ai interdit
tu	as interdit
il/elle/on	a interdit
nous	avons interdit
vous	avez interdit
ils/elles	ont interdit

IMPERFECT

j'	interdisais
tu	interdisais
il/elle/on	interdisait
nous	interdisions
vous	interdisiez
ils/elles	interdisaient

PRESENT PARTICIPLE

interdisant

PAST PARTICIPLE

interdit

EXAMPLE PHRASES

Je t'**interdis** de toucher à ça. I forbid you to touch this.

Ses parents lui **ont interdit** de sortir. His parents have forbidden him to go out.

Interdisons-leur de regarder la télé ce week-end. Let's ban them from watching TV over the weekend.

Elle nous **interdisait** de jouer avec lui. She forbade us to play with him.

---

je/j' = I   **tu** = you   **il** = he/it   **elle** = she/it   **on** = we/one   **nous** = we   **vous** = you   **ils/elles** = they

interdire

FUTURE

j'	**interdirai**
tu	**interdiras**
il/elle/on	**interdira**
nous	**interdirons**
vous	**interdirez**
ils/elles	**interdiront**

CONDITIONAL

j'	**interdirais**
tu	**interdirais**
il/elle/on	**interdirait**
nous	**interdirions**
vous	**interdiriez**
ils/elles	**interdiraient**

PAST HISTORIC

j'	**interdis**
tu	**interdis**
il/elle/on	**interdit**
nous	**interdîmes**
vous	**interdîtes**
ils/elles	**interdirent**

PLUPERFECT

j'	**avais interdit**
tu	**avais interdit**
il/elle/on	**avait interdit**
nous	**avions interdit**
vous	**aviez interdit**
ils/elles	**avaient interdit**

IMPERATIVE

interdis / interdisons / interdisez

EXAMPLE PHRASES

Si vous n'êtes pas raisonnables, je vous **interdirai** de sortir du jardin. If you're not sensible, I'll forbid you to leave the garden.

À partir de ce jour, ils nous **interdirent** de la voir. From that day on, they forbade us to see her.

Si ma fille me parlait comme ça, je lui **interdirais** de sortir avec ses copines. If my daughter spoke to me like that, I'd ban her from going out with her friends.

Elle nous **avait interdit** de lui en parler. She had forbidden us to tell him about it.

je/j' = I **tu** = you **il** = he/it **elle** = she/it **on** = we/one **nous** = we **vous** = you **ils/elles** = they

jeter (to throw)

PRESENT

je	**jette**
tu	**jettes**
il/elle/on	**jette**
nous	**jetons**
vous	**jetez**
ils/elles	**jettent**

PRESENT SUBJUNCTIVE

je	**jette**
tu	**jettes**
il/elle/on	**jette**
nous	**jetions**
vous	**jetiez**
ils/elles	**jettent**

PERFECT

j'	**ai jeté**
tu	**as jeté**
il/elle/on	**a jeté**
nous	**avons jeté**
vous	**avez jeté**
ils/elles	**ont jeté**

IMPERFECT

je	**jetais**
tu	**jetais**
il/elle/on	**jetait**
nous	**jetions**
vous	**jetiez**
ils/elles	**jetaient**

PRESENT PARTICIPLE

jetant

PAST PARTICIPLE

jeté

EXAMPLE PHRASES

Ils ne **jettent** jamais rien. They never throw anything away.

Elle **a jeté** son chewing-gum par la fenêtre. She threw her chewing gum out of the window.

Ne **jette** pas de papiers par terre. Don't throw litter on the ground.

Il faut qu'on **jette** tous ces vieux jouets cassés. We'll have to throw away all these old broken toys.

Il **jetait** toujours ses vêtements par terre. He'd always throw his clothes on the floor.

je/j' = I   tu = you   il = he/it   elle = she/it   on = we/one   **nous** = we   **vous** = you   **ils/elles** = they

jeter

FUTURE

je	**jetterai**
tu	**jetteras**
il/elle/on	**jettera**
nous	**jetterons**
vous	**jetterez**
ils/elles	**jetteront**

CONDITIONAL

je	**jetterais**
tu	**jetterais**
il/elle/on	**jetterait**
nous	**jetterions**
vous	**jetteriez**
ils/elles	**jetteraient**

PAST HISTORIC

je	**jetai**
tu	**jetas**
il/elle/on	**jeta**
nous	**jetâmes**
vous	**jetâtes**
ils/elles	**jetèrent**

PLUPERFECT

j'	**avais jeté**
tu	**avais jeté**
il/elle/on	**avait jeté**
nous	**avions jeté**
vous	**aviez jeté**
ils/elles	**avaient jeté**

IMPERATIVE

jette / jetons / jetez

EXAMPLE PHRASES

Je **jetterai** tout ça à la poubelle. I'll throw all this in the bin.

Il **jeta** sa veste sur la chaise et répondit au téléphone. He threw his jacket on the chair and answered the phone.

Je **jetterais** bien tous ces vieux magazines. I'd quite like to throw all these old magazines away.

Elle jurait qu'elle n'**avait** rien **jeté**. She swore she hadn't thrown anything away.

je/j' = I   **tu** = you   **il** = he/it   **elle** = she/it   **on** = we/one   **nous** = we   **vous** = you   **ils/elles** = they

joindre (to join)

PRESENT

je	**joins**
tu	**joins**
il/elle/on	**joint**
nous	**joignons**
vous	**joignez**
ils/elles	**joignent**

PRESENT SUBJUNCTIVE

je	**joigne**
tu	**joignes**
il/elle/on	**joigne**
nous	**joignions**
vous	**joigniez**
ils/elles	**joignent**

PERFECT

j'	**ai joint**
tu	**as joint**
il/elle/on	**a joint**
nous	**avons joint**
vous	**avez joint**
ils/elles	**ont joint**

IMPERFECT

je	**joignais**
tu	**joignais**
il/elle/on	**joignait**
nous	**joignions**
vous	**joigniez**
ils/elles	**joignaient**

PRESENT PARTICIPLE

joignant

PAST PARTICIPLE

joint

EXAMPLE PHRASES

Où est-ce qu'on peut te **joindre** ce week-end? Where can we contact you this weekend?

Il n'est pas facile à **joindre**. He's not easy to contact.

Je vous **ai joint** un plan de la ville. I have enclosed a map of the town.

joindre

FUTURE

je	**joindrai**
tu	**joindras**
il/elle/on	**joindra**
nous	**joindrons**
vous	**joindrez**
ils/elles	**joindront**

CONDITIONAL

je	**joindrais**
tu	**joindrais**
il/elle/on	**joindrait**
nous	**joindrions**
vous	**joindriez**
ils/elles	**joindraient**

PAST HISTORIC

je	**joignis**
tu	**joignis**
il/elle/on	**joignit**
nous	**joignîmes**
vous	**joignîtes**
ils/elles	**joignirent**

PLUPERFECT

j'	**avais joint**
tu	**avais joint**
il/elle/on	**avait joint**
nous	**avions joint**
vous	**aviez joint**
ils/elles	**avaient joint**

IMPERATIVE
joins / joignons / joignez

EXAMPLE PHRASES

Il **joignit** les mains et se mit à prier. He put his hands together and started to pray.

On **avait joint** les deux tables. We'd put the two tables together.

Nous **avions joint** nos efforts. It had been a joint effort.

lever (to lift)

PRESENT

je	**lève**
tu	**lèves**
il/elle/on	**lève**
nous	**levons**
vous	**levez**
ils/elles	**lèvent**

PRESENT SUBJUNCTIVE

je	**lève**
tu	**lèves**
il/elle/on	**lève**
nous	**levions**
vous	**leviez**
ils/elles	**lèvent**

PERFECT

j'	**ai levé**
tu	**as levé**
il/elle/on	**a levé**
nous	**avons levé**
vous	**avez levé**
ils/elles	**ont levé**

IMPERFECT

je	**levais**
tu	**levais**
il/elle/on	**levait**
nous	**levions**
vous	**leviez**
ils/elles	**levaient**

PRESENT PARTICIPLE
levant

PAST PARTICIPLE
levé

EXAMPLE PHRASES

Je me **lève** tous les matins à sept heures. I get up at seven every day.

Elle **a levé** la main pour répondre à la question. She put her hand up to answer the question.

Levez le doigt! Put your hand up!

Levons notre verre à ta réussite. Let's raise our glasses to your success.

lever

FUTURE

je	**lèverai**
tu	**lèveras**
il/elle/on	**lèvera**
nous	**lèverons**
vous	**lèverez**
ils/elles	**lèveront**

CONDITIONAL

je	**lèverais**
tu	**lèverais**
il/elle/on	**lèverait**
nous	**lèverions**
vous	**lèveriez**
ils/elles	**lèveraient**

PAST HISTORIC

je	**levai**
tu	**levas**
il/elle/on	**leva**
nous	**levâmes**
vous	**levâtes**
ils/elles	**levèrent**

PLUPERFECT

j'	**avais levé**
tu	**avais levé**
il/elle/on	**avait levé**
nous	**avions levé**
vous	**aviez levé**
ils/elles	**avaient levé**

IMPERATIVE

lève / levons / levez

EXAMPLE PHRASES

Je ne **lèverai** pas le petit doigt pour l'aider. I won't lift a finger to help him.

Elle **leva** les yeux et vit qu'il était en train de tricher. She looked up and saw that he was cheating.

Si mon père était encore là, il **lèverait** les bras au ciel. If my dad were still here, he'd throw his arms up in despair.

je/j' = I **tu** = you **il** = he/it **elle** = she/it **on** = we/one **nous** = we **vous** = you **ils/elles** = they

lire (to read)

PRESENT

je	**lis**
tu	**lis**
il/elle/on	**lit**
nous	**lisons**
vous	**lisez**
ils/elles	**lisent**

PRESENT SUBJUNCTIVE

je	**lise**
tu	**lises**
il/elle/on	**lise**
nous	**lisions**
vous	**lisiez**
ils/elles	**lisent**

PERFECT

j'	**ai lu**
tu	**as lu**
il/elle/on	**a lu**
nous	**avons lu**
vous	**avez lu**
ils/elles	**ont lu**

IMPERFECT

je	**lisais**
tu	**lisais**
il/elle/on	**lisait**
nous	**lisions**
vous	**lisiez**
ils/elles	**lisaient**

PRESENT PARTICIPLE

lisant

PAST PARTICIPLE

lu

EXAMPLE PHRASES

Il **lit** beaucoup. He reads a lot.

Vous **avez lu** "Madame Bovary"? Have you read "Madame Bovary"?

Lisez bien les instructions. Read the instructions carefully.

J'aimerais que tu **lises** ce livre. I'd like you to read this book.

Elle lui **lisait** une histoire. She was reading him a story.

lire

FUTURE

je	**lirai**
tu	**liras**
il/elle/on	**lira**
nous	**lirons**
vous	**lirez**
ils/elles	**liront**

CONDITIONAL

je	**lirais**
tu	**lirais**
il/elle/on	**lirait**
nous	**lirions**
vous	**liriez**
ils/elles	**liraient**

PAST HISTORIC

je	**lus**
tu	**lus**
il/elle/on	**lut**
nous	**lûmes**
vous	**lûtes**
ils/elles	**lurent**

PLUPERFECT

j'	**avais lu**
tu	**avais lu**
il/elle/on	**avait lu**
nous	**avions lu**
vous	**aviez lu**
ils/elles	**avaient lu**

IMPERATIVE

lis / lisons / lisez

EXAMPLE PHRASES

Je le **lirai** dans l'avion. I'll read it on the plane.

Il **lut** la lettre à haute voix. He read the letter aloud.

Je **lirais** plus si j'avais le temps. I'd read more if I had time.

La maîtresse s'aperçut qu'il n'**avait** pas **lu** le livre. The teacher realized that he hadn't read the book.

je/j' = I **tu** = you **il** = he/it **elle** = she/it **on** = we/one **nous** = we **vous** = you **ils/elles** = they

manger (to eat)

PRESENT		PRESENT SUBJUNCTIVE	
je	mange	je	mange
tu	manges	tu	manges
il/elle/on	mange	il/elle/on	mange
nous	mangeons	nous	mangions
vous	mangez	vous	mangiez
ils/elles	mangent	ils/elles	mangent

PERFECT		IMPERFECT	
j'	ai mangé	je	mangeais
tu	as mangé	tu	mangeais
il/elle/on	a mangé	il/elle/on	mangeait
nous	avons mangé	nous	mangions
vous	avez mangé	vous	mangiez
ils/elles	ont mangé	ils/elles	mangeaient

PRESENT PARTICIPLE	PAST PARTICIPLE
mangeant	mangé

EXAMPLE PHRASES

Nous ne **mangeons** pas souvent ensemble. We don't often eat together.

Tu **as** assez **mangé**? Have you had enough to eat?

Mange ta soupe. Eat your soup.

Il faut que je **mange** avant de partir. I have to eat before I leave.

Ils **mangeaient** en regardant la télé. They were eating while watching TV.

---

je/j' = I   tu = you   il = he/it   elle = she/it   on = we/one   nous = we   vous = you   ils/elles = they

manger

FUTURE

je	**mangerai**
tu	**mangeras**
il/elle/on	**mangera**
nous	**mangerons**
vous	**mangerez**
ils/elles	**mangeront**

CONDITIONAL

je	**mangerais**
tu	**mangerais**
il/elle/on	**mangerait**
nous	**mangerions**
vous	**mangeriez**
ils/elles	**mangeraient**

PAST HISTORIC

je	**mangeai**
tu	**mangeas**
il/elle/on	**mangea**
nous	**mangeâmes**
vous	**mangeâtes**
ils/elles	**mangèrent**

PLUPERFECT

j'	**avais mangé**
tu	**avais mangé**
il/elle/on	**avait mangé**
nous	**avions mangé**
vous	**aviez mangé**
ils/elles	**avaient mangé**

IMPERATIVE

mange / mangeons / mangez

EXAMPLE PHRASES

Je **mangerai** plus tard. I'll eat later on.

Il **mangea** rapidement et retourna travailler. He ate quickly and went back to work.

Je **mangerais** bien le reste si je n'avais pas peur de grossir. I'd gladly eat the rest if I wasn't afraid of putting on weight.

Comme ils **avaient** bien **mangé** le midi, ils ont tenu jusqu'au soir. As they had had a good lunch, they kept going until dinner time.

je/j' = I **tu** = you **il** = he/it **elle** = she/it **on** = we/one **nous** = we **vous** = you **ils/elles** = they

maudire (to curse)

PRESENT

je	maudis
tu	maudis
il/elle/on	maudit
nous	maudissons
vous	maudissez
ils/elles	maudissent

PRESENT SUBJUNCTIVE

je	maudisse
tu	maudisses
il/elle/on	maudisse
nous	maudissions
vous	maudissiez
ils/elles	maudissent

PERFECT

j'	ai maudit
tu	as maudit
il/elle/on	a maudit
nous	avons maudit
vous	avez maudit
ils/elles	ont maudit

IMPERFECT

je	maudissais
tu	maudissais
il/elle/on	maudissait
nous	maudissions
vous	maudissiez
ils/elles	maudissaient

PRESENT PARTICIPLE

maudissant

PAST PARTICIPLE

maudit

EXAMPLE PHRASES

Ils **maudissent** leurs ennemis. They curse their enemies.

Je **maudis** le jour où je l'ai rencontrée. I curse the day I met her.

Elle me **maudissait** en nettoyant mon manteau couvert de boue. She cursed me as she was cleaning my muddy coat.

Ce **maudit** stylo ne marche pas! This blasted pen doesn't work!

maudire

FUTURE

je	**maudirai**
tu	**maudiras**
il/elle/on	**maudira**
nous	**maudirons**
vous	**maudirez**
ils/elles	**maudiront**

CONDITIONAL

je	**maudirais**
tu	**maudirais**
il/elle/on	**maudirait**
nous	**maudirions**
vous	**maudiriez**
ils/elles	**maudiraient**

PAST HISTORIC

je	**maudis**
tu	**maudis**
il/elle/on	**maudit**
nous	**maudîmes**
vous	**maudîtes**
ils/elles	**maudirent**

PLUPERFECT

j'	**avais maudit**
tu	**avais maudit**
il/elle/on	**avait maudit**
nous	**avions maudit**
vous	**aviez maudit**
ils/elles	**avaient maudit**

IMPERATIVE

maudis / maudissons / maudissez

EXAMPLE PHRASES

Je les **maudirai** jusqu'à ma mort. I'll curse them to the day I die.

Il la **maudit** pour sa stupidité. He cursed her for her stupidity.

Je te **maudirais** si tu arrivais en retard. I'd curse you if you arrived late.

Nous les **avions maudits** de nous avoir laissés les attendre sous la pluie.
We had cursed them for making us wait for them in the rain.

mentir (to lie)

PRESENT

je	**mens**
tu	**mens**
il/elle/on	**ment**
nous	**mentons**
vous	**mentez**
ils/elles	**mentent**

PRESENT SUBJUNCTIVE

je	**mente**
tu	**mentes**
il/elle/on	**mente**
nous	**mentions**
vous	**mentiez**
ils/elles	**mentent**

PERFECT

j'	**ai menti**
tu	**as menti**
il/elle/on	**a menti**
nous	**avons menti**
vous	**avez menti**
ils/elles	**ont menti**

IMPERFECT

je	**mentais**
tu	**mentais**
il/elle/on	**mentait**
nous	**mentions**
vous	**mentiez**
ils/elles	**mentaient**

PRESENT PARTICIPLE

mentant

PAST PARTICIPLE

menti

EXAMPLE PHRASES

Je ne **mens** jamais. I never lie.

Il lui **a menti**. He lied to her.

Ne **mens** pas s'il te plaît. Please don't lie.

Je ne veux pas que tu me **mentes**. I don't want you to lie to me.

Elle savait qu'il **mentait**. She knew that he was lying.

mentir

FUTURE

je	**mentirai**
tu	**mentiras**
il/elle/on	**mentira**
nous	**mentirons**
vous	**mentirez**
ils/elles	**mentiront**

CONDITIONAL

je	**mentirais**
tu	**mentirais**
il/elle/on	**mentirait**
nous	**mentirions**
vous	**mentiriez**
ils/elles	**mentiraient**

PAST HISTORIC

je	**mentis**
tu	**mentis**
il/elle/on	**mentit**
nous	**mentîmes**
vous	**mentîtes**
ils/elles	**mentirent**

PLUPERFECT

j'	**avais menti**
tu	**avais menti**
il/elle/on	**avait menti**
nous	**avions menti**
vous	**aviez menti**
ils/elles	**avaient menti**

IMPERATIVE

mens / mentons / mentez

EXAMPLE PHRASES

Je **mentirai** s'il le faut. I'll lie if I have to.

Il **mentit** pour qu'on le laisse tranquille. He lied so that he'd be left alone.

Elle ne **mentirait** pas si tu ne lui faisais pas aussi peur. She wouldn't lie if you didn't frighten her so much.

Il **avait menti** pour ne pas la contrarier. He had lied in order not to upset her.

mettre (to put)

PRESENT		**PRESENT SUBJUNCTIVE**	
je	**mets**	je	**mette**
tu	**mets**	tu	**mettes**
il/elle/on	**met**	il/elle/on	**mette**
nous	**mettons**	nous	**mettions**
vous	**mettez**	vous	**mettiez**
ils/elles	**mettent**	ils/elles	**mettent**

PERFECT		**IMPERFECT**	
j'	**ai mis**	je	**mettais**
tu	**as mis**	tu	**mettais**
il/elle/on	**a mis**	il/elle/on	**mettait**
nous	**avons mis**	nous	**mettions**
vous	**avez mis**	vous	**mettiez**
ils/elles	**ont mis**	ils/elles	**mettaient**

PRESENT PARTICIPLE	**PAST PARTICIPLE**
mettant	mis

EXAMPLE PHRASES

Il **met** du gel dans ses cheveux. He puts gel in his hair.

Où est-ce que tu **as mis** les clés? Where have you put the keys?

Mets ton manteau! Put your coat on!

Il faut que je **mette** le gâteau au four. I have to put the cake in the oven.

Elle **mettait** toujours des heures à s'habiller. She would always take hours
   to get dressed.

---

je/j' = I   **tu** = you   **il** = he/it   **elle** = she/it   **on** = we/one   **nous** = we   **vous** = you   **ils/elles** = they

mettre

FUTURE

je	**mettrai**
tu	**mettras**
il/elle/on	**mettra**
nous	**mettrons**
vous	**mettrez**
ils/elles	**mettront**

CONDITIONAL

je	**mettrais**
tu	**mettrais**
il/elle/on	**mettrait**
nous	**mettrions**
vous	**mettriez**
ils/elles	**mettraient**

PAST HISTORIC

je	**mis**
tu	**mis**
il/elle/on	**mit**
nous	**mîmes**
vous	**mîtes**
ils/elles	**mirent**

PLUPERFECT

j'	**avais mis**
tu	**avais mis**
il/elle/on	**avait mis**
nous	**avions mis**
vous	**aviez mis**
ils/elles	**avaient mis**

IMPERATIVE

mets / mettons / mettez

EXAMPLE PHRASES

Je **mettrai** ma robe rose demain. I'll put on my pink dress tomorrow.

Elle **mit** la bouilloire à chauffer. She put the kettle on.

Je **mettrais** une robe si tu en mettais une aussi. I'd put on a dress if you'd put one on too.

J'**avais mis** le livre sur la table. I had put the book on the table.

monter (to go up; to take up)

PRESENT

je	**monte**
tu	**montes**
il/elle/on	**monte**
nous	**montons**
vous	**montez**
ils/elles	**montent**

PRESENT SUBJUNCTIVE

je	**monte**
tu	**montes**
il/elle/on	**monte**
nous	**montions**
vous	**montiez**
ils/elles	**montent**

PERFECT

je	**suis monté(e)**
tu	**es monté(e)**
il/elle/on	**est monté(e)**
nous	**sommes monté(e)s**
vous	**êtes monté(e)(s)**
ils/elles	**sont monté(e)s**

IMPERFECT

je	**montais**
tu	**montais**
il/elle/on	**montait**
nous	**montions**
vous	**montiez**
ils/elles	**montaient**

PRESENT PARTICIPLE

montant

PAST PARTICIPLE

monté

In the perfect and the pluperfect, use the auxiliary "avoir" when there is a direct object.

EXAMPLE PHRASES

Je **monte** ces escaliers cent fois par jour. I go up these stairs a hundred times a day.

Hier, je **suis montée** à cheval pour la première fois. Yesterday, I went horse riding for the first time.

Monte dans la voiture, je t'y emmène. Get into the car, I'll take you there.

Il s'est tordu la cheville en **montant** à une échelle. He twisted his ankle going up a ladder.

je/j' = I   **tu** = you   **il** = he/it   **elle** = she/it   **on** = we/one   **nous** = we   **vous** = you   **ils/elles** = they

monter

FUTURE

je	**monterai**
tu	**monteras**
il/elle/on	**montera**
nous	**monterons**
vous	**monterez**
ils/elles	**monteront**

CONDITIONAL

je	**monterais**
tu	**monterais**
il/elle/on	**monterait**
nous	**monterions**
vous	**monteriez**
ils/elles	**monteraient**

PAST HISTORIC

je	**montai**
tu	**montas**
il/elle/on	**monta**
nous	**montâmes**
vous	**montâtes**
ils/elles	**montèrent**

PLUPERFECT

j'	**étais monté(e)**
tu	**étais monté(e)**
il/elle/on	**était monté(e)**
nous	**étions monté(e)s**
vous	**étiez monté(e)(s)**
ils/elles	**étaient monté(e)s**

IMPERATIVE

monte / montons / montez

EXAMPLE PHRASES

Je **monterai** lui dire bonsoir dans cinq minutes. I'll go up to say goodnight to her in five minutes.

Il **monta** les escaliers en courant et sonna à la porte. He ran up the stairs and rang the bell.

Je **monterais** en haut de la tour si je n'avais pas tant le vertige. I'd go up the tower if I wasn't so scared of heights.

Comme elle était malade, je lui **avais monté** son dîner. As she was ill, I had taken her dinner up to her.

je/j' = I **tu** = you **il** = he/it **elle** = she/it **on** = we/one **nous** = we **vous** = you **ils/elles** = they

mordre (to bite)

PRESENT

je	**mords**
tu	**mords**
il/elle/on	**mord**
nous	**mordons**
vous	**mordez**
ils/elles	**mordent**

PRESENT SUBJUNCTIVE

je	**morde**
tu	**mordes**
il/elle/on	**morde**
nous	**mordions**
vous	**mordiez**
ils/elles	**mordent**

PERFECT

j'	**ai mordu**
tu	**as mordu**
il/elle/on	**a mordu**
nous	**avons mordu**
vous	**avez mordu**
ils/elles	**ont mordu**

IMPERFECT

je	**mordais**
tu	**mordais**
il/elle/on	**mordait**
nous	**mordions**
vous	**mordiez**
ils/elles	**mordaient**

PRESENT PARTICIPLE

mordant

PAST PARTICIPLE

mordu

EXAMPLE PHRASES

Il ne va pas te **mordre**! He won't bite you!
Attention, il **mord**! Watch out, he bites.
Le chien m'**a mordue**. The dog bit me.
Je me **suis mordu** la langue. I bit my tongue.

mordre

FUTURE

je	**mordrai**
tu	**mordras**
il/elle/on	**mordra**
nous	**mordrons**
vous	**mordrez**
ils/elles	**mordront**

CONDITIONAL

je	**mordrais**
tu	**mordrais**
il/elle/on	**mordrait**
nous	**mordrions**
vous	**mordriez**
ils/elles	**mordraient**

PAST HISTORIC

je	**mordis**
tu	**mordis**
il/elle/on	**mordit**
nous	**mordîmes**
vous	**mordîtes**
ils/elles	**mordirent**

PLUPERFECT

j'	**avais mordu**
tu	**avais mordu**
il/elle/on	**avait mordu**
nous	**avions mordu**
vous	**aviez mordu**
ils/elles	**avaient mordu**

IMPERATIVE

mords / mordons / mordez

EXAMPLE PHRASES

Il ne te **mordra** pas. He won't bite you.

Elle lui **mordit** le doigt et partit se cacher. She bit his finger and ran off to hide.

Il ne **mordrait** jamais personne. He would never bite anybody!

Le chien l'**avait mordu** au mollet. The dog had bitten him on the shin.

je/j' = I **tu** = you **il** = he/it **elle** = she/it **on** = we/one **nous** = we **vous** = you **ils/elles** = they

moudre (to grind)

PRESENT		**PRESENT SUBJUNCTIVE**	
je	mouds	je	moule
tu	mouds	tu	moules
il/elle/on	moud	il/elle/on	moule
nous	moulons	nous	moulions
vous	moulez	vous	mouliez
ils/elles	moulent	ils/elles	moulent

PERFECT		**IMPERFECT**	
j'	ai moulu	je	moulais
tu	as moulu	tu	moulais
il/elle/on	a moulu	il/elle/on	moulait
nous	avons moulu	nous	moulions
vous	avez moulu	vous	mouliez
ils/elles	ont moulu	ils/elles	moulaient

PRESENT PARTICIPLE
moulant

PAST PARTICIPLE
moulu

EXAMPLE PHRASES

"Qui va m'aider à **moudre** ce grain?", demanda la petite poule rousse.
   "Who will help me to grind this grain?" asked the little red hen.
Il **moud** toujours son café lui-même. He always grinds his coffee himself.
J'**ai moulu** du café pour demain matin. I've ground some coffee for
   tomorrow morning.
Le meunier **moulait** le blé à la meule. The miller ground the wheat with
   the millstone.

---

je/j' = I   tu = you   il = he/it   elle = she/it   on = we/one   nous = we   vous = you   ils/elles = they

moudre

FUTURE

je	moudrai
tu	moudras
il/elle/on	moudra
nous	moudrons
vous	moudrez
ils/elles	moudront

CONDITIONAL

je	moudrais
tu	moudrais
il/elle/on	moudrait
nous	moudrions
vous	moudriez
ils/elles	moudraient

PAST HISTORIC

je	moulus
tu	moulus
il/elle/on	moulut
nous	moulûmes
vous	moulûtes
ils/elles	moulurent

PLUPERFECT

j'	avais moulu
tu	avais moulu
il/elle/on	avait moulu
nous	avions moulu
vous	aviez moulu
ils/elles	avaient moulu

IMPERATIVE

mouds / moulons / moulez

EXAMPLE PHRASES

Je **moudrai** du café tout à l'heure. I'll grind some coffee in a moment.

Elle **moulut** un peu de poivre sur le rôti. She ground some pepper over the roast.

Si j'avais le temps je **moudrais** mon café moi-même. If I had time, I'd grind my coffee myself.

Il mesura le café qu'il **avait moulu**. He measured the coffee that he'd ground.

---

je/j' = I   tu = you   il = he/it   elle = she/it   on = we/one   nous = we   vous = you   ils/elles = they

mourir (to die)

PRESENT

je	**meurs**
tu	**meurs**
il/elle/on	**meurt**
nous	**mourons**
vous	**mourez**
ils/elles	**meurent**

PRESENT SUBJUNCTIVE

je	**meure**
tu	**meures**
il/elle/on	**meure**
nous	**mourions**
vous	**mouriez**
ils/elles	**meurent**

PERFECT

je	**suis mort(e)**
tu	**es mort(e)**
il/elle/on	**est mort(e)**
nous	**sommes mort(e)s**
vous	**êtes mort(e)(s)**
ils/elles	**sont mort(e)s**

IMPERFECT

je	**mourais**
tu	**mourais**
il/elle/on	**mourait**
nous	**mourions**
vous	**mouriez**
ils/elles	**mouraient**

PRESENT PARTICIPLE

mourant

PAST PARTICIPLE

mort

EXAMPLE PHRASES

On **meurt** de froid ici! We're freezing to death here!
Elle **est morte** en 1998. She died in 1998.
Ils **sont morts**. They're dead.
Je ne veux pas qu'il **meure**. I don't want him to die.
Nous **mourions** de froid. We were freezing to death.

je/j' = I   **tu** = you   **il** = he/it   **elle** = she/it   **on** = we/one   **nous** = we   **vous** = you   **ils/elles** = they

mourir

FUTURE

je	**mourrai**
tu	**mourras**
il/elle/on	**mourra**
nous	**mourrons**
vous	**mourrez**
ils/elles	**mourront**

CONDITIONAL

je	**mourrais**
tu	**mourrais**
il/elle/on	**mourrait**
nous	**mourrions**
vous	**mourriez**
ils/elles	**mourraient**

PAST HISTORIC

je	**mourus**
tu	**mourus**
il/elle/on	**mourut**
nous	**mourûmes**
vous	**mourûtes**
ils/elles	**moururent**

PLUPERFECT

j'	**étais mort(e)**
tu	**étais mort(e)**
il/elle/on	**était mort(e)**
nous	**étions mort(e)s**
vous	**étiez mort(e)(s)**
ils/elles	**étaient mort(e)s**

IMPERATIVE

meurs / mourons / mourez

EXAMPLE PHRASES

Si tu t'en vas, j'en **mourrai** de chagrin. If you go, I'll die of sorrow.

Il **mourut** quelques heures plus tard. He died a few hours later.

Je **mourrais** de honte si tu le lui disais. I'd die of shame if you told him about it.

Nous **étions morts** de peur. We were scared to death.

je/j' = I   **tu** = you   **il** = he/it   **elle** = she/it   **on** = we/one   **nous** = we   **vous** = you   **ils/elles** = they

naître (to be born)

PRESENT	
je	**nais**
tu	**nais**
il/elle/on	**naît**
nous	**naissons**
vous	**naissez**
ils/elles	**naissent**

PRESENT SUBJUNCTIVE	
je	**naisse**
tu	**naisses**
il/elle/on	**naisse**
nous	**naissions**
vous	**naissiez**
ils/elles	**naissent**

PERFECT	
je	**suis né(e)**
tu	**es né(e)**
il/elle/on	**est né(e)**
nous	**sommes né(e)s**
vous	**êtes né(e)(s)**
ils/elles	**sont né(e)s**

IMPERFECT	
je	**naissais**
tu	**naissais**
il/elle/on	**naissait**
nous	**naissions**
vous	**naissiez**
ils/elles	**naissaient**

PRESENT PARTICIPLE
naissant

PAST PARTICIPLE
né

EXAMPLE PHRASES

Il a l'air innocent comme l'agneau qui vient de **naître**. He looks as innocent as a newborn lamb.

Quand est-ce que tu **es né**? When were you born?

Je **suis née** le 12 février. I was born on the 12th of February.

Je ne **suis** pas **né** de la dernière pluie. I wasn't born yesterday.

naître

FUTURE

je	**naîtrai**
tu	**naîtras**
il/elle/on	**naîtra**
nous	**naîtrons**
vous	**naîtrez**
ils/elles	**naîtront**

CONDITIONAL

je	**naîtrais**
tu	**naîtrais**
il/elle/on	**naîtrait**
nous	**naîtrions**
vous	**naîtriez**
ils/elles	**naîtraient**

PAST HISTORIC

je	**naquis**
tu	**naquis**
il/elle/on	**naquit**
nous	**naquîmes**
vous	**naquîtes**
ils/elles	**naquirent**

PLUPERFECT

j'	**étais né(e)**
tu	**étais né(e)**
il/elle/on	**était né(e)**
nous	**étions né(e)s**
vous	**étiez né(e)(s)**
ils/elles	**étaient né(é)s**

IMPERATIVE

nais / naissons / naissez

EXAMPLE PHRASES

Le bébé de Delphine **naîtra** en mars. Delphine is going to have a baby in March.

Il **naquit** le 5 juillet 1909. He was born on 5 July 1909.

Ses enfants n'**étaient** pas **nés** en Écosse. Her children weren't born in Scotland.

nettoyer (to clean)

PRESENT

je	**nettoie**
tu	**nettoies**
il/elle/on	**nettoie**
nous	**nettoyons**
vous	**nettoyez**
ils/elles	**nettoient**

PRESENT SUBJUNCTIVE

je	**nettoie**
tu	**nettoies**
il/elle/on	**nettoie**
nous	**nettoyions**
vous	**nettoyiez**
ils/elles	**nettoient**

PERFECT

j'	**ai nettoyé**
tu	**as nettoyé**
il/elle/on	**a nettoyé**
nous	**avons nettoyé**
vous	**avez nettoyé**
ils/elles	**ont nettoyé**

IMPERFECT

je	**nettoyais**
tu	**nettoyais**
il/elle/on	**nettoyait**
nous	**nettoyions**
vous	**nettoyiez**
ils/elles	**nettoyaient**

PRESENT PARTICIPLE

nettoyant

PAST PARTICIPLE

nettoyé

EXAMPLE PHRASES

Je ne **nettoie** pas souvent mes lunettes. I don't clean my glasses very often.

Richard **a nettoyé** tout l'appartement. Richard has cleaned the whole flat.

Nettoie tes chaussures avant de les ranger. Clean your shoes before putting them away.

J'aimerais que vous **nettoyiez** ta chambre. I'd like you to clean your room.

Elle **nettoyait** le sol en écoutant la radio. She was cleaning the floor while listening to the radio.

---

je/j' = I **tu** = you **il** = he/it **elle** = she/it **on** = we/one **nous** = we **vous** = you **ils/elles** = they

nettoyer

FUTURE

je	**nettoierai**
tu	**nettoieras**
il/elle/on	**nettoiera**
nous	**nettoierons**
vous	**nettoierez**
ils/elles	**nettoieront**

CONDITIONAL

je	**nettoierais**
tu	**nettoierais**
il/elle/on	**nettoierait**
nous	**nettoierions**
vous	**nettoieriez**
ils/elles	**nettoieraient**

PAST HISTORIC

je	**nettoyai**
tu	**nettoyas**
il/elle/on	**nettoya**
nous	**nettoyâmes**
vous	**nettoyâtes**
ils/elles	**nettoyèrent**

PLUPERFECT

j'	**avais nettoyé**
tu	**avais nettoyé**
il/elle/on	**avait nettoyé**
nous	**avions nettoyé**
vous	**aviez nettoyé**
ils/elles	**avaient nettoyé**

IMPERATIVE

nettoie / nettoyons / nettoyez

EXAMPLE PHRASES

Je **nettoierai** tout ça ce soir. I'll clean everything this evening.

Elle **nettoya** le miroir et s'y regarda longuement. She cleaned the mirror
and looked at herself for a long time.

Il **nettoierait** sa chambre tout seul si je l'encourageais à le faire. He'd clean
his bedroom himself if I encouraged him to do it.

Quand je suis rentrée , ils **avaient** tout **nettoyé**. When I got back, they'd
cleaned everything up.

je/j' = I **tu** = you **il** = he/it **elle** = she/it **on** = we/one **nous** = we **vous** = you **ils/elles** = they

obéir (to obey)

PRESENT

j'	obéis
tu	obéis
il/elle/on	obéit
nous	obéissons
vous	obéissez
ils/elles	obéissent

PRESENT SUBJUNCTIVE

j'	obéisse
tu	obéisses
il/elle/on	obéisse
nous	obéissions
vous	obéissiez
ils/elles	obéissent

PERFECT

j'	ai obéi
tu	as obéi
il/elle/on	a obéi
nous	avons obéi
vous	avez obéi
ils/elles	ont obéi

IMPERFECT

j'	obéissais
tu	obéissais
il/elle/on	obéissait
nous	obéissions
vous	obéissiez
ils/elles	obéissaient

PRESENT PARTICIPLE

obéissant

PAST PARTICIPLE

obéi

EXAMPLE PHRASES

Je n'**obéis** pas toujours à mes parents. I don't always obey my parents.

J'aimerais que tu **obéisses** quand je te demande de faire quelque chose.
   I'd like you to do it when I ask you to do something.

Mon chien n'**obéissait** jamais. My dog never obeyed commands.

obéir

FUTURE

j'	obéirai
tu	obéiras
il/elle/on	obéira
nous	obéirons
vous	obéirez
ils/elles	obéiront

CONDITIONAL

j'	obéirais
tu	obéirais
il/elle/on	obéirait
nous	obéirions
vous	obéiriez
ils/elles	obéiraient

PAST HISTORIC

j'	obéis
tu	obéis
il/elle/on	obéit
nous	obéîmes
vous	obéîtes
ils/elles	obéirent

PLUPERFECT

j'	avais obéi
tu	avais obéi
il/elle/on	avait obéi
nous	avions obéi
vous	aviez obéi
ils/elles	avaient obéi

IMPERATIVE

obéis / obéissons / obéissez

EXAMPLE PHRASES

Il n'**obéira** jamais si tu lui parles comme ça. He'll never obey if you speak to him like that.

Ils **obéirent** sans se plaindre. They obeyed without complaining.

Ils ne lui **obéiraient** pas s'ils ne l'aimaient pas. They wouldn't obey her if they didn't like her.

Comme elle n'avait pas le choix, elle **avait obéi** à ses ordres. As she didn't have any choice, she'd obeyed his orders.

je/j' = I   tu = you   il = he/it   elle = she/it   on = we/one   nous = we   vous = you   ils/elles = they

offrir (to offer)

PRESENT

j'	offre
tu	offres
il/elle/on	offre
nous	offrons
vous	offrez
ils/elles	offrent

PRESENT SUBJUNCTIVE

j'	offre
tu	offres
il/elle/on	offre
nous	offrions
vous	offriez
ils/elles	offrent

PERFECT

j'	ai offert
tu	as offert
il/elle/on	a offert
nous	avons offert
vous	avez offert
ils/elles	ont offert

IMPERFECT

j'	offrais
tu	offrais
il/elle/on	offrait
nous	offrions
vous	offriez
ils/elles	offraient

PRESENT PARTICIPLE

offrant

PAST PARTICIPLE

offert

EXAMPLE PHRASES

Viens, je t'**offre** à boire. Come on, I'll buy you a drink.

Paul m'**a offert** du parfum pour mon anniversaire. Paul gave me some
   perfume for my birthday.

Offre-lui des fleurs. Give her some flowers.

Il **offrait** souvent de me raccompagner. He would often offer me a lift back.

offrir

FUTURE

j'	**offrirai**
tu	**offriras**
il/elle/on	**offrira**
nous	**offrirons**
vous	**offrirez**
ils/elles	**offriront**

CONDITIONAL

j'	**offrirais**
tu	**offrirais**
il/elle/on	**offrirait**
nous	**offririons**
vous	**offririez**
ils/elles	**offriraient**

PAST HISTORIC

j'	**offris**
tu	**offris**
il/elle/on	**offrit**
nous	**offrîmes**
vous	**offrîtes**
ils/elles	**offrirent**

PLUPERFECT

j'	**avais offert**
tu	**avais offert**
il/elle/on	**avait offert**
nous	**avions offert**
vous	**aviez offert**
ils/elles	**avaient offert**

IMPERATIVE
offre / offrons / offrez

EXAMPLE PHRASES

Je lui **offrirai** une voiture pour ses 21 ans. I'll buy her a car for her 21st birthday.

Il lui **offrit** de l'aider. He offered to help her.

S'il était plus aimable, je lui **offrirais** de l'aider. If he were more pleasant, I'd offer to help him.

On lui **avait offert** un poste de secrétaire. They had offered her a secretarial post.

ouvrir (to open)

PRESENT

j'	**ouvre**
tu	**ouvres**
il/elle/on	**ouvre**
nous	**ouvrons**
vous	**ouvrez**
ils/elles	**ouvrent**

PRESENT SUBJUNCTIVE

j'	**ouvre**
tu	**ouvres**
il/elle/on	**ouvre**
nous	**ouvrions**
vous	**ouvriez**
ils/elles	**ouvrent**

PERFECT

j'	**ai ouvert**
tu	**as ouvert**
il/elle/on	**a ouvert**
nous	**avons ouvert**
vous	**avez ouvert**
ils/elles	**ont ouvert**

IMPERFECT

j'	**ouvrais**
tu	**ouvrais**
il/elle/on	**ouvrait**
nous	**ouvrions**
vous	**ouvriez**
ils/elles	**ouvraient**

PRESENT PARTICIPLE
ouvrant

PAST PARTICIPLE
ouvert

EXAMPLE PHRASES

Est-ce que tu pourrais **ouvrir** la fenêtre? Could you open the window?

Elle **a ouvert** la porte. She opened the door.

La porte s'**est ouverte**. The door opened.

Ouvre la porte, s'il te plaît. Open the door, please.

Ouvrez vos livres à la page 10. Open your books at page 10.

Je me suis coupé en **ouvrant** une boîte de conserve. I cut myself opening a tin.

---

ouvrir

FUTURE

j'	**ouvrirai**
tu	**ouvriras**
il/elle/on	**ouvrira**
nous	**ouvrirons**
vous	**ouvrirez**
ils/elles	**ouvriront**

CONDITIONAL

j'	**ouvrirais**
tu	**ouvrirais**
il/elle/on	**ouvrirait**
nous	**ouvririons**
vous	**ouvririez**
ils/elles	**ouvriraient**

PAST HISTORIC

j'	**ouvris**
tu	**ouvris**
il/elle/on	**ouvrit**
nous	**ouvrîmes**
vous	**ouvrîtes**
ils/elles	**ouvrirent**

PLUPERFECT

j'	**avais ouvert**
tu	**avais ouvert**
il/elle/on	**avait ouvert**
nous	**avions ouvert**
vous	**aviez ouvert**
ils/elles	**avaient ouvert**

IMPERATIVE
ouvre / ouvrons / ouvrez

EXAMPLE PHRASES

J'**ouvrirai** la fenêtre tout à l'heure. I'll open the window in a moment.

Elle **ouvrit** les yeux et lui sourit. She opened her eyes and smiled at him.

J'**ouvrirais** la fenêtre s'il ne faisait pas si froid. I would open the window if it weren't so cold.

Ils **avaient ouvert** tous leurs cadeaux de Noël. They had opened all their Christmas presents.

je/j' = I **tu** = you **il** = he/it **elle** = she/it **on** = we/one **nous** = we **vous** = you **ils/elles** = they

paraître (to appear)

PRESENT

je	**parais**
tu	**parais**
il/elle/on	**paraît**
nous	**paraissons**
vous	**paraissez**
ils/elles	**paraissent**

PRESENT SUBJUNCTIVE

je	**paraisse**
tu	**paraisses**
il/elle/on	**paraisse**
nous	**paraissions**
vous	**paraissiez**
ils/elles	**paraissent**

PERFECT

j'	**ai paru**
tu	**as paru**
il/elle/on	**a paru**
nous	**avons paru**
vous	**avez paru**
ils/elles	**ont paru**

IMPERFECT

je	**paraissais**
tu	**paraissais**
il/elle/on	**paraissait**
nous	**paraissions**
vous	**paraissiez**
ils/elles	**paraissaient**

PRESENT PARTICIPLE
paraissant

PAST PARTICIPLE
paru

EXAMPLE PHRASES

Gisèle **paraît** plus jeune que son âge. Gisèle doesn't look her age.

Il **paraît** qu'il fait chaud toute l'année là-bas. Apparently it's hot all year round over there.

Il m'**a paru** angoissé. I thought he looked stressed.

Elle **paraissait** fatiguée. She seemed tired.

paraître

FUTURE

je	**paraîtrai**
tu	**paraîtras**
il/elle/on	**paraîtra**
nous	**paraîtrons**
vous	**paraîtrez**
ils/elles	**paraîtront**

CONDITIONAL

je	**paraîtrais**
tu	**paraîtrais**
il/elle/on	**paraîtrait**
nous	**paraîtrions**
vous	**paraîtriez**
ils/elles	**paraîtraient**

PAST HISTORIC

je	**parus**
tu	**parus**
il/elle/on	**parut**
nous	**parûmes**
vous	**parûtes**
ils/elles	**parurent**

PLUPERFECT

j'	**avais paru**
tu	**avais paru**
il/elle/on	**avait paru**
nous	**avions paru**
vous	**aviez paru**
ils/elles	**avaient paru**

IMPERATIVE

parais / paraissons / paraissez

EXAMPLE PHRASES

Cet article **paraîtra** le mois prochain. This article will be published next month.

Il **parut** gêné. He looked embarrassed.

Cela **paraîtrait** étrange si je venais sans mon mari. It would look strange if I came without my husband.

Il **avait paru** pressé de partir. He had seemed in a hurry to leave.

---

je/j' = I **tu** = you **il** = he/it **elle** = she/it **on** = we/one **nous** = we **vous** = you **ils/elles** = they

partir (to go; to leave)

PRESENT

je	**pars**
tu	**pars**
il/elle/on	**part**
nous	**partons**
vous	**partez**
ils/elles	**partent**

PRESENT SUBJUNCTIVE

je	**parte**
tu	**partes**
il/elle/on	**parte**
nous	**partions**
vous	**partiez**
ils/elles	**partent**

PERFECT

je	**suis parti(e)**
tu	**es parti(e)**
il/elle/on	**est parti(e)**
nous	**sommes parti(e)s**
vous	**êtes parti(e)(s)**
ils/elles	**sont parti(e)s**

IMPERFECT

je	**partais**
tu	**partais**
il/elle/on	**partait**
nous	**partions**
vous	**partiez**
ils/elles	**partaient**

PRESENT PARTICIPLE

partant

PAST PARTICIPLE

parti

EXAMPLE PHRASES

On **part** en vacances le 15 août. We're going on holiday on the 15th of August.

Elle **est partie** tôt ce matin. She left early this morning.

Ne **partez** pas sans moi. Don't leave without me!

Il faut qu'on **parte** de bonne heure. We have to leave early.

Il **partait** à huit heures tous les matins. He left at eight o'clock every morning.

---

je/j' = I   **tu** = you   **il** = he/it   **elle** = she/it   **on** = we/one   **nous** = we   **vous** = you   **ils/elles** = they

partir

FUTURE

je	**partirai**
tu	**partiras**
il/elle/on	**partira**
nous	**partirons**
vous	**partirez**
ils/elles	**partiront**

CONDITIONAL

je	**partirais**
tu	**partirais**
il/elle/on	**partirait**
nous	**partirions**
vous	**partiriez**
ils/elles	**partiraient**

PAST HISTORIC

je	**partis**
tu	**partis**
il/elle/on	**partit**
nous	**partîmes**
vous	**partîtes**
ils/elles	**partirent**

PLUPERFECT

j'	**étais parti(e)**
tu	**étais parti(e)**
il/elle/on	**était parti(e)**
nous	**étions parti(e)s**
vous	**étiez parti(e)(s)**
ils/elles	**étaient parti(e)s**

IMPERATIVE

pars / partons / partez

EXAMPLE PHRASES

Nous **partirons** demain. We'll leave tomorrow.

Il **partit** sans rien dire. He left without saying a word.

Je ne **partirais** pas sans dire au revoir. I wouldn't leave without saying goodbye.

Quand je suis arrivée, ils **étaient** déjà **partis**. When I arrived, they had already left.

je/j' = I **tu** = you **il** = he/it **elle** = she/it **on** = we/one **nous** = we **vous** = you **ils/elles** = they

passer (to pass)

PRESENT	
je	**passe**
tu	**passes**
il/elle/on	**passe**
nous	**passons**
vous	**passez**
ils/elles	**passent**

PRESENT SUBJUNCTIVE	
je	**passe**
tu	**passes**
il/elle/on	**passe**
nous	**passions**
vous	**passiez**
ils/elles	**passent**

PERFECT	
je	**suis passé(e)**
tu	**es passé(e)**
il/elle/on	**est passé(e)**
nous	**sommes passé(e)s**
vous	**êtes passé(e)(s)**
ils/elles	**sont passé(e)s**

IMPERFECT	
je	**passais**
tu	**passais**
il/elle/on	**passait**
nous	**passions**
vous	**passiez**
ils/elles	**passaient**

PRESENT PARTICIPLE
passant

PAST PARTICIPLE
passé

In the perfect and the pluperfect, use the auxiliary "avoir" when there is a direct object.

EXAMPLE PHRASES

Je vais **passer** les vacances chez mes grands-parents. I'm going to spend the holidays at my grandparents' house.

L'histoire se **passe** au Mexique. The story takes place in Mexico.

Il **a passé** son examen en juin. He sat his exam in June.

Elle **est passée** me dire bonjour. She came by to say hello.

Passe-moi le pain, s'il te plaît. Pass me the bread please.

Ils **passaient** leur temps à regarder la télé. They spent their time watching TV.

passer

FUTURE

je	**passerai**
tu	**passeras**
il/elle/on	**passera**
nous	**passerons**
vous	**passerez**
ils/elles	**passeront**

CONDITIONAL

je	**passerais**
tu	**passerais**
il/elle/on	**passerait**
nous	**passerions**
vous	**passeriez**
ils/elles	**passeraient**

PAST HISTORIC

je	**passai**
tu	**passas**
il/elle/on	**passa**
nous	**passâmes**
vous	**passâtes**
ils/elles	**passèrent**

PLUPERFECT

j'	**étais passé(e)**
tu	**étais passé(e)**
il/elle/on	**était passé(e)**
nous	**étions passé(e)s**
vous	**étiez passé(e)(s)**
ils/elles	**étaient passé(e)s**

IMPERATIVE
passe / passons / passez

EXAMPLE PHRASES

Je **passerai** te voir ce soir. I'll come to see you tonight.

Elle **passa** la soirée à emballer les cadeaux de Noël. She spent the evening wrapping up the Christmas presents.

Ils **passeraient** plus de temps à jouer dehors s'il faisait moins mauvais.
    They'd spend more time playing outside if the weather weren't so bad.

Les mois **avaient passé**. Months had passed.

je/j' = I **tu** = you **il** = he/it **elle** = she/it **on** = we/one **nous** = we **vous** = you **ils/elles** = they

payer (to pay)

PRESENT

je	**paye**
tu	**payes**
il/elle/on	**paye**
nous	**payons**
vous	**payez**
ils/elles	**payent**

PRESENT SUBJUNCTIVE

je	**paye**
tu	**payes**
il/elle/on	**paye**
nous	**payions**
vous	**payiez**
ils/elles	**payent**

PERFECT

j'	**ai payé**
tu	**as payé**
il/elle/on	**a payé**
nous	**avons payé**
vous	**avez payé**
ils/elles	**ont payé**

IMPERFECT

je	**payais**
tu	**payais**
il/elle/on	**payait**
nous	**payions**
vous	**payiez**
ils/elles	**payaient**

PRESENT PARTICIPLE

payant

PAST PARTICIPLE

payé

EXAMPLE PHRASES

Les étudiants **payent** moitié prix. Students pay half price.

Tu l'**as payé** combien? How much did you pay for it?

Il faut que je **paye** l'électricien. I have to pay the electrician.

Il ne **payait** jamais son loyer. He never paid his rent.

payer

FUTURE

je	**payerai**
tu	**payeras**
il/elle/on	**payera**
nous	**payerons**
vous	**payerez**
ils/elles	**payeront**

CONDITIONAL

je	**payerais**
tu	**payerais**
il/elle/on	**payerait**
nous	**payerions**
vous	**payeriez**
ils/elles	**payeraient**

PAST HISTORIC

je	**payai**
tu	**payas**
il/elle/on	**paya**
nous	**payâmes**
vous	**payâtes**
ils/elles	**payèrent**

PLUPERFECT

j'	**avais payé**
tu	**avais payé**
il/elle/on	**avait payé**
nous	**avions payé**
vous	**aviez payé**
ils/elles	**avaient payé**

IMPERATIVE

paye / payons / payez

EXAMPLE PHRASES

Je vous **payerai** demain. I'll pay you tomorrow.

Il **paya** la note et partit. He paid the bill and left.

Je lui ai dit que je la **payerais** la prochaine fois. I told him that I would pay him the next time.

Sa patronne ne l'**avait** pas **payée** depuis deux mois. Her boss hadn't paid her for the last two months.

peindre (to paint)

PRESENT		PRESENT SUBJUNCTIVE	
je	**peins**	je	**peigne**
tu	**peins**	tu	**peignes**
il/elle/on	**peint**	il/elle/on	**peigne**
nous	**peignons**	nous	**peignions**
vous	**peignez**	vous	**peigniez**
ils/elles	**peignent**	ils/elles	**peignent**

PERFECT		IMPERFECT	
j'	**ai peint**	je	**peignais**
tu	**as peint**	tu	**peignais**
il/elle/on	**a peint**	il/elle/on	**peignait**
nous	**avons peint**	nous	**peignions**
vous	**avez peint**	vous	**peigniez**
ils/elles	**ont peint**	ils/elles	**peignaient**

PRESENT PARTICIPLE
peignant

PAST PARTICIPLE
peint

EXAMPLE PHRASES

Il ne **peint** plus depuis son opération. He hasn't painted since his operation.

On **a peint** l'entrée en bleu clair. We painted the hall light blue.

Ce tableau **a été peint** en 1913. This picture was painted in 1913.

Il **peignait** toujours des paysages. He always painted landscapes.

peindre

FUTURE

je	**peindrai**
tu	**peindras**
il/elle/on	**peindra**
nous	**peindrons**
vous	**peindrez**
ils/elles	**peindront**

CONDITIONAL

je	**peindrais**
tu	**peindrais**
il/elle/on	**peindrait**
nous	**peindrions**
vous	**peindriez**
ils/elles	**peindraient**

PAST HISTORIC

je	**peignis**
tu	**peignis**
il/elle/on	**peignit**
nous	**peignîmes**
vous	**peignîtes**
ils/elles	**peignirent**

PLUPERFECT

j'	**avais peint**
tu	**avais peint**
il/elle/on	**avait peint**
nous	**avions peint**
vous	**aviez peint**
ils/elles	**avaient peint**

IMPERATIVE
peins / peignons / peignez

EXAMPLE PHRASES

Je **peindrai** le plafond demain. I'll paint the ceiling tomorrow.

Il **peignit** les volets en rose. He painted the shutters pink.

Si j'étais toi, je **peindrais** les murs avant de poser le carrelage. If I were you, I would paint the walls before laying the tiles.

Elle n'**avait peint** que la moitié de la pièce. She'd only painted half of the room.

perdre (to lose)

PRESENT		PRESENT SUBJUNCTIVE	
je	**perds**	je	**perde**
tu	**perds**	tu	**perdes**
il/elle/on	**perd**	il/elle/on	**perde**
nous	**perdons**	nous	**perdions**
vous	**perdez**	vous	**perdiez**
ils/elles	**perdent**	ils/elles	**perdent**

PERFECT		IMPERFECT	
j'	**ai perdu**	je	**perdais**
tu	**as perdu**	tu	**perdais**
il/elle/on	**a perdu**	il/elle/on	**perdait**
nous	**avons perdu**	nous	**perdions**
vous	**avez perdu**	vous	**perdiez**
ils/elles	**ont perdu**	ils/elles	**perdaient**

PRESENT PARTICIPLE	PAST PARTICIPLE
perdant	perdu

EXAMPLE PHRASES

Si tu te **perds**, appelle-moi. Call me if you get lost.

L'Italie **a perdu** un à zéro. Italy lost one-nil.

J'**ai perdu** mon porte-monnaie dans le métro. I lost my purse on the underground.

Ne **perds** pas encore tes gants. Don't lose your gloves again.

Il ne faut pas que je **perde** son adresse. I mustn't lose his address.

Il **perdait** toujours ses affaires. He was always losing his things.

perdre

FUTURE

je	**perdrai**
tu	**perdras**
il/elle/on	**perdra**
nous	**perdrons**
vous	**perdrez**
ils/elles	**perdront**

CONDITIONAL

je	**perdrais**
tu	**perdrais**
il/elle/on	**perdrait**
nous	**perdrions**
vous	**perdriez**
ils/elles	**perdraient**

PAST HISTORIC

je	**perdis**
tu	**perdis**
il/elle/on	**perdit**
nous	**perdîmes**
vous	**perdîtes**
ils/elles	**perdirent**

PLUPERFECT

j'	**avais perdu**
tu	**avais perdu**
il/elle/on	**avait perdu**
nous	**avions perdu**
vous	**aviez perdu**
ils/elles	**avaient perdu**

IMPERATIVE

perds / perdons / perdez

EXAMPLE PHRASES

Je **perdrai** forcément contre lui. I'll obviously lose against him.

Il **perdit** patience et se mit à crier. He lost his patience and began to shout.

Tu ne **perdrais** pas tes affaires si tu faisais plus attention. You wouldn't lose your things if you were more careful.

Elle **avait perdu** la mémoire depuis son accident. She had lost her memory after her accident.

plaire (to please)

PRESENT		PRESENT SUBJUNCTIVE	
je	**plais**	je	**plaise**
tu	**plais**	tu	**plaises**
il/elle/on	**plaît**	il/elle/on	**plaise**
nous	**plaisons**	nous	**plaisions**
vous	**plaisez**	vous	**plaisiez**
ils/elles	**plaisent**	ils/elles	**plaisent**

PERFECT		IMPERFECT	
j'	**ai plu**	je	**plaisais**
tu	**as plu**	tu	**plaisais**
il/elle/on	**a plu**	il/elle/on	**plaisait**
nous	**avons plu**	nous	**plaisions**
vous	**avez plu**	vous	**plaisiez**
ils/elles	**ont plu**	ils/elles	**plaisaient**

PRESENT PARTICIPLE	PAST PARTICIPLE
plaisant	plu

EXAMPLE PHRASES

Le menu ne me **plaît** pas. I don't like the menu.

s'il te **plaît**. please

s'il vous **plaît**. please

Ça t'**a plu**, le film? Did you like the film?

La robe noire me **plaisait** beaucoup. I really liked the black dress.

plaire

FUTURE

je	**plairai**
tu	**plairas**
il/elle/on	**plaira**
nous	**plairons**
vous	**plairez**
ils/elles	**plairont**

CONDITIONAL

je	**plairais**
tu	**plairais**
il/elle/on	**plairait**
nous	**plairions**
vous	**plairiez**
ils/elles	**plairaient**

PAST HISTORIC

je	**plus**
tu	**plus**
il/elle/on	**plut**
nous	**plûmes**
vous	**plûtes**
ils/elles	**plurent**

PLUPERFECT

j'	**avais plu**
tu	**avais plu**
il/elle/on	**avait plu**
nous	**avions plu**
vous	**aviez plu**
ils/elles	**avaient plu**

IMPERATIVE

plais / plaisons / plaisez

EXAMPLE PHRASES

Ce film ne lui **plaira** pas. He won't like this film.

Elle lui **plut** immédiatement. He liked her straight away.

Ça te **plairait** d'aller à la mer? Would you like to go to the seaside?

Cette remarque ne lui **avait** pas **plu**. He hadn't liked that remark.

je/j' = I **tu** = you **il** = he/it **elle** = she/it **on** = we/one **nous** = we **vous** = you **ils/elles** = they

pleuvoir (to rain)

PRESENT
   il **pleut**

PRESENT SUBJUNCTIVE
   il **pleuve**

PERFECT
   il **a plu**

IMPERFECT
   il **pleuvait**

PRESENT PARTICIPLE
pleuvant

PAST PARTICIPLE
plu

EXAMPLE PHRASES

Il **pleut** beaucoup à Glasgow. It rains a lot in Glasgow.

Il **a plu** toute la journée. It rained all day long.

J'ai peur qu'il **pleuve** cet après-midi. I'm afraid it might rain this afternoon.

Il **pleuvait** tellement qu'ils décidèrent de rester chez eux. It rained so much that they decided to stay at home.

---

je/j' = I   tu = you   il = he/it   elle = she/it   on = we/one   nous = we   vous = you   ils/elles = they

pleuvoir

FUTURE

il **pleuvra**

CONDITIONAL

il **pleuvrait**

PAST HISTORIC

il **plut**

PLUPERFECT

il **avait plu**

IMPERATIVE

not used

EXAMPLE PHRASES

J'espère qu'il ne **pleuvra** pas demain. I hope it won't rain tomorrow.

Il **plut** pendant quarante jours et quarante nuits. It rained for forty days and forty nights.

Il **pleuvrait** probablement si je ne prenais pas mon parapluie. It will probably rain if I don't take my umbrella.

Il n'**avait** pas **plu** de tout l'été. It hadn't rained all summer.

pouvoir (to be able)

PRESENT

je	**peux**
tu	**peux**
il/elle/on	**peut**
nous	**pouvons**
vous	**pouvez**
ils/elles	**peuvent**

PRESENT SUBJUNCTIVE

je	**puisse**
tu	**puisses**
il/elle/on	**puisse**
nous	**puissions**
vous	**puissiez**
ils/elles	**puissent**

PERFECT

j'	**ai pu**
tu	**as pu**
il/elle/on	**a pu**
nous	**avons pu**
vous	**avez pu**
ils/elles	**ont pu**

IMPERFECT

je	**pouvais**
tu	**pouvais**
il/elle/on	**pouvait**
nous	**pouvions**
vous	**pouviez**
ils/elles	**pouvaient**

PRESENT PARTICIPLE

pouvant

PAST PARTICIPLE

pu

EXAMPLE PHRASES

Je **peux** vous aider? Can I help you?

J'ai fait tout ce que j'**ai pu**. I did all I could.

Nous avons changé la date du baptême de Clara pour que tu **puisses** venir.

　　We've changed the date of Clara's christening so that you're able to come.

Elle ne **pouvait** pas s'empêcher de rire. She couldn't help laughing.

pouvoir

FUTURE

je	**pourrai**
tu	**pourras**
il/elle/on	**pourra**
nous	**pourrons**
vous	**pourrez**
ils/elles	**pourront**

CONDITIONAL

je	**pourrais**
tu	**pourrais**
il/elle/on	**pourrait**
nous	**pourrions**
vous	**pourriez**
ils/elles	**pourraient**

PAST HISTORIC

je	**pus**
tu	**pus**
il/elle/on	**put**
nous	**pûmes**
vous	**pûtes**
ils/elles	**purent**

PLUPERFECT

j'	**avais pu**
tu	**avais pu**
il/elle/on	**avait pu**
nous	**avions pu**
vous	**aviez pu**
ils/elles	**avaient pu**

IMPERATIVE

not used

EXAMPLE PHRASES

Je ne **pourrai** pas venir samedi. I won't be able to come on Saturday.

Il ne **put** se souvenir de son nom. He couldn't remember her name.

Je **pourrais** te prêter ma robe si tu voulais. I could lend you my dress if you like.

Il n'**avait** pas **pu** les rejoindre. He hadn't been able to join them.

je/j' = I   **tu** = you   **il** = he/it   **elle** = she/it   **on** = we/one   **nous** = we   **vous** = you   **ils/elles** = they

prendre (to take)

PRESENT

je	**prends**
tu	**prends**
il/elle/on	**prend**
nous	**prenons**
vous	**prenez**
ils/elles	**prennent**

PRESENT SUBJUNCTIVE

je	**prenne**
tu	**prennes**
il/elle/on	**prenne**
nous	**prenions**
vous	**preniez**
ils/elles	**prennent**

PERFECT

j'	**ai pris**
tu	**as pris**
il/elle/on	**a pris**
nous	**avons pris**
vous	**avez pris**
ils/elles	**ont pris**

IMPERFECT

je	**prenais**
tu	**prenais**
il/elle/on	**prenait**
nous	**prenions**
vous	**preniez**
ils/elles	**prenaient**

PRESENT PARTICIPLE

prenant

PAST PARTICIPLE

pris

EXAMPLE PHRASES

N'oublie pas de **prendre** ton passeport. Don't forget to take your passport.

Pour qui est-ce qu'il se **prend**? Who does he think he is?

J'**ai pris** plein de photos. I took lots of pictures.

Prends ton appareil photo. Take your camera.

Il faut que je **prenne** mes affaires de gym. I have to take my gym kit.

Il **prenait** le bus à huit heures le matin. He got the bus at eight in the morning.

---

je/j' = I   **tu** = you   **il** = he/it   **elle** = she/it   **on** = we/one   **nous** = we   **vous** = you   **ils/elles** = they

prendre

FUTURE

je	**prendrai**
tu	**prendras**
il/elle/on	**prendra**
nous	**prendrons**
vous	**prendrez**
ils/elles	**prendront**

CONDITIONAL

je	**prendrais**
tu	**prendrais**
il/elle/on	**prendrait**
nous	**prendrions**
vous	**prendriez**
ils/elles	**prendraient**

PAST HISTORIC

je	**pris**
tu	**pris**
il/elle/on	**prit**
nous	**prîmes**
vous	**prîtes**
ils/elles	**prirent**

PLUPERFECT

j'	**avais pris**
tu	**avais pris**
il/elle/on	**avait pris**
nous	**avions pris**
vous	**aviez pris**
ils/elles	**avaient pris**

IMPERATIVE

prends / prenons / prenez

EXAMPLE PHRASES

Il **prendra** le train de 8h20. He'll take the 8.20 train.

Elle **prit** son sac et partit. She took her bag and left.

Si j'habitais ici, je **prendrais** le bus pour aller travailler. If I lived here, I'd take the bus to work.

Il n'**avait** jamais **pris** l'avion. He'd never travelled by plane.

protéger (to protect)

PRESENT

je	**protège**
tu	**protèges**
il/elle/on	**protège**
nous	**protégeons**
vous	**protégez**
ils/elles	**protègent**

PRESENT SUBJUNCTIVE

je	**protège**
tu	**protèges**
il/elle/on	**protège**
nous	**protégions**
vous	**protégiez**
ils/elles	**protègent**

PERFECT

j'	**ai protégé**
tu	**as protégé**
il/elle/on	**a protégé**
nous	**avons protégé**
vous	**avez protégé**
ils/elles	**ont protégé**

IMPERFECT

je	**protégeais**
tu	**protégeais**
il/elle/on	**protégeait**
nous	**protégions**
vous	**protégiez**
ils/elles	**protégeaient**

PRESENT PARTICIPLE

protégeant

PAST PARTICIPLE

protégé

EXAMPLE PHRASES

Ne crains rien, je te **protège**. Don't be scared, I'm looking after you.

Le champ **est protégé** du vent par la colline. The field is sheltered from the wind by the hill.

Protège ton livre de la pluie. Protect your book from the rain.

Je voudrais une tente qui **protège** bien contre le froid. I'd like a tent which protects you from the cold.

Il me **protégeait** contre tous ceux qui m'embêtaient. He protected me from all those who annoyed me.

je/j' = I   **tu** = you   **il** = he/it   **elle** = she/it   **on** = we/one   **nous** = we   **vous** = you   **ils/elles** = they

protéger

FUTURE

je	**protégerai**
tu	**protégeras**
il/elle/on	**protégera**
nous	**protégerons**
vous	**protégerez**
ils/elles	**protégeront**

CONDITIONAL

je	**protégerais**
tu	**protégerais**
il/elle/on	**protégerait**
nous	**protégerions**
vous	**protégeriez**
ils/elles	**protégeraient**

PAST HISTORIC

je	**protégeai**
tu	**protégeas**
il/elle/on	**protégea**
nous	**protégeâmes**
vous	**protégeâtes**
ils/elles	**protégèrent**

PLUPERFECT

j'	**avais protégé**
tu	**avais protégé**
il/elle/on	**avait protégé**
nous	**avions protégé**
vous	**aviez protégé**
ils/elles	**avaient protégé**

IMPERATIVE

protège / protégeons / protégez

EXAMPLE PHRASES

Ce manteau te **protégera** bien du froid. This coat will protect you from the cold.

Il se **protégea** le visage avec ses mains. He protected his face with his hands.

Cette crème te **protégerait** mieux les mains. This cream would protect your hands better.

Il **avait** toujours **protégé** sa petite sœur à l'école. He'd always protected his little sister at school.

---

je/j' = I   **tu** = you   **il** = he/it   **elle** = she/it   **on** = we/one   **nous** = we   **vous** = you   **ils/elles** = they

recevoir (to receive)

PRESENT

je	**reçois**
tu	**reçois**
il/elle/on	**reçoit**
nous	**recevons**
vous	**recevez**
ils/elles	**reçoivent**

PRESENT SUBJUNCTIVE

je	**reçoive**
tu	**reçoives**
il/elle/on	**reçoive**
nous	**recevions**
vous	**receviez**
ils/elles	**reçoivent**

PERFECT

j'	**ai reçu**
tu	**as reçu**
il/elle/on	**a reçu**
nous	**avons reçu**
vous	**avez reçu**
ils/elles	**ont reçu**

IMPERFECT

je	**recevais**
tu	**recevais**
il/elle/on	**recevait**
nous	**recevions**
vous	**receviez**
ils/elles	**recevaient**

PRESENT PARTICIPLE

recevant

PAST PARTICIPLE

reçu

EXAMPLE PHRASES

Je ne **reçois** jamais de courrier. I never get any mail.

Elle **a reçu** une lettre de Charlotte. She received a letter from Charlotte.

Recevez, Monsieur, mes salutations. Yours sincerely.

J'attendais que tu **reçoives** l'invitation pour t'emmener choisir un cadeau.
   I was waiting for you to get the invitation before I took you to choose
   a present.

Il **recevait** d'étranges messages. He was getting strange messages.

recevoir

FUTURE

je	**recevrai**
tu	**recevras**
il/elle/on	**recevra**
nous	**recevrons**
vous	**recevrez**
ils/elles	**recevront**

CONDITIONAL

je	**recevrais**
tu	**recevrais**
il/elle/on	**recevrait**
nous	**recevrions**
vous	**recevriez**
ils/elles	**recevraient**

PAST HISTORIC

je	**reçus**
tu	**reçus**
il/elle/on	**reçut**
nous	**reçûmes**
vous	**reçûtes**
ils/elles	**reçurent**

PLUPERFECT

j'	**avais reçu**
tu	**avais reçu**
il/elle/on	**avait reçu**
nous	**avions reçu**
vous	**aviez reçu**
ils/elles	**avaient reçu**

IMPERATIVE

reçois / recevons / recevez

EXAMPLE PHRASES

Elle **recevra** une réponse la semaine prochaine. She'll get an answer next week.

Il **reçut** une lettre anonyme. He received an anonymous letter.

Tu ne **recevrais** pas autant de monde si ta maison n'était pas aussi grande.
    You wouldn't entertain so many people if your house weren't so big.

Cela faisait une semaine qu'il n'**avait** pas **reçu** de courrier. He hadn't had any
    mail for a week.

---

réfléchir (to think)

PRESENT

je	**réfléchis**
tu	**réfléchis**
il/elle/on	**réfléchit**
nous	**réfléchissons**
vous	**réfléchissez**
ils/elles	**réfléchissent**

PRESENT SUBJUNCTIVE

je	**réfléchisse**
tu	**réfléchisses**
il/elle/on	**réfléchisse**
nous	**réfléchissions**
vous	**réfléchissiez**
ils/elles	**réfléchissent**

PERFECT

j'	**ai réfléchi**
tu	**as réfléchi**
il/elle/on	**a réfléchi**
nous	**avons réfléchi**
vous	**avez réfléchi**
ils/elles	**ont réfléchi**

IMPERFECT

je	**réfléchissais**
tu	**réfléchissais**
il/elle/on	**réfléchissait**
nous	**réfléchissions**
vous	**réfléchissiez**
ils/elles	**réfléchissaient**

PRESENT PARTICIPLE
réfléchissant

PAST PARTICIPLE
réfléchi

EXAMPLE PHRASES
Il est en train de **réfléchir**. He's thinking.

Je vais **réfléchir** à ta proposition. I'll think about your suggestion.

Réfléchissez avant de répondre. Think before answering.

Il faut que j'y **réfléchisse**. I'll have to think about it.

réfléchir

FUTURE

je	**réfléchirai**
tu	**réfléchiras**
il/elle/on	**réfléchira**
nous	**réfléchirons**
vous	**réfléchirez**
ils/elles	**réfléchiront**

CONDITIONAL

je	**réfléchirais**
tu	**réfléchirais**
il/elle/on	**réfléchirait**
nous	**réfléchirions**
vous	**réfléchiriez**
ils/elles	**réfléchiraient**

PAST HISTORIC

je	**réfléchis**
tu	**réfléchis**
il/elle/on	**réfléchit**
nous	**réfléchîmes**
vous	**réfléchîtes**
ils/elles	**réfléchirent**

PLUPERFECT

j'	**avais réfléchi**
tu	**avais réfléchi**
il/elle/on	**avait réfléchi**
nous	**avions réfléchi**
vous	**aviez réfléchi**
ils/elles	**avaient réfléchi**

IMPERATIVE

réfléchis / réfléchissons / réfléchissez

EXAMPLE PHRASES

J'y **réfléchirai** et nous en reparlerons lors de notre prochaine réunion. I'll think about it and we'll talk about it at our next meeting.

Il **réfléchit** longuement avant de parler. He thought for a long time before he spoke.

Si j'étais toi, j'y **réfléchirais** encore un peu. If I were you, I'd give it more thought.

Ils **avaient** bien **réfléchi** et ils avaient décidé de vendre la maison. They had thought it over and they had decided to sell the house.

je/j' = I **tu** = you **il** = he/it **elle** = she/it **on** = we/one **nous** = we **vous** = you **ils/elles** = they

rentrer (to go back; to go in)

PRESENT		PRESENT SUBJUNCTIVE	
je	rentre	je	rentre
tu	rentres	tu	rentres
il/elle/on	rentre	il/elle/on	rentre
nous	rentrons	nous	rentrions
vous	rentrez	vous	rentriez
ils/elles	rentrent	ils/elles	rentrent

PERFECT		IMPERFECT	
je	suis rentré(e)	je	rentrais
tu	es rentré(e)	tu	rentrais
il/elle/on	est rentré(e)	il/elle/on	rentrait
nous	sommes rentré(e)s	nous	rentrions
vous	êtes rentré(e)(s)	vous	rentriez
ils/elles	sont rentré(e)s	ils/elles	rentraient

PRESENT PARTICIPLE	PAST PARTICIPLE
rentrant	rentré

In the perfect and the pluperfect, use the auxiliary "avoir" when there is a direct object.

EXAMPLE PHRASES

Je **rentre** déjeuner à midi. I go home for lunch.

À quelle heure est-ce qu'elle **est rentrée**? What time did she get in?

Ne **rentre** pas trop tard. Don't come home too late.

Il faut que je **rentre** de bonne heure aujourd'hui. I have to go home early today.

Il ne **rentrait** jamais avant neuf heures le soir. He never came home before
nine in the evening.

rentrer

FUTURE

je	rentrerai
tu	rentreras
il/elle/on	rentrera
nous	rentrerons
vous	rentrerez
ils/elles	rentreront

CONDITIONAL

je	rentrerais
tu	rentrerais
il/elle/on	rentrerait
nous	rentrerions
vous	rentreriez
ils/elles	rentreraient

PAST HISTORIC

je	rentrai
tu	rentras
il/elle/on	rentra
nous	rentrâmes
vous	rentrâtes
ils/elles	rentrèrent

PLUPERFECT

j'	étais rentré(e)
tu	étais rentré(e)
il/elle/on	était rentré(e)
nous	étions rentré(e)s
vous	étiez rentré(e)(s)
ils/elles	étaient rentré(e)s

IMPERATIVE

rentre / rentrons / rentrez

EXAMPLE PHRASES

Nous ne **rentrerons** pas tard. We won't come home late.

Il **rentra** chez lui en courant. He ran all the way home.

Si je n'avais pas peur de me perdre, je **rentrerais** sans toi. If I weren't afraid I'd get lost, I'd go home without you.

Ils **étaient rentrés** dans le magasin. They'd gone into the shop.

Il **avait** déjà **rentré** la voiture dans le garage. He'd already put the car into the garage.

je/j' = I **tu** = you **il** = he/it **elle** = she/it **on** = we/one **nous** = we **vous** = you **ils/elles** = they

répondre (to answer)

PRESENT

je	**réponds**
tu	**réponds**
il/elle/on	**répond**
nous	**répondons**
vous	**répondez**
ils/elles	**répondent**

PRESENT SUBJUNCTIVE

je	**réponde**
tu	**répondes**
il/elle/on	**réponde**
nous	**répondions**
vous	**répondiez**
ils/elles	**répondent**

PERFECT

j'	**ai répondu**
tu	**as répondu**
il/elle/on	**a répondu**
nous	**avons répondu**
vous	**avez répondu**
ils/elles	**ont répondu**

IMPERFECT

je	**répondais**
tu	**répondais**
il/elle/on	**répondait**
nous	**répondions**
vous	**répondiez**
ils/elles	**répondaient**

PRESENT PARTICIPLE

répondant

PAST PARTICIPLE

répondu

EXAMPLE PHRASES

Ça ne **répond** pas. There's no reply.

C'est elle qui **a répondu** au téléphone. She answered the phone.

Lisez le texte et **répondez** aux questions. Read the text and answer the questions.

J'attendais que tu **répondes** à ma lettre. I was waiting for you to reply to my letter.

Il ne **répondait** jamais au téléphone le soir. He never answered the phone in the evening.

je/j' = I   **tu** = you   **il** = he/it   **elle** = she/it   **on** = we/one   **nous** = we   **vous** = you   **ils/elles** = they

répondre

FUTURE

je	**répondrai**
tu	**répondras**
il/elle/on	**répondra**
nous	**répondrons**
vous	**répondrez**
ils/elles	**répondront**

CONDITIONAL

je	**répondrais**
tu	**répondrais**
il/elle/on	**répondrait**
nous	**répondrions**
vous	**répondriez**
ils/elles	**répondraient**

PAST HISTORIC

je	**répondis**
tu	**répondis**
il/elle/on	**répondit**
nous	**répondîmes**
vous	**répondîtes**
ils/elles	**répondirent**

PLUPERFECT

j'	**avais répondu**
tu	**avais répondu**
il/elle/on	**avait répondu**
nous	**avions répondu**
vous	**aviez répondu**
ils/elles	**avaient répondu**

IMPERATIVE

réponds / répondons / répondez

EXAMPLE PHRASES

Je **répondrai** à son message ce soir. I'll reply to his message this evening.

"Je ne sais pas," **répondit**-elle. I don't know, she answered.

Il ne te **répondrait** pas comme ça si tu étais plus stricte. He wouldn't answer back like that if you were stricter.

Je n'**avais** pas encore **répondu** à son invitation. I hadn't replied to her invitation yet.

je/j' = I   **tu** = you   **il** = he/it   **elle** = she/it   **on** = we/one   **nous** = we   **vous** = you   **ils/elles** = they

résoudre (to solve; to resolve)

PRESENT

je	**résous**
tu	**résous**
il/elle/on	**résout**
nous	**résolvons**
vous	**résolvez**
ils/elles	**résolvent**

PRESENT SUBJUNCTIVE

je	**résolve**
tu	**résolves**
il/elle/on	**résolve**
nous	**résolvions**
vous	**résolviez**
ils/elles	**résolvent**

PERFECT

j'	**ai résolu**
tu	**as résolu**
il/elle/on	**a résolu**
nous	**avons résolu**
vous	**avez résolu**
ils/elles	**ont résolu**

IMPERFECT

je	**résolvais**
tu	**résolvais**
il/elle/on	**résolvait**
nous	**résolvions**
vous	**résolviez**
ils/elles	**résolvaient**

PRESENT PARTICIPLE
résolvant

PAST PARTICIPLE
résolu

EXAMPLE PHRASES

C'est un problème qui sera difficile à **résoudre**. This problem will be difficult to solve.

La violence ne **résout** rien. Violence doesn't solve anything.

J'**ai résolu** le problème. I've solved the problem.

J'aimerais que vous **résolviez** la question aujourd'hui. I'd like you to resolve the question today.

résoudre

FUTURE

je **résoudrai**

tu **résoudras**

il/elle/on **résoudra**

nous **résoudrons**

vous **résoudrez**

ils/elles **résoudront**

CONDITIONAL

je **résoudrais**

tu **résoudrais**

il/elle/on **résoudrait**

nous **résoudrions**

vous **résoudriez**

ils/elles **résoudraient**

PAST HISTORIC

je **résolus**

tu **résolus**

il/elle/on **résolut**

nous **résolûmes**

vous **résolûtes**

ils/elles **résolurent**

PLUPERFECT

j' **avais résolu**

tu **avais résolu**

il/elle/on **avait résolu**

nous **avions résolu**

vous **aviez résolu**

ils/elles **avaient résolu**

IMPERATIVE

résous / résolvons / résolvez

EXAMPLE PHRASES

Son refus de s'excuser ne **résoudra** pas la querelle. His refusal to apologize won't resolve the quarrel.

Il **résolut** l'énigme en quelques minutes. He solved the riddle in a few minutes.

C'est un problème qui se **résoudrait** rapidement s'il n'y avait pas déjà d'autres problèmes. This problem could be solved quickly if there weren't already other problems.

À la fin de la réunion, nous **avions résolu** la question. By the end of the meeting, we had resolved the question.

je/j' = I **tu** = you **il** = he/it **elle** = she/it **on** = we/one **nous** = we **vous** = you **ils/elles** = they

rester (to stay)

PRESENT

je	**reste**
tu	**restes**
il/elle/on	**reste**
nous	**restons**
vous	**restez**
ils/elles	**restent**

PRESENT SUBJUNCTIVE

je	**reste**
tu	**restes**
il/elle/on	**reste**
nous	**restions**
vous	**restiez**
ils/elles	**restent**

PERFECT

je	**suis resté(e)**
tu	**es resté(e)**
il/elle/on	**est resté(e)**
nous	**sommes resté(e)s**
vous	**êtes resté(e)(s)**
ils/elles	**sont resté(e)s**

IMPERFECT

je	**restais**
tu	**restais**
il/elle/on	**restait**
nous	**restions**
vous	**restiez**
ils/elles	**restaient**

PRESENT PARTICIPLE

restant

PAST PARTICIPLE

resté

EXAMPLE PHRASES

Cet été, je **reste** en Écosse. I'm staying in Scotland this summer.

Ils ne **sont** pas **restés** très longtemps. They didn't stay very long.

Reste ici! Stay here!

Elle aimerait que Marianne **reste** dormir ce soir. She'd like Marianne to stay for a sleepover tonight.

Il leur **restait** encore un peu d'argent. They still had some money left.

je/j' = I   **tu** = you   **il** = he/it   **elle** = she/it   **on** = we/one   **nous** = we   **vous** = you   **ils/elles** = they

rester

FUTURE

je	**resterai**
tu	**resteras**
il/elle/on	**restera**
nous	**resterons**
vous	**resterez**
ils/elles	**resteront**

CONDITIONAL

je	**resterais**
tu	**resterais**
il/elle/on	**resterait**
nous	**resterions**
vous	**resteriez**
ils/elles	**resteraient**

PAST HISTORIC

je	**restai**
tu	**restas**
il/elle/on	**resta**
nous	**restâmes**
vous	**restâtes**
ils/elles	**restèrent**

PLUPERFECT

j'	**étais resté(e)**
tu	**étais resté(e)**
il/elle/on	**était resté(e)**
nous	**étions resté(e)s**
vous	**étiez resté(e)(s)**
ils/elles	**étaient resté(e)s**

IMPERATIVE

reste / restons / restez

EXAMPLE PHRASES

Si tu finis les biscuits il n'en **restera** plus pour ce soir. If you finish the biscuits there won't be any left for tonight.

Il **resta** dans sa chambre toute la soirée. He stayed in his bedroom all evening.

Si c'était à moi de choisir, je **resterais** à la maison. If it were my choice, I'd stay home.

Nous **étions restés** à la maison pour regarder le match de football. We'd stayed home to watch the football match.

je/j' = I **tu** = you **il** = he/it **elle** = she/it **on** = we/one **nous** = we **vous** = you **ils/elles** = they

retourner (to return; to turn)

PRESENT

je	**retourne**
tu	**retournes**
il/elle/on	**retourne**
nous	**retournons**
vous	**retournez**
ils/elles	**retournent**

PRESENT SUBJUNCTIVE

je	**retourne**
tu	**retournes**
il/elle/on	**retourne**
nous	**retournions**
vous	**retourniez**
ils/elles	**retournent**

PERFECT

je	**suis retourné(e)**
tu	**es retourné(e)**
il/elle/on	**est retourné(e)**
nous	**sommes retourné(e)s**
vous	**êtes retourné(e)(s)**
ils/elles	**sont retourné(e)s**

IMPERFECT

je	**retournais**
tu	**retournais**
il/elle/on	**retournait**
nous	**retournions**
vous	**retourniez**
ils/elles	**retournaient**

PRESENT PARTICIPLE

retournant

PAST PARTICIPLE

retourné

In the perfect and the pluperfect, use the auxiliary "avoir" when there is a direct object.

EXAMPLE PHRASES

J'aimerais bien **retourner** en Italie un jour. I'd like to go back to Italy one day.

Cet été, nous **retournons** en Grèce. We're going back to Greece this summer.

Est-ce que tu **es retournée** à Londres? Have you ever been back to London?

Zoë, **retourne**-toi! Turn around Zoë!

Il va falloir que je **retourne** voir le film. I'll have to go back to see the film.

Elle **retournait** rarement dans son pays natal. She rarely went back to her native country.

je/j' = I   **tu** = you   **il** = he/it   **elle** = she/it   **on** = we/one   **nous** = we   **vous** = you   **ils/elles** = they

retourner

FUTURE

je	**retournerai**
tu	**retourneras**
il/elle/on	**retournera**
nous	**retournerons**
vous	**retournerez**
ils/elles	**retourneront**

CONDITIONAL

je	**retournerais**
tu	**retournerais**
il/elle/on	**retournerait**
nous	**retournerions**
vous	**retourneriez**
ils/elles	**retourneraient**

PAST HISTORIC

je	**retournai**
tu	**retournas**
il/elle/on	**retourna**
nous	**retournâmes**
vous	**retournâtes**
ils/elles	**retournèrent**

PLUPERFECT

j'	**étais retourné(e)**
tu	**étais retourné(e)**
il/elle/on	**était retourné(e)**
nous	**étions retourné(e)s**
vous	**étiez retourné(e)(s)**
ils/elles	**étaient retourné(e)s**

IMPERATIVE

retourne / retournons / retournez

EXAMPLE PHRASES

Je ne **retournerai** jamais les voir. I'll never go back to see them.

Elle déjeuna rapidement et **retourna** travailler. She had a quick lunch and went back to work.

Il disait qu'il ne **retournerait** jamais vivre avec elle. He said that he would never go back to live with her.

Elle **avait retourné** la carte pour vérifier. She had turned the card over to check.

je/j' = I **tu** = you **il** = he/it **elle** = she/it **on** = we/one **nous** = we **vous** = you **ils/elles** = they

réussir (to be successful)

PRESENT

je	**réussis**
tu	**réussis**
il/elle/on	**réussit**
nous	**réussissons**
vous	**réussissez**
ils/elles	**réussissent**

PRESENT SUBJUNCTIVE

je	**réussisse**
tu	**réussisses**
il/elle/on	**réussisse**
nous	**réussissions**
vous	**réussissiez**
ils/elles	**réussissent**

PERFECT

j'	**ai réussi**
tu	**as réussi**
il/elle/on	**a réussi**
nous	**avons réussi**
vous	**avez réussi**
ils/elles	**ont réussi**

IMPERFECT

je	**réussissais**
tu	**réussissais**
il/elle/on	**réussissait**
nous	**réussissions**
vous	**réussissiez**
ils/elles	**réussissaient**

PRESENT PARTICIPLE
réussissant

PAST PARTICIPLE
réussi

EXAMPLE PHRASES

Il faut se battre pour **réussir** dans la vie. You have to fight to be successful in life.

Tous ses enfants **ont** très bien **réussi**. All her children are very successful.

J'aimerais qu'il **réussisse** à son permis de conduire. I'd like him to pass his driving test.

Elle **réussissait** toujours à me faire rire quand j'étais triste. She always managed to make me laugh when I was sad.

je/j' = I   **tu** = you   **il** = he/it   **elle** = she/it   **on** = we/one   **nous** = we   **vous** = you   **ils/elles** = they

réussir

FUTURE

je	**réussirai**
tu	**réussiras**
il/elle/on	**réussira**
nous	**réussirons**
vous	**réussirez**
ils/elles	**réussiront**

CONDITIONAL

je	**réussirais**
tu	**réussirais**
il/elle/on	**réussirait**
nous	**réussirions**
vous	**réussiriez**
ils/elles	**réussiraient**

PAST HISTORIC

je	**réussis**
tu	**réussis**
il/elle/on	**réussit**
nous	**réussîmes**
vous	**réussîtes**
ils/elles	**réussirent**

PLUPERFECT

j'	**avais réussi**
tu	**avais réussi**
il/elle/on	**avait réussi**
nous	**avions réussi**
vous	**aviez réussi**
ils/elles	**avaient réussi**

IMPERATIVE

réussis / réussissons / réussissez

EXAMPLE PHRASES

Je suis sûr que tu **réussiras** à ton examen. I'm sure you'll pass your exam.

Finalement, elle **réussit** à le convaincre. She eventually managed to convince him.

Je **réussirais** peut-être mes gâteaux si j'avais un four qui marchait. My cakes might turn out fine if I had an oven that worked.

Elle **avait réussi** à battre le record du monde. She had succeeded in beating the world record.

je/j' = I **tu** = you **il** = he/it **elle** = she/it **on** = we/one **nous** = we **vous** = you **ils/elles** = they

se réveiller (to wake up)

PRESENT		PRESENT SUBJUNCTIVE	
je	**me réveille**	je	**me réveille**
tu	**te réveilles**	tu	**te réveilles**
il/elle/on	**se réveille**	il/elle/on	**se réveille**
nous	**nous réveillons**	nous	**nous réveillions**
vous	**vous réveillez**	vous	**vous réveilliez**
ils/elles	**se réveillent**	ils/elles	**se réveillent**

PERFECT		IMPERFECT	
je	**me suis réveillé(e)**	je	**me réveillais**
tu	**t'es réveillé(e)**	tu	**te réveillais**
il/elle/on	**s'est réveillé(e)**	il/elle/on	**se réveillait**
nous	**nous sommes réveillé(e)s**	nous	**nous réveillions**
vous	**vous êtes réveillé(e)(s)**	vous	**vous réveilliez**
ils/elles	**se sont réveillé(e)s**	ils/elles	**se réveillaient**

PRESENT PARTICIPLE
se réveillant

PAST PARTICIPLE
réveillé

EXAMPLE PHRASES

Je **me réveille** à sept heures tous les matins. I wake up at seven every morning.

Il **s'est réveillé** en retard. He overslept.

Réveille-toi: il est huit heures! Wake up - it's eight!

Il faut que je **me réveille** à cinq heures demain matin. I have to get up at five tomorrow morning.

Elle **se réveillait** toujours avant moi. She always woke up before me.

---

je/j' = I   **tu** = you   **il** = he/it   **elle** = she/it   **on** = we/one   **nous** = we   **vous** = you   **ils/elles** = they

se réveiller

FUTURE

je	**me réveillerai**
tu	**te réveilleras**
il/elle/on	**se réveillera**
nous	**nous réveillerons**
vous	**vous réveillerez**
ils/elles	**se réveilleront**

CONDITIONAL

je	**me réveillerais**
tu	**te réveillerais**
il/elle/on	**se réveillerait**
nous	**nous réveillerions**
vous	**vous réveilleriez**
ils/elles	**se réveilleraient**

PAST HISTORIC

je	**me réveillai**
tu	**te réveillas**
il/elle/on	**se réveilla**
nous	**nous reveillâmes**
vous	**vous réveillâtes**
ils/elles	**se réveillèrent**

PLUPERFECT

je	**m'étais réveill(e)**
tu	**t'étais réveill(e)**
il/elle/on	**s'était réveillé(e)**
nous	**nous étions réveill(e)s**
vous	**vous étiez réveillé(e)(s)**
ils/elles	**s'étaient réveillé(e)s**

IMPERATIVE

réveille-toi / réveillons-nous / réveillez-nous

EXAMPLE PHRASES

Louise ne **se réveillera** probablement pas avant neuf heures. Louise probably won't wake up before nine.

Elle **se réveilla** en sursaut. She woke up with a start.

Je ne **me réveillerais** pas sans mon réveil. I wouldn't wake up without my alarm clock.

Elle ne **s'était** pas **réveillée** quand je l'avais appelée. She hadn't woken up when I had called her.

je/j' = I **tu** = you **il** = he/it **elle** = she/it **on** = we/one **nous** = we **vous** = you **ils/elles** = they

revenir (to come back)

PRESENT		PRESENT SUBJUNCTIVE	
je	**reviens**	je	**revienne**
tu	**reviens**	tu	**reviennes**
il/elle/on	**revient**	il/elle/on	**revienne**
nous	**revenons**	nous	**revenions**
vous	**revenez**	vous	**reveniez**
ils/elles	**reviennent**	ils/elles	**reviennent**

PERFECT		IMPERFECT	
je	**suis revenu(e)**	je	**revenais**
tu	**es revenu(e)**	tu	**revenais**
il/elle/on	**est revenu(e)**	il/elle/on	**revenait**
nous	**sommes revenu(e)s**	nous	**revenions**
vous	**êtes revenu(e)(s)**	vous	**reveniez**
ils/elles	**sont revenu(e)s**	ils/elles	**revenaient**

PRESENT PARTICIPLE
revenant

PAST PARTICIPLE
revenu

EXAMPLE PHRASES

Je **reviens** dans cinq minutes! I'll be back in five minutes!

Ça me **revient**! It's coming back to me now!

Mon chat n'**est** toujours pas **revenu**. My cat still hasn't come back.

Philippe! **Reviens** immédiatement! Philippe! Come back immediately!

J'aimerais qu'il **revienne** me voir. I'd like him to come back to see me.

Son chien se promenait souvent loin de chez lui mais il **revenait** toujours.

His dog often wandered far away from his house, but he'd always come back.

---

je/j' = I   **tu** = you   **il** = he/it   **elle** = she/it   **on** = we/one   **nous** = we   **vous** = you   **ils/elles** = they

revenir

FUTURE

je	**reviendrai**
tu	**reviendras**
il/elle/on	**reviendra**
nous	**reviendrons**
vous	**reviendrez**
ils/elles	**reviendront**

CONDITIONAL

je	**reviendrais**
tu	**reviendrais**
il/elle/on	**reviendrait**
nous	**reviendrions**
vous	**reviendriez**
ils/elles	**reviendraient**

PAST HISTORIC

je	**revins**
tu	**revins**
il/elle/on	**revint**
nous	**revînmes**
vous	**revîntes**
ils/elles	**revinrent**

PLUPERFECT

j'	**étais revenu(e)**
tu	**étais revenu(e)**
il/elle/on	**était revenu(e)**
nous	**étions revenu(e)s**
vous	**étiez revenu(e)(s)**
ils/elles	**étaient revenu(e)s**

IMPERATIVE
reviens / revenons / revenez

EXAMPLE PHRASES

Je ne **reviendrai** jamais ici. I'll never come back here.

Il **revint** nous voir le lendemain. He came back to see us the next day.

Elle ne **reviendrait** pas si elle avait le choix. She wouldn't come back if she had the choice.

Ils **étaient revenus** le soir même avec leur fille. They had come back that same evening with their daughter.

---

je/j' = I **tu** = you **il** = he/it **elle** = she/it **on** = we/one **nous** = we **vous** = you **ils/elles** = they

rire (to laugh)

PRESENT

je	**ris**
tu	**ris**
il/elle/on	**rit**
nous	**rions**
vous	**riez**
ils/elles	**rient**

PRESENT SUBJUNCTIVE

je	**rie**
tu	**ries**
il/elle/on	**rie**
nous	**riions**
vous	**riiez**
ils/elles	**rient**

PERFECT

j'	**ai ri**
tu	**as ri**
il/elle/on	**a ri**
nous	**avons ri**
vous	**avez ri**
ils/elles	**ont ri**

IMPERFECT

je	**riais**
tu	**riais**
il/elle/on	**riait**
nous	**riions**
vous	**riiez**
ils/elles	**riaient**

PRESENT PARTICIPLE

riant

PAST PARTICIPLE

ri

EXAMPLE PHRASES

C'était juste pour **rire**. It was only for a laugh.

Elle **rit** toujours de mes plaisanteries. She always laughs at my jokes.

On **a** bien **ri**. We had a good laugh.

Ne **ris** pas, ce n'est pas drôle! Don't laugh, it's not funny!

Je n'aime pas qu'on **rie** derrière mon dos. I don't like it when people laugh behind my back.

rire

FUTURE

je	**rirai**
tu	**riras**
il/elle/on	**rira**
nous	**rirons**
vous	**rirez**
ils/elles	**riront**

CONDITIONAL

je	**rirais**
tu	**rirais**
il/elle/on	**rirait**
nous	**ririons**
vous	**ririez**
ils/elles	**riraient**

PAST HISTORIC

je	**ris**
tu	**ris**
il/elle/on	**rit**
nous	**rîmes**
vous	**rîtes**
ils/elles	**rirent**

PLUPERFECT

j'	**avais ri**
tu	**avais ri**
il/elle/on	**avait ri**
nous	**avions ri**
vous	**aviez ri**
ils/elles	**avaient ri**

IMPERATIVE

ris / rions / riez

EXAMPLE PHRASES

Tu ne **riras** pas tant quand ce sera ton tour. You won't be laughing so much when it's your turn.

Elle **rit** quand il lui raconta l'histoire. She laughed when he told her the story.

Il ne **rirait** pas s'il savait où tu es allé. He wouldn't be laughing if he knew where you've been.

Ils **avaient ri** quand elle leur avait raconté ce qui s'était passé. They had laughed when she had told them what had happened.

je/j' = I   **tu** = you   **il** = he/it   **elle** = she/it   **on** = we/one   **nous** = we   **vous** = you   **ils/elles** = they

rompre (to break; to split up)

PRESENT

je	**romps**
tu	**romps**
il/elle/on	**rompt**
nous	**rompons**
vous	**rompez**
ils/elles	**rompent**

PRESENT SUBJUNCTIVE

je	**rompe**
tu	**rompes**
il/elle/on	**rompe**
nous	**rompions**
vous	**rompiez**
ils/elles	**rompent**

PERFECT

j'	**ai rompu**
tu	**as rompu**
il/elle/on	**a rompu**
nous	**avons rompu**
vous	**avez rompu**
ils/elles	**ont rompu**

IMPERFECT

je	**rompais**
tu	**rompais**
il/elle/on	**rompait**
nous	**rompions**
vous	**rompiez**
ils/elles	**rompaient**

PRESENT PARTICIPLE

rompant

PAST PARTICIPLE

rompu

EXAMPLE PHRASES

Elle **a rompu** le silence. She broke the silence.

Paul et Jo **ont rompu**. Paul and Jo have split up.

Ils ont tiré sur la corde jusqu'à ce qu'elle **rompe**. They pulled on the rope until it broke.

rompre

FUTURE

je	**romprai**
tu	**rompras**
il/elle/on	**rompra**
nous	**romprons**
vous	**romprez**
ils/elles	**rompront**

CONDITIONAL

je	**romprais**
tu	**romprais**
il/elle/on	**romprait**
nous	**romprions**
vous	**rompriez**
ils/elles	**rompraient**

PAST HISTORIC

je	**rompis**
tu	**rompis**
il/elle/on	**rompit**
nous	**rompîmes**
vous	**rompîtes**
ils/elles	**rompirent**

PLUPERFECT

j'	**avais rompu**
tu	**avais rompu**
il/elle/on	**avait rompu**
nous	**avions rompu**
vous	**aviez rompu**
ils/elles	**avaient rompu**

IMPERATIVE
romps / rompons / rompez

EXAMPLE PHRASES

Il **rompit** le silence en entrant. He broke the silence when he came in.

Le charme **était rompu**. The spell was broken.

Il **avait** déjà **rompu** avec Alice quand il a rencontré Christine. He'd already split up with Alice when he met Christine.

je/j' = I **tu** = you **il** = he/it **elle** = she/it **on** = we/one **nous** = we **vous** = you **ils/elles** = they

savoir (to know)

PRESENT

je	**sais**
tu	**sais**
il/elle/on	**sait**
nous	**savons**
vous	**savez**
ils/elles	**savent**

PRESENT SUBJUNCTIVE

je	**sache**
tu	**saches**
il/elle/on	**sache**
nous	**sachions**
vous	**sachiez**
ils/elles	**sachent**

PERFECT

j'	**ai su**
tu	**as su**
il/elle/on	**a su**
nous	**avons su**
vous	**avez su**
ils/elles	**ont su**

IMPERFECT

je	**savais**
tu	**savais**
il/elle/on	**savait**
nous	**savions**
vous	**saviez**
ils/elles	**savaient**

PRESENT PARTICIPLE
sachant

PAST PARTICIPLE
su

EXAMPLE PHRASES

Tu **sais** ce que tu vas faire l'année prochaine? Do you know what you're going to do next year?

Je ne **sais** pas. I don't know.

Elle ne **sait** pas nager. She can't swim.

Je voulais qu'il le **sache**. I wanted him to know about it.

Tu **savais** que son père était enseignant? Did you know that her father was a teacher?

---

je/j' = I   **tu** = you   **il** = he/it   **elle** = she/it   **on** = we/one   **nous** = we   **vous** = you   **ils/elles** = they

savoir

FUTURE

je	**saurai**
tu	**sauras**
il/elle/on	**saura**
nous	**saurons**
vous	**saurez**
ils/elles	**sauront**

CONDITIONAL

je	**saurais**
tu	**saurais**
il/elle/on	**saurait**
nous	**saurions**
vous	**sauriez**
ils/elles	**sauraient**

PAST HISTORIC

je	**sus**
tu	**sus**
il/elle/on	**sut**
nous	**sûmes**
vous	**sûtes**
ils/elles	**surent**

PLUPERFECT

j'	**avais su**
tu	**avais su**
il/elle/on	**avait su**
nous	**avions su**
vous	**aviez su**
ils/elles	**avaient su**

IMPERATIVE

sache / sachons / sachez

EXAMPLE PHRASES

Elle ne **saura** pas où on est. She won't know where we are.

Il ne le **sut** que beaucoup plus tard. He only knew about it a lot later.

Tous ces enfants **sauraient** lire si on leur apprenait. All these children would be able to read if they were taught.

Ils ne l'**avaient su** que beaucoup plus tard. They hadn't known about it until a lot later.

---

je/j' = I **tu** = you **il** = he/it **elle** = she/it **on** = we/one **nous** = we **vous** = you **ils/elles** = they

sentir (to smell; to feel)

PRESENT

je	**sens**
tu	**sens**
il/elle/on	**sent**
nous	**sentons**
vous	**sentez**
ils/elles	**sentent**

PRESENT SUBJUNCTIVE

je	**sente**
tu	**sentes**
il/elle/on	**sente**
nous	**sentions**
vous	**sentiez**
ils/elles	**sentent**

PERFECT

j'	**ai senti**
tu	**as senti**
il/elle/on	**a senti**
nous	**avons senti**
vous	**avez senti**
ils/elles	**ont senti**

IMPERFECT

je	**sentais**
tu	**sentais**
il/elle/on	**sentait**
nous	**sentions**
vous	**sentiez**
ils/elles	**sentaient**

PRESENT PARTICIPLE
sentant

PAST PARTICIPLE
senti

EXAMPLE PHRASES

Ça **sent** bon ici. It smells nice here.

Elle ne se **sent** pas bien. She's not feeling well.

Je n'**ai** rien **senti**. I didn't feel a thing.

Sens ces fleurs. Smell these flowers.

Ça **sentait** mauvais. It smelt bad.

sentir

FUTURE

je	**sentirai**
tu	**sentiras**
il/elle/on	**sentira**
nous	**sentirons**
vous	**sentirez**
ils/elles	**sentiront**

CONDITIONAL

je	**sentirais**
tu	**sentirais**
il/elle/on	**sentirait**
nous	**sentirions**
vous	**sentiriez**
ils/elles	**sentiraient**

PAST HISTORIC

je	**sentis**
tu	**sentis**
il/elle/on	**sentit**
nous	**sentîmes**
vous	**sentîtes**
ils/elles	**sentirent**

PLUPERFECT

j'	**avais senti**
tu	**avais senti**
il/elle/on	**avait senti**
nous	**avions senti**
vous	**aviez senti**
ils/elles	**avaient senti**

IMPERATIVE

sens / sentons / sentez

EXAMPLE PHRASES

Ne vous inquiétez pas: vous ne **sentirez** rien. Don't worry – you won't feel a thing.

Il **sentit** que ce n'était pas le bon moment. He felt that it wasn't the right time.

Elle se **sentirait** mieux si elle se reposait. She'd feel better if she rested.

Il n'**avait** rien **senti** pendant l'opération. He hadn't felt a thing during the operation.

servir (to serve; to be of use to)

PRESENT

je	**sers**
tu	**sers**
il/elle/on	**sert**
nous	**servons**
vous	**servez**
ils/elles	**servent**

PRESENT SUBJUNCTIVE

je	**serve**
tu	**serves**
il/elle/on	**serve**
nous	**servions**
vous	**serviez**
ils/elles	**servent**

PERFECT

j'	**ai servi**
tu	**as servi**
il/elle/on	**a servi**
nous	**avons servi**
vous	**avez servi**
ils/elles	**ont servi**

IMPERFECT

je	**servais**
tu	**servais**
il/elle/on	**servait**
nous	**servions**
vous	**serviez**
ils/elles	**servaient**

PRESENT PARTICIPLE

servant

PAST PARTICIPLE

servi

EXAMPLE PHRASES

On vous **sert**? Are you being served?

Ça **sert** à quoi ce bouton? What is this button for?

Servez-vous. Help yourself.

Il faut que je **serve** la soupe. I have to serve the soup.

Ça ne **servait** à rien de le supplier. It was no use begging him.

servir

FUTURE

je	**servirai**
tu	**serviras**
il/elle/on	**servira**
nous	**servirons**
vous	**servirez**
ils/elles	**serviront**

CONDITIONAL

je	**servirais**
tu	**servirais**
il/elle/on	**servirait**
nous	**servirions**
vous	**serviriez**
ils/elles	**serviraient**

PAST HISTORIC

je	**servis**
tu	**servis**
il/elle/on	**servit**
nous	**servîmes**
vous	**servîtes**
ils/elles	**servirent**

PLUPERFECT

j'	**avais servi**
tu	**avais servi**
il/elle/on	**avait servi**
nous	**avions servi**
vous	**aviez servi**
ils/elles	**avaient servi**

IMPERATIVE

sers / servons / servez

EXAMPLE PHRASES

Ces boîtes te **serviront** quand tu déménageras. You'll find these boxes useful when you move house.

Elle leur **servit** des profiteroles en dessert. She served them profiteroles for dessert.

Ça ne **servirait** à rien d'y aller maintenant. It would serve no purpose to go there now.

Cette valise n'**avait** pas **servi** depuis dix ans. This suitcase hadn't been used for ten years.

je/j' = I   **tu** = you   **il** = he/it   **elle** = she/it   **on** = we/one   **nous** = we   **vous** = you   **ils/elles** = they

sortir (to go out; to take out)

PRESENT		**PRESENT SUBJUNCTIVE**	
je	**sors**	je	**sorte**
tu	**sors**	tu	**sortes**
il/elle/on	**sort**	il/elle/on	**sorte**
nous	**sortons**	nous	**sortions**
vous	**sortez**	vous	**sortiez**
ils/elles	**sortent**	ils/elles	**sortent**

PERFECT		**IMPERFECT**	
je	**suis sorti(e)**	je	**sortais**
tu	**es sorti(e)**	tu	**sortais**
il/elle/on	**est sorti(e)**	il/elle/on	**sortait**
nous	**sommes sorti(e)s**	nous	**sortions**
vous	**êtes sorti(e)(s)**	vous	**sortiez**
ils/elles	**sont sorti(e)s**	ils/elles	**sortaient**

PRESENT PARTICIPLE	**PAST PARTICIPLE**
sortant	sorti

In the perfect and the imperfect, use the auxiliary "avoir" when there is a direct object.

EXAMPLE PHRASES

Aurélie **sort** avec Bruno. Aurélie is going out with Bruno.

Je ne **suis** pas **sortie** ce week-end. I didn't go out this weekend.

Je n'**ai** pas **sorti** le chien parce qu'il pleuvait. I didn't take the dog out for a walk because it was raining.

Sortez en silence. Go out quietly.

Je ne veux pas que tu **sortes** habillée comme ça. I don't want you to go out dressed like that.

Il **sortait** quand c'est arrivé. He was going out when it happened.

je/j' = I **tu** = you **il** = he/it **elle** = she/it **on** = we/one **nous** = we **vous** = you **ils/elles** = they

sortir

FUTURE

je	**sortirai**
tu	**sortiras**
il/elle/on	**sortira**
nous	**sortirons**
vous	**sortirez**
ils/elles	**sortiront**

CONDITIONAL

je	**sortirais**
tu	**sortirais**
il/elle/on	**sortirait**
nous	**sortirions**
vous	**sortiriez**
ils/elles	**sortiraient**

PAST HISTORIC

je	**sortis**
tu	**sortis**
il/elle/on	**sortit**
nous	**sortîmes**
vous	**sortîtes**
ils/elles	**sortirent**

PLUPERFECT

j'	**étais sorti(e)**
tu	**étais sorti(e)**
il/elle/on	**était sorti(e)**
nous	**étions sorti(e)s**
vous	**étiez sorti(e)(s)**
ils/elles	**étaient sorti(e)s**

IMPERATIVE

sors / sortons / sortez

EXAMPLE PHRASES

Je **sortirai** la poubelle en partant. I'll take out the bin on my way out.

Il **sortit** une photo de sa poche. He took a photo out of his pocket.

Elle ne **sortirait** jamais de chez elle si son mari ne l'y obligeait pas.
   She'd never leave her house if her husband didn't force her.

Elle **était sortie** de l'hôpital la veille. She had come out of hospital the day
   before.

---

je/j' = I **tu** = you **il** = he/it **elle** = she/it **on** = we/one **nous** = we **vous** = you **ils/elles** = they

souffrir (to be in pain)

PRESENT

je	**souffre**
tu	**souffres**
il/elle/on	**souffre**
nous	**souffrons**
vous	**souffrez**
ils/elles	**souffrent**

PRESENT SUBJUNCTIVE

je	**souffre**
tu	**souffres**
il/elle/on	**souffre**
nous	**souffrions**
vous	**souffriez**
ils/elles	**souffrent**

PERFECT

j'	**ai souffert**
tu	**as souffert**
il/elle/on	**a souffert**
nous	**avons souffert**
vous	**avez souffert**
ils/elles	**ont souffert**

IMPERFECT

j'	**souffrais**
tu	**souffrais**
il/elle/on	**souffrait**
nous	**souffrions**
vous	**souffriez**
ils/elles	**souffraient**

PRESENT PARTICIPLE

souffrant

PAST PARTICIPLE

souffert

EXAMPLE PHRASES

Il **souffre** beaucoup. He's in a lot of pain.

Elle **a** beaucoup **souffert** quand il l'a quittée. She suffered a lot when he left her.

Souffre en silence. Suffer in silence.

J'ai peur qu'il ne **souffre**. I'm scared he might be suffering.

Il **souffrait** de ne plus la voir. It pained him not to see her any more.

souffrir

FUTURE

je	**souffrirai**
tu	**souffriras**
il/elle/on	**souffrira**
nous	**souffrirons**
vous	**souffrirez**
ils/elles	**souffriront**

CONDITIONAL

je	**souffrirais**
tu	**souffrirais**
il/elle/on	**souffrirait**
nous	**souffririons**
vous	**souffririez**
ils/elles	**souffriraient**

PAST HISTORIC

je	**souffris**
tu	**souffris**
il/elle/on	**souffrit**
nous	**souffrîmes**
vous	**souffrîtes**
ils/elles	**souffrirent**

PLUPERFECT

j'	**avais souffert**
tu	**avais souffert**
il/elle/on	**avait souffert**
nous	**avions souffert**
vous	**aviez souffert**
ils/elles	**avaient souffert**

IMPERATIVE

souffre / souffrons / souffrez

EXAMPLE PHRASES

Je te promets que tu ne **souffriras** pas trop. I promise that you won't be in too much pain.

Ils **souffrirent** en silence. They suffered in silence.

Elle ne **souffrirait** pas tant si elle prenait son médicament. She wouldn't suffer so much if she took her medicine.

Elle **avait** beaucoup **souffert** durant son enfance. She had suffered a lot during her childhood.

---

je/j' = I **tu** = you **il** = he/it **elle** = she/it **on** = we/one **nous** = we **vous** = you **ils/elles** = they

se souvenir (to remember)

PRESENT		**PRESENT SUBJUNCTIVE**	
je	**me souviens**	je	**me souvienne**
tu	**te souviens**	tu	**te souviennes**
il/elle/on	**se souvient**	il/elle/on	**se souvienne**
nous	**nous souvenons**	nous	**nous souvenions**
vous	**vous souvenez**	vous	**vous souveniez**
ils/elles	**se souviennent**	ils/elles	**se souviennent**

PERFECT		**IMPERFECT**	
je	**me suis souvenu(e)**	je	**me souvenais**
tu	**t'es souvenu(e)**	tu	**te souvenais**
il/elle/on	**s'est souvenu(e)**	il/elle/on	**se souvenait**
nous	**nous sommes souvenu(e)s**	nous	**nous souvenions**
vous	**vous êtes souvenu(e)(s)**	vous	**vous souveniez**
ils/elles	**se sont souvenu(e)s**	ils/elles	**se souvenaient**

PRESENT PARTICIPLE
se souvenant

PAST PARTICIPLE
souvenu

EXAMPLE PHRASES

Je ne **me souviens** pas de son adresse. I can't remember his address.

Te souviens-tu du jour où Pierre s'est cassé le bras? Do you remember the day when Pierre broke his arm?

Souviens-toi: il neigeait ce jour-là. Remember – it was snowing that day.

Je ne crois pas qu'elle **s'en souvienne**. I don't think that she remembers it.

Il ne **se souvenait** pas où il avait mis ses clés. He couldn't remember where he'd put his keys.

---

je/j' = I   **tu** = you   **il** = he/it   **elle** = she/it   **on** = we/one   **nous** = we   **vous** = you   **ils/elles** = they

se souvenir

FUTURE

je	**me souviendrai**
tu	**te souviendras**
il/elle/on	**se souviendra**
nous	**nous souviendrons**
vous	**vous souviendrez**
ils/elles	**se souviendront**

CONDITIONAL

je	**me souviendrais**
tu	**te souviendrais**
il/elle/on	**se souviendrait**
nous	**nous souviendrions**
vous	**vous souviendriez**
ils/elles	**se souviendraient**

PAST HISTORIC

je	**me souvins**
tu	**te souvins**
il/elle/on	**se souvint**
nous	**nous souvînmes**
vous	**vous souvîntes**
ils/elles	**se souvinrent**

PLUPERFECT

je	**m'étais souvenu(e)**
tu	**t'étais souvenu(e)**
il/elle/on	**s'était souvenu(e)**
nous	**nous étions souvenu(e)s**
vous	**vous étiez souvenu(e)(s)**
ils/elles	**s'étaient souvenu(e)s**

IMPERATIVE

souviens-toi / souvenons-nous / souvenez-nous

EXAMPLE PHRASES

Fais-lui une liste, sinon il ne **se souviendra** pas de ce qu'il doit acheter.
  Make him a list, otherwise he won't remember what he has to buy.
Elle **se souvint** qu'elle leur avait promis une surprise. She remembered that
  she'd promised them a surprise.
Si je ne prenais pas de notes, je ne **me souviendrais** pas de mes cours.
  If I didn't take notes, I wouldn't remember my lessons.
Il **s'était souvenu** un peu tard de son anniversaire. He had remembered her
  birthday a little late.

je/j' = I   **tu** = you   **il** = he/it   **elle** = she/it   **on** = we/one   **nous** = we   **vous** = you   **ils/elles** = they

suffire (to be enough)

PRESENT

je	**suffis**
tu	**suffis**
il/elle/on	**suffit**
nous	**suffisons**
vous	**suffisez**
ils/elles	**suffisent**

PRESENT SUBJUNCTIVE

je	**suffise**
tu	**suffises**
il/elle/on	**suffise**
nous	**suffisions**
vous	**suffisiez**
ils/elles	**suffisent**

PERFECT

j'	**ai suffi**
tu	**as suffi**
il/elle/on	**a suffi**
nous	**avons suffi**
vous	**avez suffi**
ils/elles	**ont suffi**

IMPERFECT

je	**suffisais**
tu	**suffisais**
il/elle/on	**suffisait**
nous	**suffisions**
vous	**suffisiez**
ils/elles	**suffisaient**

PRESENT PARTICIPLE
suffisant

PAST PARTICIPLE
suffi

EXAMPLE PHRASES

Ça **suffit**! That's enough!

Ses jouets lui **suffisent**. His toys are enough for him.

Une séance avec l'ostéopathe **a suffi** pour me soulager. One session with the osteopath was enough to ease the pain.

Il **suffisait** de me le demander. You only had to ask.

suffire

FUTURE

je	**suffirai**
tu	**suffiras**
il/elle/on	**suffira**
nous	**suffirons**
vous	**suffirez**
ils/elles	**suffiront**

CONDITIONAL

je	**suffirais**
tu	**suffirais**
il/elle/on	**suffirait**
nous	**suffirions**
vous	**suffiriez**
ils/elles	**suffiraient**

PAST HISTORIC

je	**suffis**
tu	**suffis**
il/elle/on	**suffit**
nous	**suffîmes**
vous	**suffîtes**
ils/elles	**suffirent**

PLUPERFECT

j'	**avais suffi**
tu	**avais suffi**
il/elle/on	**avait suffi**
nous	**avions suffi**
vous	**aviez suffi**
ils/elles	**avaient suffi**

IMPERATIVE
suffis / suffisons / suffisez

EXAMPLE PHRASES

Ça te **suffira**, dix euros? Will ten euros be enough?

Sa promesse lui **suffit**: il lui faisait confiance. Her promise was enough for him – he trusted her.

Il **suffirait** de se dépêcher un peu pour le rattraper. We'd only have to hurry a little to catch up with him.

Il nous **avait suffi** d'aller à la bibliothèque municipale pour trouver le livre. We only had to go to the community library to find the book.

je/j' = I   **tu** = you   **il** = he/it   **elle** = she/it   **on** = we/one   **nous** = we   **vous** = you   **ils/elles** = they

suivre (to follow)

PRESENT

je	**suis**
tu	**suis**
il/elle/on	**suit**
nous	**suivons**
vous	**suivez**
ils/elles	**suivent**

PRESENT SUBJUNCTIVE

je	**suive**
tu	**suives**
il/elle/on	**suive**
nous	**suivions**
vous	**suiviez**
ils/elles	**suivent**

PERFECT

j'	**ai suivi**
tu	**as suivi**
il/elle/on	**a suivi**
nous	**avons suivi**
vous	**avez suivi**
ils/elles	**ont suivi**

IMPERFECT

je	**suivais**
tu	**suivais**
il/elle/on	**suivait**
nous	**suivions**
vous	**suiviez**
ils/elles	**suivaient**

PRESENT PARTICIPLE

suivant

PAST PARTICIPLE

suivi

EXAMPLE PHRASES

Elle n'arrive pas à **suivre** en maths. She can't keep up in maths.

Mon chat me **suit** partout dans la maison. My cat follows me all around the house.

Il **a suivi** un cours d'allemand pendant six mois. He did a German course for six months.

Je n'aime pas qu'il me **suive** partout comme un petit chien. I don't like him following me everywhere like a dog.

Ils nous **suivaient** à vélo. They were cycling behind us.

je/j' = I   **tu** = you   **il** = he/it   **elle** = she/it   **on** = we/one   **nous** = we   **vous** = you   **ils/elles** = they

suivre

FUTURE

je	**suivrai**
tu	**suivras**
il/elle/on	**suivra**
nous	**suivrons**
vous	**suivrez**
ils/elles	**suivront**

CONDITIONAL

je	**suivrais**
tu	**suivrais**
il/elle/on	**suivrait**
nous	**suivrions**
vous	**suivriez**
ils/elles	**suivraient**

PAST HISTORIC

je	**suivis**
tu	**suivis**
il/elle/on	**suivit**
nous	**suivîmes**
vous	**suivîtes**
ils/elles	**suivirent**

PLUPERFECT

j'	**avais suivi**
tu	**avais suivi**
il/elle/on	**avait suivi**
nous	**avions suivi**
vous	**aviez suivi**
ils/elles	**avaient suivi**

IMPERATIVE

suis / suivons / suivez

EXAMPLE PHRASES

Je vous **suivrai** de loin. I'll follow you at a distance.

Elle le **suivit** dans son bureau. She followed him into his office.

Il lui dit qu'il la **suivrait** en voiture. He told her that he would follow her in his car.

Je n'**avais** pas bien **suivi** les derniers événements. I hadn't really been following the latest events.

Suivez-moi. Follow me.

je/j' = I **tu** = you **il** = he/it **elle** = she/it **on** = we/one **nous** = we **vous** = you **ils/elles** = they

se taire (to stop talking)

PRESENT

je	**me tais**
tu	**te tais**
il/elle/on	**se tait**
nous	**nous taisons**
vous	**vous taisez**
ils/elles	**se taisent**

PRESENT SUBJUNCTIVE

je	**me taise**
tu	**te taises**
il/elle/on	**se taise**
nous	**nous taisions**
vous	**vous taisiez**
ils/elles	**se taisent**

PERFECT

je	**me suis tu(e)**
tu	**t'es tu(e)**
il/elle/on	**s'est tu(e)**
nous	**nous sommes tu(e)s**
vous	**vous êtes tu(e)(s)**
ils/elles	**se sont tu(e)s**

IMPERFECT

je	**me taisais**
tu	**te taisais**
il/elle/on	**se taisait**
nous	**nous taisions**
vous	**vous taisiez**
ils/elles	**se taisaient**

PRESENT PARTICIPLE
se taisant

PAST PARTICIPLE
tu

EXAMPLE PHRASES

Je préfère **me taire** quand ils se disputent. I prefer to keep quiet when they argue.

Il **s'est tu**. He stopped talking.

Sophie, **tais-toi**! Be quiet, Sophie!

Taisez-vous! Be quiet!

se taire

FUTURE

je	**me tairai**
tu	**te tairas**
il/elle/on	**se taira**
nous	**nous tairons**
vous	**vous tairez**
ils/elles	**se tairont**

CONDITIONAL

je	**me tairais**
tu	**te tairais**
il/elle/on	**se tairait**
nous	**nous tairions**
vous	**vous tairiez**
ils/elles	**se tairaient**

PAST HISTORIC

je	**me tus**
tu	**te tus**
il/elle/on	**se tut**
nous	**nous tûmes**
vous	**vous tûtes**
ils/elles	**se turent**

PLUPERFECT

je	**m'étais tu(e)**
tu	**t'étais tu(e)**
il/elle/on	**s'était tu(e)**
nous	**nous étions tu(e)s**
vous	**vous étiez tu(e)(s)**
ils/elles	**s'étaient tu(e)s**

IMPERATIVE

tais-toi / taisons-nous / taisez-vous

EXAMPLE PHRASES

Je **me tairai** si tu me laisses finir ma phrase. I'll stop talking if you let me finish my sentence.

Elle **se tut**. She stopped talking.

Je me **tairais** si j'étais sûr que tu n'allais pas inventer un mensonge. I'd stop talking if I were sure that you wouldn't invent some lie.

Il **s'était tu** et tout resta silencieux pendant quelques minutes. He had stopped talking and for a few minutes all was silent.

je/j' = I   tu = you   il = he/it   elle = she/it   on = we/one   nous = we   vous = you   ils/elles = they

tenir (to hold)

PRESENT

je	**tiens**
tu	**tiens**
il/elle/on	**tient**
nous	**tenons**
vous	**tenez**
ils/elles	**tiennent**

PRESENT SUBJUNCTIVE

je	**tienne**
tu	**tiennes**
il/elle/on	**tienne**
nous	**tenions**
vous	**teniez**
ils/elles	**tiennent**

PERFECT

j'	**ai tenu**
tu	**as tenu**
il/elle/on	**a tenu**
nous	**avons tenu**
vous	**avez tenu**
ils/elles	**ont tenu**

IMPERFECT

je	**tenais**
tu	**tenais**
il/elle/on	**tenait**
nous	**tenions**
vous	**teniez**
ils/elles	**tenaient**

PRESENT PARTICIPLE

tenant

PAST PARTICIPLE

tenu

EXAMPLE PHRASES

Il **tient** de son père. He takes after his father.

Tiens-moi la main. Hold my hand.

Tiens, prends mon stylo. Here, have my pen.

Tiens-toi droit! Sit up straight!

Elle **tenait** beaucoup à son chat. She was really attached to her cat.

tenir

FUTURE

je	**tiendrai**
tu	**tiendras**
il/elle/on	**tiendra**
nous	**tiendrons**
vous	**tiendrez**
ils/elles	**tiendront**

CONDITIONAL

je	**tiendrais**
tu	**tiendrais**
il/elle/on	**tiendrait**
nous	**tiendrions**
vous	**tiendriez**
ils/elles	**tiendraient**

PAST HISTORIC

je	**tins**
tu	**tins**
il/elle/on	**tint**
nous	**tînmes**
vous	**tîntes**
ils/elles	**tinrent**

PLUPERFECT

j'	**avais tenu**
tu	**avais tenu**
il/elle/on	**avait tenu**
nous	**avions tenu**
vous	**aviez tenu**
ils/elles	**avaient tenu**

IMPERATIVE
tiens / tenons / tenez

EXAMPLE PHRASES

Vous ne pourrez pas tomber car je vous **tiendrai** le bras. There's no chance of you falling as I'll be holding your arm.

Il **tint** sa promesse. He kept his promise.

Il ne me **tiendrait** pas la main s'il voyait un de ses copains. He wouldn't hold my hand if he saw one of his friends.

Elle **avait tenu** à y aller. She insisted on going.

je/j' = I   **tu** = you   **il** = he/it   **elle** = she/it   **on** = we/one   **nous** = we   **vous** = you   **ils/elles** = they

tomber (to fall)

PRESENT

je	**tombe**
tu	**tombes**
il/elle/on	**tombe**
nous	**tombons**
vous	**tombez**
ils/elles	**tombent**

PRESENT SUBJUNCTIVE

je	**tombe**
tu	**tombes**
il/elle/on	**tombe**
nous	**tombions**
vous	**tombiez**
ils/elles	**tombent**

PERFECT

je	**suis tombé(e)**
tu	**es tombé(e)**
il/elle/on	**est tombé(e)**
nous	**sommes tombé(e)s**
vous	**êtes tombé(e)(s)**
ils/elles	**sont tombé(e)s**

IMPERFECT

je	**tombais**
tu	**tombais**
il/elle/on	**tombait**
nous	**tombions**
vous	**tombiez**
ils/elles	**tombaient**

PRESENT PARTICIPLE

tombant

PAST PARTICIPLE

tombé

EXAMPLE PHRASES

Attention, tu vas **tomber**! Be careful, you'll fall!

Ça **tombe** bien. That's lucky.

Nicole **est tombée** de cheval. Nicole fell off her horse.

Il **tombait** de sommeil. He was asleep on his feet.

Elle s'est fait mal en **tombant** dans l'escalier. She hurt herself falling down the stairs.

tomber

FUTURE

je	**tomberai**
tu	**tomberas**
il/elle/on	**tombera**
nous	**tomberons**
vous	**tomberez**
ils/elles	**tomberont**

CONDITIONAL

je	**tomberais**
tu	**tomberais**
il/elle/on	**tomberait**
nous	**tomberions**
vous	**tomberiez**
ils/elles	**tomberaient**

PAST HISTORIC

je	**tombai**
tu	**tombas**
il/elle/on	**tomba**
nous	**tombâmes**
vous	**tombâtes**
ils/elles	**tombèrent**

PLUPERFECT

j'	**étais tombé(e)**
tu	**étais tombé(e)**
il/elle/on	**était tombé(e)**
nous	**étions tombé(e)s**
vous	**étiez tombé(e)(s)**
ils/elles	**étaient tombé(e)s**

IMPERATIVE

tombe / tombons / tombez

EXAMPLE PHRASES

J'espère qu'il ne **tombera** pas de son cheval. I hope he won't fall off his horse.

La tasse **tomba** par terre et se cassa. The cup fell on the floor and broke.

Tu ne **tomberais** pas si souvent si tu regardais où tu marches. You wouldn't fall so often if you watched where you were going.

Il **était** mal **tombé** et s'était cassé le bras. He'd had a bad fall and had broken his arm.

je/j' = I **tu** = you **il** = he/it **elle** = she/it **on** = we/one **nous** = we **vous** = you **ils/elles** = they

traire (to milk)

PRESENT

je	**trais**
tu	**trais**
il/elle/on	**trait**
nous	**trayons**
vous	**trayez**
ils/elles	**traient**

PRESENT SUBJUNCTIVE

je	**traie**
tu	**traies**
il/elle/on	**traie**
nous	**trayions**
vous	**trayiez**
ils/elles	**traient**

PERFECT

j'	**ai trait**
tu	**as trait**
il/elle/on	**a trait**
nous	**avons trait**
vous	**avez trait**
ils/elles	**ont trait**

IMPERFECT

je	**trayais**
tu	**trayais**
il/elle/on	**trayait**
nous	**trayions**
vous	**trayiez**
ils/elles	**trayaient**

PRESENT PARTICIPLE

trayant .

PAST PARTICIPLE

trait

EXAMPLE PHRASES

À la ferme, on a appris à **traire** les vaches. We learnt to milk cows on the farm.

Elle **trait** les vaches à six heures du matin. She milks the cows at six am.

Nous **avons trait** les vaches. We milked the cows.

Il faut qu'elle **traie** les vaches de bonne heure tous les matins. She has to milk the cows early every morning.

On **trayait** les vaches avant d'aller à l'école. We milked the cows before going to school.

je/j' = I **tu** = you **il** = he/it **elle** = she/it **on** = we/one **nous** = we **vous** = you **ils/elles** = they

traire

FUTURE

je	**trairai**
tu	**trairas**
il/elle/on	**traira**
nous	**trairons**
vous	**trairez**
ils/elles	**trairont**

CONDITIONAL

je	**trairais**
tu	**trairais**
il/elle/on	**trairait**
nous	**trairions**
vous	**trairiez**
ils/elles	**trairaient**

PAST HISTORIC

not used

PLUPERFECT

j'	**avais trait**
tu	**avais trait**
il/elle/on	**avait trait**
nous	**avions trait**
vous	**aviez trait**
ils/elles	**avaient trait**

IMPERATIVE

trais / trayons / trayez

EXAMPLE PHRASES

Je **trairai** les vaches pour toi quand tu seras parti. I'll milk the cows for you when you're away.

Je **trairais** les brebis si je savais comment faire. I'd milk the ewes if I knew what to do.

Cela faisait longtemps qu'elle n'**avait** pas **trait** une vache. She hadn't milked a cow for a long time.

je/j' = I **tu** = you **il** = he/it **elle** = she/it **on** = we/one **nous** = we **vous** = you **ils/elles** = they

vaincre (to defeat)

PRESENT

je	**vaincs**
tu	**vaincs**
il/elle/on	**vainc**
nous	**vainquons**
vous	**vainquez**
ils/elles	**vainquent**

PRESENT SUBJUNCTIVE

je	**vainque**
tu	**vainques**
il/elle/on	**vainque**
nous	**vainquions**
vous	**vainquiez**
ils/elles	**vainquent**

PERFECT

j'	**ai vaincu**
tu	**as vaincu**
il/elle/on	**a vaincu**
nous	**avons vaincu**
vous	**avez vaincu**
ils/elles	**ont vaincu**

IMPERFECT

je	**vainquais**
tu	**vainquais**
il/elle/on	**vainquait**
nous	**vainquions**
vous	**vainquiez**
ils/elles	**vainquaient**

PRESENT PARTICIPLE

vainquant

PAST PARTICIPLE

vaincu

EXAMPLE PHRASES

Il a réussi à **vaincre** sa timidité. He managed to overcome his shyness.

L'armée **a été vaincue**. The army was defeated.

La France **a vaincu** la Corée trois buts à deux. France beat Korea three goals to two.

vaincre

FUTURE

je	**vaincrai**
tu	**vaincras**
il/elle/on	**vaincra**
nous	**vaincrons**
vous	**vaincrez**
ils/elles	**vaincront**

CONDITIONAL

je	**vaincrais**
tu	**vaincrais**
il/elle/on	**vaincrait**
nous	**vaincrions**
vous	**vaincriez**
ils/elles	**vaincraient**

PAST HISTORIC

je	**vainquis**
tu	**vainquis**
il/elle/on	**vainquit**
nous	**vainquîmes**
vous	**vainquîtes**
ils/elles	**vainquirent**

PLUPERFECT

j'	**avais vaincu**
tu	**avais vaincu**
il/elle/on	**avait vaincu**
nous	**avions vaincu**
vous	**aviez vaincu**
ils/elles	**avaient vaincu**

IMPERATIVE

vaincs / vainquons / vainquez

EXAMPLE PHRASES

Tu ne **vaincras** pas ta peur en restant dans ta chambre. You won't overcome
your fear if you stay in your bedroom.

Ils **vainquirent** l'armée ennemie après une bataille acharnée. They defeated
the enemy army after a fierce battle.

Elle **avait** déjà **vaincu** cette adversaire. She'd already beaten this opponent.

valoir (to be worth)

PRESENT

je	**vaux**
tu	**vaux**
il/elle/on	**vaut**
nous	**valons**
vous	**valez**
ils/elles	**valent**

PRESENT SUBJUNCTIVE

je	**vaille**
tu	**vailles**
il/elle/on	**vaille**
nous	**valions**
vous	**valiez**
ils/elles	**vaillent**

PERFECT

j'	**ai valu**
tu	**as valu**
il/elle/on	**a valu**
nous	**avons valu**
vous	**avez valu**
ils/elles	**ont valu**

IMPERFECT

je	**valais**
tu	**valais**
il/elle/on	**valait**
nous	**valions**
vous	**valiez**
ils/elles	**valaient**

PRESENT PARTICIPLE

valant

PAST PARTICIPLE

valu

EXAMPLE PHRASES

Ça **vaut** combien? How much is it worth?

Ça ne **vaut** pas la peine de s'inquiéter. It's not worth worrying about.

Cette voiture **vaut** très cher. That car's worth a lot of money.

Il **valait** mieux ne pas y penser. It was best not to think about it.

---

je/j' = I   **tu** = you   **il** = he/it   **elle** = she/it   **on** = we/one   **nous** = we   **vous** = you   **ils/elles** = they

valoir

FUTURE

je	**vaudrai**
tu	**vaudras**
il/elle/on	**vaudra**
nous	**vaudrons**
vous	**vaudrez**
ils/elles	**vaudront**

CONDITIONAL

je	**vaudrais**
tu	**vaudrais**
il/elle/on	**vaudrait**
nous	**vaudrions**
vous	**vaudriez**
ils/elles	**vaudraient**

PAST HISTORIC

je	**valus**
tu	**valus**
il/elle/on	**valut**
nous	**valûmes**
vous	**valûtes**
ils/elles	**valurent**

PLUPERFECT

j'	**avais valu**
tu	**avais valu**
il/elle/on	**avait valu**
nous	**avions valu**
vous	**aviez valu**
ils/elles	**avaient valu**

IMPERATIVE

vaux / valons / valez

EXAMPLE PHRASES

Ça **vaudra** sûrement la peine d'y aller. It will probably be worth going.

Ça **vaudrait** la peine d'essayer. It would be worth a try.

Il **vaudrait** mieux que tu demandes la permission. You'd be best to ask for permission.

Son insolence lui **avait valu** une punition. His cheek had earned him a punishment.

je/j' = I **tu** = you **il** = he/it **elle** = she/it **on** = we/one **nous** = we **vous** = you **ils/elles** = they

vendre (to sell)

PRESENT		**PRESENT SUBJUNCTIVE**	
je	**vends**	je	**vende**
tu	**vends**	tu	**vendes**
il/elle/on	**vend**	il/elle/on	**vende**
nous	**vendons**	nous	**vendions**
vous	**vendez**	vous	**vendiez**
ils/elles	**vendent**	ils/elles	**vendent**

PERFECT		**IMPERFECT**	
j'	**ai vendu**	je	**vendais**
tu	**as vendu**	tu	**vendais**
il/elle/on	**a vendu**	il/elle/on	**vendait**
nous	**avons vendu**	nous	**vendions**
vous	**avez vendu**	vous	**vendiez**
ils/elles	**ont vendu**	ils/elles	**vendaient**

PRESENT PARTICIPLE
vendant

PAST PARTICIPLE
vendu

EXAMPLE PHRASES

Elle voudrait **vendre** sa voiture. She would like to sell her car.

Est-ce que vous **vendez** des piles? Do you sell batteries?

Il m'**a vendu** son vélo pour cinquante euros. He sold me his bike for fifty euros.

Il **vendait** des glaces sur la plage. He sold ice creams on the beach.

je/j' = I   **tu** = you   **il** = he/it   **elle** = she/it   **on** = we/one   **nous** = we   **vous** = you   **ils/elles** = they

vendre

FUTURE

je	**vendrai**
tu	**vendras**
il/elle/on	**vendra**
nous	**vendrons**
vous	**vendrez**
ils/elles	**vendront**

CONDITIONAL

je	**vendrais**
tu	**vendrais**
il/elle/on	**vendrait**
nous	**vendrions**
vous	**vendriez**
ils/elles	**vendraient**

PAST HISTORIC

je	**vendis**
tu	**vendis**
il/elle/on	**vendit**
nous	**vendîmes**
vous	**vendîtes**
ils/elles	**vendirent**

PLUPERFECT

j'	**avais vendu**
tu	**avais vendu**
il/elle/on	**avait vendu**
nous	**avions vendu**
vous	**aviez vendu**
ils/elles	**avaient vendu**

IMPERATIVE

vends / vendons / vendez

EXAMPLE PHRASES

Tu ne **vendras** rien à ce prix-là. You'll never sell anything at that price.

Elle **vendit** son appartement et partit vivre en Provence. She sold her flat and went to live in Provence.

Je ne **vendrais** pas ce piano pour tout l'or du monde. I wouldn't sell this piano for all the gold in the world.

Il **avait** déjà **vendu** sa maison. He'd already sold his house.

je/j' = I **tu** = you **il** = he/it **elle** = she/it **on** = we/one **nous** = we **vous** = you **ils/elles** = they

venir (to come)

PRESENT

je	**viens**
tu	**viens**
il/elle/on	**vient**
nous	**venons**
vous	**venez**
ils/elles	**viennent**

PRESENT SUBJUNCTIVE

je	**vienne**
tu	**viennes**
il/elle/on	**vienne**
nous	**venions**
vous	**veniez**
ils/elles	**viennent**

PERFECT

je	**suis venu(e)**
tu	**es venu(e)**
il/elle/on	**est venu(e)**
nous	**sommes venu(e)s**
vous	**êtes venu(e)(s)**
ils/elles	**sont venu(e)s**

IMPERFECT

je	**venais**
tu	**venais**
il/elle/on	**venait**
nous	**venions**
vous	**veniez**
ils/elles	**venaient**

PRESENT PARTICIPLE

venant

PAST PARTICIPLE

venu

EXAMPLE PHRASES

Fatou et Malik **viennent** du Sénégal. Fatou and Malik come from Sénégal.

Ils **sont venus** la voir ce matin. They came to see her this morning.

Viens avec moi! Come with me!

Elle aimerait que tu **viennes** à son mariage. She'd like you to come to her wedding.

Je **venais** de finir mes devoirs quand ils sont arrivés. I'd just finished my homework when they arrived.

je/j' = I   **tu** = you   **il** = he/it   **elle** = she/it   **on** = we/one   **nous** = we   **vous** = you   **ils/elles** = they

venir

FUTURE

je **viendrai**

tu **viendras**

il/elle/on **viendra**

nous **viendrons**

vous **viendrez**

ils/elles **viendront**

CONDITIONAL

je **viendrais**

tu **viendrais**

il/elle/on **viendrait**

nous **viendrions**

vous **viendriez**

ils/elles **viendraient**

PAST HISTORIC

je **vins**

tu **vins**

il/elle/on **vint**

nous **vînmes**

vous **vîntes**

ils/elles **vinrent**

PLUPERFECT

j' **étais venu(e)**

tu **étais venu(e)**

il/elle/on **était venu(e)**

nous **étions venu(e)s**

vous **étiez venu(e)(s)**

ils/elles **étaient venu(e)s**

IMPERATIVE

viens / venons / venez

EXAMPLE PHRASES

Elle ne **viendra** pas cette année. She won't be coming this year.

Il **vint** nous voir après la messe. He came to see us after mass.

Elle **viendrait** avec nous si elle n'avait pas tant de travail. She'd come with
us if she didn't have so much work.

Ils **étaient venus** nous annoncer leur fiançailles. They had come to tell us
that they had got engaged.

je/j' = I **tu** = you **il** = he/it **elle** = she/it **on** = we/one **nous** = we **vous** = you **ils/elles** = they

vêtir (to dress)

PRESENT

je **vêts**

tu **vêts**

il/elle/on **vêt**

nous **vêtons**

vous **vêtez**

ils/elles **vêtent**

PRESENT SUBJUNCTIVE

je **vête**

tu **vêtes**

il/elle/on **vête**

nous **vêtions**

vous **vêtiez**

ils/elles **vêtent**

PERFECT

j' **ai vêtu**

tu **as vêtu**

il/elle/on **a vêtu**

nous **avons vêtu**

vous **avez vêtu**

ils/elles **ont vêtu**

IMPERFECT

je **vêtais**

tu **vêtais**

il/elle/on **vêtait**

nous **vêtions**

vous **vêtiez**

ils/elles **vêtaient**

PRESENT PARTICIPLE

vêtant

PAST PARTICIPLE

vêtu

EXAMPLE PHRASES

Il faut se lever, se laver et se **vêtir** en dix minutes. You have to get up, get washed and get dressed in ten minutes.

Vous n'**êtes** pas **vêtus** suffisamment chaudement pour aller jouer dehors. You're not dressed warmly enough to go and play outside.

Tu **es** bizarrement **vêtu** aujourd'hui! You are strangely dressed today!

Nous vîmes une mariée tout de blanc **vêtue**. We saw a bride all dressed in white.

vêtir

FUTURE

je **vêtirai**
tu **vêtiras**
il/elle/on **vêtira**
nous **vêtirons**
vous **vêtirez**
ils/elles **vêtiront**

CONDITIONAL

je **vêtirais**
tu **vêtirais**
il/elle/on **vêtirait**
nous **vêtirions**
vous **vêtiriez**
ils/elles **vêtiraient**

PAST HISTORIC

je **vêtis**
tu **vêtis**
il/elle/on **vêtit**
nous **vêtîmes**
vous **vêtîtes**
ils/elles **vêtirent**

PLUPERFECT

j' **avais vêtu**
tu **avais vêtu**
il/elle/on **avait vêtu**
nous **avions vêtu**
vous **aviez vêtu**
ils/elles **avaient vêtu**

IMPERATIVE

vêts / vêtons / vêtez

EXAMPLE PHRASES

Il **était vêtu** d'un pantalon et d'un pull. He was wearing trousers and a jumper.

Nous **étions** chaudement **vêtus**. We were warmly dressed.

Il **était** toujours bien **vêtu**. He was always well dressed.

Ils n'**étaient** pas **vêtus** de façon adéquate pour aller marcher dans les montagnes.
   They weren't properly dressed to go hill-walking.

vivre (to live)

PRESENT

je	**vis**
tu	**vis**
il/elle/on	**vit**
nous	**vivons**
vous	**vivez**
ils/elles	**vivent**

PRESENT SUBJUNCTIVE

je	**vive**
tu	**vives**
il/elle/on	**vive**
nous	**vivions**
vous	**viviez**
ils/elles	**vivent**

PERFECT

j'	**ai vécu**
tu	**as vécu**
il/elle/on	**a vécu**
nous	**avons vécu**
vous	**avez vécu**
ils/elles	**ont vécu**

IMPERFECT

je	**vivais**
tu	**vivais**
il/elle/on	**vivait**
nous	**vivions**
vous	**viviez**
ils/elles	**vivaient**

PRESENT PARTICIPLE
vivant

PAST PARTICIPLE
vécu

EXAMPLE PHRASES

Et ton grand-père? Il **vit** encore? What about your grandfather? Is he still alive?

Les gorilles **vivent** surtout dans la forêt. Gorillas mostly live in the forest.

Il **a vécu** dix ans à Lyon. He lived in Lyons for ten years.

Cela ne faisait pas longtemps qu'ils **vivaient** ensemble. They hadn't lived
  together for long.

vivre

FUTURE

je	**vivrai**
tu	**vivras**
il/elle/on	**vivra**
nous	**vivrons**
vous	**vivrez**
ils/elles	**vivront**

CONDITIONAL

je	**vivrais**
tu	**vivrais**
il/elle/on	**vivrait**
nous	**vivrions**
vous	**vivriez**
ils/elles	**vivraient**

PAST HISTORIC

je	**vécus**
tu	**vécus**
il/elle/on	**vécut**
nous	**vécûmes**
vous	**vécûtes**
ils/elles	**vécurent**

PLUPERFECT

j'	**avais vécu**
tu	**avais vécu**
il/elle/on	**avait vécu**
nous	**avions vécu**
vous	**aviez vécu**
ils/elles	**avaient vécu**

IMPERATIVE

vis / vivons / vivez

EXAMPLE PHRASES

Vivras-tu avec ta sœur quand tu feras tes études à Paris? Will you live with your sister when you're studying in Paris?

Elle **vécut** d'abord en Espagne, puis en Italie. She lived in Spain first and then in Italy.

S'ils n'avaient pas d'enfants, ils ne **vivraient** plus ensemble depuis longtemps. If they didn't have children they would have stopped living together long ago.

Ils n'**avaient** jamais **vécu** à la campagne. They'd never lived in the countryside.

je/j' = I **tu** = you **il** = he/it **elle** = she/it **on** = we/one **nous** = we **vous** = you **ils/elles** = they

voir (to see)

PRESENT

je	**vois**
tu	**vois**
il/elle/on	**voit**
nous	**voyons**
vous	**voyez**
ils/elles	**voient**

PRESENT SUBJUNCTIVE

je	**voie**
tu	**voies**
il/elle/on	**voie**
nous	**voyions**
vous	**voyiez**
ils/elles	**voient**

PERFECT

j'	**ai vu**
tu	**as vu**
il/elle/on	**a vu**
nous	**avons vu**
vous	**avez vu**
ils/elles	**ont vu**

IMPERFECT

je	**voyais**
tu	**voyais**
il/elle/on	**voyait**
nous	**voyions**
vous	**voyiez**
ils/elles	**voyaient**

PRESENT PARTICIPLE

voyant

PAST PARTICIPLE

vu

EXAMPLE PHRASES

Venez me **voir** quand vous serez à Paris. Come and see me when you're in Paris.

Est-ce que cette tache se **voit**? Does that stain show?

Est-ce que tu l'**as vu**? Have you seen him?

Il ne **voyait** rien sans ses lunettes. He couldn't see anything without his glasses.

---

je/j' = I   **tu** = you   **il** = he/it   **elle** = she/it   **on** = we/one   **nous** = we   **vous** = you   **ils/elles** = they

voir

FUTURE

je	**verrai**
tu	**verras**
il/elle/on	**verra**
nous	**verrons**
vous	**verrez**
ils/elles	**verront**

CONDITIONAL

je	**verrais**
tu	**verrais**
il/elle/on	**verrait**
nous	**verrions**
vous	**verriez**
ils/elles	**verraient**

PAST HISTORIC

je	**vis**
tu	**vis**
il/elle/on	**vit**
nous	**vîmes**
vous	**vîtes**
ils/elles	**virent**

PLUPERFECT

j'	**avais vu**
tu	**avais vu**
il/elle/on	**avait vu**
nous	**avions vu**
vous	**aviez vu**
ils/elles	**avaient vu**

IMPERATIVE

vois / voyons / voyez

EXAMPLE PHRASES

Tu **verras** que je ne t'ai pas menti. You'll see that I didn't lie to you.

Il la **vit** arriver de loin. He saw her arrive from a long way off.

Il savait qu'il ne la **verrait** pas avant le lendemain. He knew that he wouldn't see her until the next day.

Ils ne l'**avaient** pas **vue** depuis son accident. They hadn't seen her since her accident.

je/j' = I **tu** = you **il** = he/it **elle** = she/it **on** = we/one **nous** = we **vous** = you **ils/elles** = they

vouloir (to want)

PRESENT

je	**veux**
tu	**veux**
il/elle/on	**veut**
nous	**voulons**
vous	**voulez**
ils/elles	**veulent**

PRESENT SUBJUNCTIVE

je	**veuille**
tu	**veuilles**
il/elle/on	**veuille**
nous	**voulions**
vous	**vouliez**
ils/elles	**veuillent**

PERFECT

j'	**ai voulu**
tu	**as voulu**
il/elle/on	**a voulu**
nous	**avons voulu**
vous	**avez voulu**
ils/elles	**ont voulu**

IMPERFECT

je	**voulais**
tu	**voulais**
il/elle/on	**voulait**
nous	**voulions**
vous	**vouliez**
ils/elles	**voulaient**

PRESENT PARTICIPLE
voulant

PAST PARTICIPLE
voulu

EXAMPLE PHRASES

Elle **veut** un vélo pour Noël. She wants a bike for Christmas.

Veux-tu que je t'aide? Do you want me to help you?

Il n'**a** pas **voulu** te déranger. He didn't want to disturb you.

Ils **voulaient** aller au cinéma. They wanted to go to the cinema.

je/j' = I   **tu** = you   **il** = he/it   **elle** = she/it   **on** = we/one   **nous** = we   **vous** = you   **ils/elles** = they

vouloir

FUTURE

je	**voudrai**
tu	**voudras**
il/elle/on	**voudra**
nous	**voudrons**
vous	**voudrez**
ils/elles	**voudront**

CONDITIONAL

je	**voudrais**
tu	**voudrais**
il/elle/on	**voudrait**
nous	**voudrions**
vous	**voudriez**
ils/elles	**voudraient**

PAST HISTORIC

je	**voulus**
tu	**voulus**
il/elle/on	**voulut**
nous	**voulûmes**
vous	**voulûtes**
ils/elles	**voulurent**

PLUPERFECT

j'	**avais voulu**
tu	**avais voulu**
il/elle/on	**avait voulu**
nous	**avions voulu**
vous	**aviez voulu**
ils/elles	**avaient voulu**

IMPERATIVE

veuille / veuillons / veuillez

EXAMPLE PHRASES

Ils ne **voudront** pas partir trop tard. They won't want to leave too late.

Elle ne **voulut** pas les inquiéter. She didn't want to worry them.

Tu **voudrais** une tasse de thé? Would you like a cup of tea?

Il n'**avait** pas **voulu** partir sans lui dire au revoir. He hadn't wanted to leave without saying goodbye to her.

je/j' = I   **tu** = you   **il** = he/it   **elle** = she/it   **on** = we/one   **nous** = we   **vous** = you   **ils/elles** = they

se vouvoyer (to address each other as "vous")

PRESENT
on **se vouvoie**
nous **nous vouvoyons**
vous **vous vouvoyez**
ils/elles **se vouvoient**

PRESENT SUBJUNCTIVE
on **se vouvoie**
nous **nous vouvoyions**
vous **vous vouvoyiez**
ils/elles **se vouvoient**

PERFECT
on **s'est vouvoyé**
nous **nous sommes vouvoyé(e)s**
vous **vous êtes vouvoyé(e)s**
ils/elles **se sont vouvoyé(e)s**

IMPERFECT
on **se vouvoyait**
nous **nous vouvoyions**
vous **vous vouvoyiez**
ils/elles **se vouvoyaient**

PRESENT PARTICIPLE
se vouvoyant

PAST PARTICIPLE
vouvoyé

EXAMPLE PHRASES
Avec Hélène, on **se vouvoie** encore. Hélène and I are still addressing each other as "**vous**".

Vous **vous êtes** toujours **vouvoyés** avec Michel? Have you and Michel always addressed each other as "**vous**"?

Je préférerais qu'on **se vouvoie**. I'd rather we addressed each other as "**vous**".

Ils ne **se vouvoyaient** plus. They weren't addressing each other as "**vous**" any more.

---

je/j' = I   **tu** = you   **il** = he/it   **elle** = she/it   **on** = we/one   **nous** = we   **vous** = you   **ils/elles** = they

se vouvoyer

FUTURE

on	**se vouvoiera**
nous	**nous vouvoierons**
vous	**vous vouvoierez**
ils/elles	**se vouvoieront**

CONDITIONAL

on	**se vouvoierait**
nous	**nous vouvoierions**
vous	**vous vouvoieriez**
ils/elles	**se vouvoieraient**

PAST HISTORIC

on	**se vouvoya**
nous	**nous vouvoyâmes**
vous	**vous vouvoyâtes**
ils/elles	**se vouvoyèrent**

PLUPERFECT

on	**s'était vouvoyé**
nous	**nous étions vouvoyé(e)s**
vous	**vous étiez vouvoyé(e)s**
ils/elles	**s'étaient vouvoyé(e)s**

IMPERATIVE

not used

EXAMPLE PHRASES

Je te parie qu'ils **se vouvoieront**. I bet they'll address each other as "**vous**".

Ils **se vouvoyèrent** les premiers jours. They addressed each other as "**vous**" for the first few days.

On **se vouvoierait** encore si je n'avais rien dit. We'd still be addressing each other as "**vous**" if I hadn't said anything.

Nous **nous étions vouvoyés** au début. We'd addressed each other as "**vous**" at the beginning.

---

je/j' = I **tu** = you **il** = he/it **elle** = she/it **on** = we/one **nous** = we **vous** = you **ils/elles** = they

How to use the Verb Index

The verbs in bold are the model verbs which you will find in the verb tables. All the other verbs follow one of these patterns, so the number next to each verb indicates which pattern fits this particular verb. For example, **aider** (*to help*) follows the same pattern as **donner** (number 70 in the verb tables). All the verbs are in alphabetical order. For reflexive verbs like **s'asseoir** (*to sit down*) or **se taire** (*to stop talking*), look under **asseoir** or **taire**, not under **s'** or **se**.

Superior numbers (¹, ² etc) refer you to notes on page 240. These notes explain any differences between the verbs and their model.

With the exception of reflexive verbs which *always* take **être**, all verbs have the same auxiliary (**être** or **avoir**) as their model verb. There are a few exceptions which are indicated by a superior number ¹ or ². An asterisk (*) means that the verb takes **avoir** when it is used with a direct object, and **être** when it isn't. For more information on verbs that take either **avoir** or **être**, see pages 48–50.

abaisser	70	accueillir	56	agir	100	**amuser (s')**	**8**
abandonner	70	accumuler	70	agiter	70	analyser	70
abattre	26	accuser	70	agrandir	100	anéantir	100
abêtir	100	acharner (s')	70	agréer	48	angoisser	70
abîmer	70	acheminer	70	ahurir	100	animer	70
abolir	100	**acheter**	**2**	aider	70	annexer	70
abonder	70	achever	114	aigrir	100	annoncer	32
abonner	70	**acquérir**	**4**	aiguiser	70	annoter	70
aborder	70	actionner	70	aimanter	70	annuler	70
aboutir	100	activer	70	aimer	70	anoblir	100
aboyer	136	adapter	70	ajouter	70	anticiper	70
abréger	164	additionner	70	ajuster	70	apaiser	70
abreuver	70	adhérer	86	alarmer	70	**apercevoir**	**10**
abriter	70	adjoindre	112	alerter	70	apitoyer	136
abrutir	100	admettre	124	alimenter	70	aplatir	100
absenter (s')	70	admirer	70	allécher	86	apparaître²	144
absorber	70	adopter	70	alléger	164	appareiller	70
absoudre⁴	174	adorer	70	alléguer	86	apparenter	70
abstenir (s')	208	adosser	70	**aller**	**6**	apparier	50
abstraire	212	adoucir	100	allier	50	appartenir	208
abuser	70	adresser	70	allumer	70	appauvrir	100
accabler	70	advenir³	220	altérer	86	**appeler**	**12**
accaparer	70	aérer	86	alterner	70	applaudir	100
accéder	86	affaiblir	100	alunir	100	appliquer	70
accélérer	86	affairer (s')	70	amaigrir	100	apporter	70
accepter	70	affaisser (s')	70	ambitionner	70	apprécier	50
accompagner	70	affamer	70	améliorer	70	apprendre	162
accomplir	100	affermir	100	aménager	118	apprêter	70
accorder	70	afficher	70	amener	114	apprivoiser	70
accoter	70	affirmer	70	ameuter	70	approcher	70
accoucher	70	affliger	118	amincir	100	approfondir	100
accouder (s')	70	affoler	70	amoindrir	100	approprier	50
accourir⁵	44	affranchir	100	amollir	100	approuver	70
accoutumer	70	affréter	86	amonceler	12	**appuyer**	**14**
accrocher	70	affronter	70	amorcer	32	arc-bouter	70
accroître⁶	54	agacer	32	amplifier	50	argenter	70
accroupir (s')	100	agenouiller (s')	70	amputer	70	arguer	70

armer	70	balafrer	70	brandir	100	chérir	100
arpenter	70	balancer	32	branler	70	chiffrer	70
arracher	70	balayer	150	braquer	70	choisir	100
arranger	118	balbutier	50	braver	70	chômer	70
arrêter	70	baliser	70	bredouiller	70	choquer	70
arriver	**16**	bannir	100	breveter	12	choyer	136
arrondir	100	baptiser	70	bricoler	70	chuchoter	70
arroser	70	baratiner	70	brider	70	circoncire[8]	202
asphyxier	50	barbouiller	70	briguer	70	circonscrire	74
aspirer	70	barioler	70	briller	70	circonvenir[1]	220
assagir	100	barrer	70	brimer	70	circuler	70
assainir	100	barricader	70	briser	70	cirer	70
assassiner	70	basculer	70	broder	70	ciseler	2
assembler	70	baser	70	broncher	70	citer	70
assener	114	batailler	70	brosser	70	clarifier	50
asseoir (s')	**18**	batifoler	70	brouiller	70	classer	70
asservir	100	bâtir	100	broyer	136	classifier	50
assiéger	164	**battre**	**26**	brûler	70	cligner	70
assigner	70	bavarder	70	brunir	100	clignoter	70
assimiler	70	baver	70	buter	70	clouer	70
assister	70	bêcher	70	cabrer (se)	70	coder	70
associer	50	becqueter	110	cacher	70	codifier	50
assombrir	100	bégayer	150	cadrer	70	cogner	70
assommer	70	bêler	70	cajoler	70	coiffer	70
assortir	100	bénéficier	50	calculer	70	coincer	32
assoupir	100	bénir	100	caler	70	coïncider	70
assouplir	100	bercer	32	câliner	70	collaborer	70
assourdir	100	berner	70	calmer	70	collectionner	70
assujettir	100	beugler	70	calomnier	50	coller	70
assumer	70	beurrer	70	calquer	70	coloniser	70
assurer	70	biaiser	70	camper	70	colorer	70
astiquer	70	bichonner	70	capituler	70	colorier	50
astreindre	152	biffer	70	capter	70	combattre	26
atermoyer	136	blaguer	70	captiver	70	combler	70
attabler (s')	70	blâmer	70	capturer	70	commander	70
attacher	70	blanchir	100	caractériser	70	commémorer	70
attaquer	70	blaser	70	caresser	70	**commencer**	**32**
atteindre	**20**	blêmir	100	caricaturer	70	commettre	124
atteler	12	blesser	70	caser	70	communier	50
attendre	**22**	bloquer	70	casser	70	communiquer	70
attendrir	100	blottir (se)	100	cataloguer	70	comparaître	144
atterrir	100	**boire**	**28**	catapulter	70	comparer	70
attirer	70	boiter	70	causer	70	compenser	70
attraper	70	bombarder	70	céder	86	complaire	156
attribuer	70	bondir	100	ceindre	152	compléter	86
augmenter	70	bonifier	50	célébrer	86	complimenter	70
autoriser	70	border	70	celer	2	compliquer	70
avachir (s')	100	borner	70	censurer	70	comporter	70
avaler	70	boucher	70	cercler	70	composer	70
avancer	32	boucler	70	certifier	50	composter	70
avantager	118	bouder	70	cesser	70	comprendre	162
aventurer	70	bouffer	70	chagriner	70	compromettre	124
avertir	100	bouffir	100	chahuter	70	compter	70
aveugler	70	bouger	118	chamailler	70	concéder	86
avilir	100	**bouillir**	**30**	chanceler	12	concentrer	70
aviser	70	bouleverser	70	changer	118	concerner	70
aviver	70	boulonner	70	chanter	70	concevoir	166
avoir	**24**	bourdonner	70	chantonner	70	concilier	50
avouer	70	bourrer	70	charger	118	**conclure**	**34**
bâcler	70	boursoufler	70	charmer	70	concourir	44
bafouer	70	bousculer	70	charrier	50	concurrencer	32
bagarrer (se)	70	bousiller	70	chasser	70	condamner	70
baigner	70	boutonner	70	châtier	50	condenser	70
bâiller	70	braconner	70	chatouiller	70	condescendre[1]	62
baiser	70	brailler	70	chauffer	70	**conduire**	**36**
baisser	70	braire[7]	212	chausser	70	conférer	86
balader (se)	70	brancher	70	chercher	70	confier	50

Notes

1 Auxiliary = **avoir**.

2 Auxiliary = **être**.

3 Only infinitive and 3rd persons of each tense used.

4 Past participle: **absous, absoute**.

5 Conjugated with either **avoir** or **être**.

6 No circumflex on: **j'accrois, tu accrois**, and **accru**.

7 Hardly used except in the infinitive and the 3rd persons of the present, future and conditional.

8 Past participle: **circoncis**.

9 Past participle: **confit**.

10 No circumflex on: **je décrois, tu décrois**, and **décru**.

11 When **demeurer** means to live, the auxiliary is **avoir**; when it means to remain, the auxiliary is **être**.

12 Past participle: **dissous, dissoute**.

13 Present participle: **faillant**; past participle: **failli**; future: **je faillirai**, etc; conditional: **je faillirais**, etc. NB: **J'ai failli tomber** = I nearly fell.

14 When **fleurir** means to prosper, the present participle is **florissant**, and the imperfect is **florissait**.

15 Past participle: **frit**; used mainly in the present tense singular and in compound tenses.

16 Past participle: **inclus**.

17 Past participle: **mû, mue, mus, mues**.

18 Past participle: **nui**.

19 In questions, **je peux** can be replaced by **je puis: Puis-je vous aider?** May I help you?

20 Subjunctive: **je prévale**, etc.

21 Future: **je prévoirai**, etc; conditional: **je prévoirais**, etc.

22 Used only in the infinitive, present and past participles, and compound tenses.

23 Past participle: **relui**.

24 No past participle, no compound tenses.